PRAISE FOR *UNHITTABLE*

"I started following PitchingNinja back in college and loved how he broke down the pitching side of the game. He considers all aspects of the game: our training, our thought process, and how pitching has evolved over the years. *Unhittable* gives insight into the technology, mindset, and work behind being a pitcher in today's game."
—Tarik Skubal, 2024 and 2025 Cy Young Award winner and pitcher for the Detroit Tigers

"Rob Friedman is my favorite baseball analyst. With his deep expertise and unique sense of humor, he has done more than anyone to rekindle my love for America's pastime. *Unhittable* is a masterpiece of history and analysis that will help fans understand why we're living in a golden age of pitching, and how a combination of science and human wisdom has created the greatest generation of pitchers that baseball has ever seen."
—Derek Thompson, contributing writer at *The Atlantic* and coauthor of the *New York Times* bestseller *Abundance*

"Long before social media, let alone televised games, baseball players and fans alike marveled at the movement or speed of projectiles as they hurtled toward the plate. Now we are in the golden age to appreciate pitching. Rob has played a part in this revolution, bringing the art of pitching to the masses."
—Sarah Langs, writer and analyst at MLB.com

"Pitching has advanced more in the last decade than it has in the previous century, and Friedman explains how, in riveting detail. In *Unhittable*, the pages move like a 100-mph fastball. Friedman masterfully captures the state of the game's most important position."
—Travis Sawchik, *New York Times* bestselling author of *Big Data Baseball* and *The MVP Machine*

"For tons of baseball fans, the whole experience of watching MLB pretty much splits into two eras: before they found PitchingNinja and after. As pitching has taken over modern baseball, Rob walks you through exactly why and how the game has basically turned hitting into a nearly impossible task. *Unhittable* tackles this shift, using real stories from the pitchers on the mound, and gives fans who've never thrown a ball or stood in the batter's box a real appreciation for just how insane the game they're obsessed with actually is."

—Jimmy "Jomboy" O'Brien, founder of Jomboy Media and host of the *Talkin' Baseball* podcast

UNHITTABLE

= ((13*HR)
- (3*BB+HBP))
(2*K))/IP + CONSTANT
48.4% Whiff Rate

wOBA = (unintentional BB factor x
/IP + CONSTANT   IP = ((13*HR)
                x HBP + 1B factor x 1B + 2

lgERA - (((13*lgHR)
unintentional   - 5.6 degree VAA
8" induced vertical break
6" horizontal break   13*H
mph   K))/IP
              3214 R
                        8.4
             - 5.6 degree
              FIP C   t =
         lgERA - (((13*lgHR)
              (3*lgBB+lgHB
                (*lgK))/I

UNHITTABLE

How Technology, Mavericks, and
Innovators Engineered Baseball's
New Era of Pitching Dominance

ROB FRIEDMAN

HARPER
An Imprint of HarperCollins*Publishers*

Without limiting the exclusive rights of any author, contributor or the publisher of this publication, any unauthorized use of this publication to train generative artificial intelligence (AI) technologies is expressly prohibited. HarperCollins also exercise their rights under Article 4(3) of the Digital Single Market Directive 2019/790 and expressly reserve this publication from the text and data mining exception.

UNHITTABLE. Copyright © 2026 by PitchingNinja LLC. All rights reserved. No part of this book may be used or reproduced in any manner whatsoever without written permission except in the case of brief quotations embodied in critical articles and reviews. For information, address HarperCollins Publishers, 195 Broadway, New York, NY 10007. In Europe, HarperCollins Publishers, Macken House, 39/40 Mayor Street Upper, Dublin 1, D01 C9W8, Ireland.

HarperCollins books may be purchased for educational, business, or sales promotional use. For information, please email the Special Markets Department at SPsales@harpercollins.com.

hc.com

FIRST EDITION

Title page photograph © PM Images/Getty Images

Library of Congress Cataloging-in-Publication Data has been applied for.

ISBN 978-0-06-345676-1

Printed in the United States of America

26 27 28 29 30 LBC 5 4 3 2 1

To Jack, who got me into this mess and helped re-spark my love for baseball, and to Madeline, who kept me grounded with her trash talk while proving it's never too late to learn to pitch. And to Patricia, who deserves a medal for encouraging me to chase this wild idea in the first place.

You go to the ballpark and you see the pitcher standing there in the middle of the diamond. . . . He stands on a hill like a king with the grass of the infield cut away all around him. He's the center of attraction. He gets the third out and walks comfortably off the mound toward the dugout with the knowledge that he was better than the other side. Everybody else runs off the field, but the pitcher walks, lingering in the eye and the mind of fans.

—Tom Seaver, quoted in *The Last Icon: Tom Seaver and His Times*, by Steven Travers

CONTENTS

Preface: How Outsiders Hacked Pitching's Code   xi

Introduction: Welcome to the Age of Unhittable   xvii

Chapter 1	1
Chapter 2	10
Chapter 3	19
Chapter 4	26
Chapter 5	35
Chapter 6	45
Chapter 7	54
Chapter 8	61
Chapter 9	74
Chapter 10	86
Chapter 11	98

Chapter 12	108
Chapter 13	116
Chapter 14	123
Chapter 15	134
Chapter 16	146
Chapter 17	154
Chapter 18	166
Chapter 19	181
Chapter 20	190
Chapter 21	201
Chapter 22	220
Chapter 23	232
Chapter 24	241
Acknowledgments	245
Notes	247
Index	253

PREFACE
How Outsiders Hacked Pitching's Code

Although my life now revolves around baseball, I didn't take the typical path to the sport's inner circle. I wasn't a standout player. I loved the game, played as a kid, but I was never the kind of athlete who turned heads. My early career had nothing to do with baseball. I was a lawyer.

I graduated at the top of my class from Emory Law School, practiced law for several years, and eventually became general counsel of a cable modem and telephony company called Arris. Then I co-founded a startup called Digital Envoy, which developed one of the first commercial geolocation technologies. Over the next two decades, we built it into a global data powerhouse, reshaping how online businesses understood their users. I spent my days dealing with contracts, code, and analytics—not curveballs.

But no matter how far I got from the field, baseball never really left me. And when my son, Jack, started playing, I found myself pulled back into the game—this time not as a player, but as a dad with a camera.

I started by photographing Jack's games. It was just a hobby. I enjoyed the creative challenge, and it gave me a way to connect with other parents. But as I reviewed the pictures, I began noticing patterns—mechanical issues in throws or swings that showed up clearly in still frames. I shared a few observations, casually at first. That led to more conversations, more questions. Eventually someone asked me, "Why don't you just coach?"

At first, I laughed it off. I wasn't a former pro. I hadn't pitched in college. Who was I to tell anyone how to throw a baseball? I had coached my daughter, Madeline, in softball, but softball pitching always felt like its own mysterious universe. Still, the coaching spark was there—and curiosity took over. If I was going to do this, I didn't want to recycle the same half-remembered clichés I'd heard growing up. I'm a visual and analytical learner by nature, so I needed to know not just what worked—but why it worked. So I started digging—reading articles, watching videos, asking questions on message boards. I fell down the rabbit hole of pitching mechanics, and I never really came out.

By 2008 or so, I stumbled onto the Let's Talk Pitching message board. It was one of the only places online where people were obsessively breaking down the science of throwing a baseball. It became my classroom. That board, it turned out, was a quiet launchpad for the coming pitching revolution.

Back then, we were all nobodies. Just a group of hyper-curious coaches, players, dads, engineers, and data nerds arguing about Tim Lincecum's stride or Nolan Ryan's arm path. But among those usernames were people who would go on to change the sport. Kyle Boddy was just starting to test his data-driven training ideas. Ben Brewster was still an aspiring pitcher trying to figure out the golden truths of pitching and prove the doubters wrong. Paul Nyman, an engineer with a contrarian streak, was constantly challenging everyone's assumptions. Influential and soon-to-be influential coaches Eric Cressey, Lantz Wheeler, Alan Jaeger—they were all there, too. The conversations could get heated. But it was the kind of heat that sharpens things.

That forum lit a fire in me.

Everything I learned there, I brought to the field. I coached Jack, and then other players. My philosophy was simple: Get a little better every day. That applied to the kids I coached, but also to me. I was constantly reading, learning, and tinkering. I believed that if you outworked people—especially in the off-hours, when nobody else was grinding—those gains would add up. I saw the results. My players improved. Their confidence grew. And they started to separate themselves from the pack.

As Jack's pitching career progressed, so did my coaching. I worked with travel teams, coached at East Cobb Baseball, and later volunteered as a pitching coach at Paideia High School. What began as a way to help my son became something bigger—a way to give back to the sport, and a way to keep learning.

Jack worked hard and showed promise. His fastball touched 95 mph and he earned a scholarship to Georgia Tech. But baseball has a cruel side. In high school, during a game where he struck out the final batter, I saw him glance toward the dugout. There was something in his eyes—a look I'll never forget. Pain. That moment marked the beginning of a labrum injury that eventually ended his career. He'd later hit a game-winning home run in that same game. Bittersweet doesn't even begin to cover it.

That injury changed me. It sharpened my focus. It reminded me how fragile this game is, how quickly everything can vanish. And it deepened my commitment to helping pitchers succeed without breaking down. I wanted to understand the link between performance and injury. I wanted to keep others from going through what Jack had.

I also realized how lucky we were to be able to access the kind of coaching and information that helped Jack reach that level. Not every family can afford it. The cost of private lessons, travel teams, gear, hotel rooms—it adds up fast. Baseball shouldn't be a rich kid's sport. I never wanted a kid to sit with their parents years later wondering "what if" because they couldn't afford a pitching coach.

That's why I created PitchingNinja and later FlatGround. I wanted to make high-quality pitching education and exposure free and accessible to everyone. I didn't start with any grand plan. In 2014, I joined Twitter and started posting videos and insights because it felt like a natural extension of everything I was doing. I figured maybe a few dozen people—players, coaches, parents—would find it helpful.

I called the account PitchingNinja. The name came partly from my wife's Japanese heritage and partly from a moment when Jack, wearing a bandana on a cold day, looked like a ninja on the mound. A coach joked about it. Jack hated the nickname. I leaned into it. I was the team's pitching coach, after all. Why not own it?

To my surprise, the account took off. MLB pitchers loved the breakdowns. Coaches appreciated the details. Fans loved the nasty pitch clips. It turned into a hub—not just for entertainment, but for education and exposure. And through FlatGround, it became a way for unsigned players to get noticed by scouts and schools. That part matters to me more than anything. If even one kid gets a shot they wouldn't have otherwise had, it's worth it.

Along my coaching journey, I was an early adopter—drawn to tools that actually made pitchers better. Weighted balls. Pocket Radar. Rapsodo. Motion capture. The same principle that drove my business career—measure what matters—applied perfectly to pitching. If you can measure it, you can improve it. If you can improve it, you can maximize your talent.

My journey even took my son and me to the Texas Baseball Ranch, where I picked the brain of Brent Strom, a grizzled coaching veteran who could turn pitching mechanics into teen comedy. To Jack and his friends, he gave this unforgettable lesson on glute engagement: "Just imagine trying to hold in a fart in class. What muscles are you using?"

I saw early what places like Driveline Baseball and Tread Athletics were building. When my son, Jack, trained with Tread in its early days, they handed him a customized plan: strength training, mobility work, nutrition, throwing drills—all tailored to his specific needs. Over time, Jack added sixty pounds of explosive strength, shot up several inches, and went from topping out at 77 mph to touching 95.

That kind of transformation doesn't happen by accident. It happens when data, effort, and belief collide. What you're holding is the product of that collision. It's personal, but it's not just about me or Jack. It's about the outsiders who helped bring baseball into a new era. The ones who didn't wait for permission. The ones who challenged the old-school myths. The ones who refused to accept "because that's how we've always done it" as an answer.

Some were engineers. Some were pitchers. Some were biomechanists, coders, strength coaches, or dads with cameras. But all of them had the same drive: to figure out how to make pitching better. Smarter. Safer. Nastier.

They didn't just improve pitching. They redefined it.

This book is their story—and mine. It's a celebration of the mavericks, the nerds, and the rebels who rewrote baseball's code.

Let's get started.

INTRODUCTION
Welcome to the Age of Unhittable

There's a moment of quiet before a pitch.

The pitcher stands alone, sixty feet, six inches away, gripping the ball like a magician holding his trick. The crowd buzzes, but the air feels still, as if everyone senses that something devastating is about to happen. The batter digs in, helmet tilted forward, bat twitching like a coiled spring.

And then it comes.

A slider breaks two feet in the blink of an eye and drops off the table. The batter swings. The crowd gasps. The ball slaps the catcher's mitt with a pop, and all the hitter can do is shake his head.

It's the kind of pitch that makes people lean back in their seats and say, "No chance." But this isn't luck. This pitch wasn't born in a backyard or shaped only by feel. It was built. Designed. Engineered to be unhittable.

Baseball hasn't always been this way. For most of its 175-year history, pitching was simpler and rougher around the edges. There were legends, of course—Walter Johnson throwing bullets before radar guns existed, Bob Feller racing a motorcycle, Nolan Ryan lighting up the gun into his forties. But for all their dominance, they were mostly guessing. They were feeling their way through the game.

Pitchers used to be artists, relying on instinct, toughness, and maybe a little sweat or spitball magic. Coaching was vague. If you had a fastball, great. A curveball? Even better. Want to get better? Figure it out. Spin rate, vertical break, and release height weren't part of the conversation. It was more grit and trial and error than science.

That has changed.

Today's pitchers are biomechanical engineers in cleats. Their deliveries are studied frame by frame. Their grips are optimized. Their arsenals are built to tunnel, spin, fade, rise, and vanish.

The mound is no longer just a battlefield—it is a laboratory.

Kids now train to throw like scientists. They may dream about being the next Nolan Ryan. But they're studying Rapsodo charts, analyzing iPhone video, tweaking finger pressure to vary spin efficiency. They are searching for any edge they can find.

The tools are everywhere. Edgertronic cameras capture video at over one thousand frames per second. Motion capture rigs track the body down to the millimeter. Pitching machines replicate the exact release point and movement of big-league arms. A pitcher today has access to more information about one throw than an old school Hall of Famer had in a lifetime.

It's hard to say exactly when the revolution started. Maybe it was Tom House mapping mechanics with biomechanics before anyone else cared. Maybe it was Trevor Bauer, a pitcher as known for challenging convention as hitters, deciding he didn't want to just play the game—he wanted to decode it. Maybe it was Kyle Boddy testing training ideas in a Washington warehouse. However it began, it's now everywhere.

Fastballs are faster. Sliders are sharper. New pitches are no longer stumbled upon; they're engineered with intent. Pitchers throw harder, longer, and with more deception than at any point in the game's history. Pull up a highlight reel. Every night, a new pitch goes viral. A curveball that defies physics. A sweeper that disappears behind a left-handed batter. A splitter that vanishes under the barrel.

This is the era of pitch design, biomechanics, and constant innovation.

But there's a problem.

For every pitcher who has evolved into a high-tech weapon, there is a hitter left behind. Strikeouts are at an all-time high. Offense is shrinking. Games are tilting toward the guys on the mound, and the balance that once defined baseball has started to collapse.

For generations, baseball has been a game of tension between hitter and pitcher. Babe Ruth shifted the balance with home runs. Bob Gibson took it back with a 1.12 ERA in 1968. The steroid era tilted it toward offense again. The best hitters and pitchers in history have traded blows for over a century.

Now? Pitchers are winning. And it's not close.

What follows is the story of how that happened.

It's a look inside the world of outsiders who rewrote the code—nerds, coaches, and athletes who refused to accept the old ways. It's about underground pitching facilities where velocity reigns, motion capture labs that build pitchers like machines, and kids who followed the data until their stuff became too filthy to ignore.

It's about how social media turned pitch design into a shared language. How one viral slider can inspire thousands. How a culture that once prioritized throwing strikes evolved into one that thrives on missing bats.

And it's about what happens next.

Because no matter how dominant pitchers have become, hitters aren't standing still. A new generation is quietly preparing its counterpunch.

They're adapting because they have no choice.

They're training with advanced machines like Trajekt, which replicate elite pitchers down to their delivery, release point, and spin profile. They're studying heat maps, refining their swings through biomechanics, and using motion sensors to track how energy moves through their bodies. Optimizing angles. Shortening paths. Anticipating movement instead of reacting to it.

Brent Rooker, one of the league's top power hitters, put it bluntly: "Even the worst pitch now is still nasty because they've optimized everything. You used to face guys with one elite pitch. Now, every guy has three or four."

Even Hall of Famers I've spoken with, who used to feast on elite pitching of their day, admit they'd have a hard time competing now. That's how nasty it's gotten.

That's the reality hitters face. Every at-bat feels like survival. But rather than complain, they're building new weapons. Custom-designed bats. Personalized swings tailored to body type and movement patterns. Even their mindset is changing. The best hitters aren't just reacting anymore. They're training differently, anticipating more, and stepping into the box with a plan to strike back.

They're not there yet. But they're getting closer.

And the same tools that turned pitchers into high-tech monsters are now creeping into the batter's box—one swing at a time.

This is what happens when tradition collides with technology. When feel meets force plates. When some of the brightest minds in sports science set their sights on the oldest game in America.

This is how pitching became unhittable.

Can pitchers keep pushing the limits through technology? Or are they pushing too far?

Can hitters ever catch up?

Welcome to baseball's new frontier.

UNHITTABLE

1

In the early 1990s, Randy Johnson was struggling to harness his potential. Standing six feet ten with a fastball that could blow the doors off any hitter, Johnson had all the physical gifts to be great. But his mechanics were a mess, his control was wildly inconsistent, and he led the league in walks three times early in his career. Critics questioned whether Johnson could ever turn his raw talent into sustained dominance. He'd made an All-Star team, but hadn't seen a single Cy Young downballot vote, even when he led the American League (AL) in strikeouts.

That's when the team of Nolan Ryan and Tom House stepped in, offering their expertise to help Johnson transform from a scatter-armed thrower into one of the most unhittable pitchers the game has ever seen.

Tom House first met Randy Johnson during a pivotal moment in Johnson's career, when the towering left-hander was struggling with command despite his electric fastball. House recounted sitting with Nolan Ryan in the dugout during pregame workouts in Seattle. As they watched Johnson unleashing thunderous fastballs in the bullpen, including some sailing onto the field, Ryan and House immediately recognized his raw gifts—and the glaring issues holding him back.

Johnson, clearly frustrated, approached House directly and admitted, "Tom, I'm doing terrible. I can't throw strikes. In fact, I'm getting a little worried." Sensing an opportunity to help someone make the most of their abundant talent, even if it was an opposing pitcher, Ryan invited Johnson to join a training session with House the next day. That conversation set the stage for a transformation that would ultimately turn Johnson into one of the most unhittable pitchers in baseball history.

Ryan and House brought Johnson into their system, one that combined mechanical refinement, strength training, and mental preparation. Ryan had already worked with House to extend and recharge his own career, so he immediately recognized the parallels between his early struggles and Johnson's. Johnson's unique frame and overpowering delivery were both his greatest weapons and his biggest hurdles. Using video analysis, House meticulously broke down Johnson's mechanics frame by frame, identifying inefficiencies that were robbing him of both velocity and command.

One glaring issue stood out: Johnson's landing-foot placement. With his long legs and towering frame, Johnson wasn't landing consistently, which threw off his balance and caused his release point to vary from pitch to pitch. This inconsistency made it nearly impossible for him to control his fastball. House focused on stabilizing Johnson's landing and aligning his stride, ensuring his body worked in harmony rather than by fighting itself. By creating a more repeatable delivery, Johnson could finally unlock the full potential of his fastball without sacrificing accuracy.

Ryan's mentorship played an equally pivotal role. As someone who had faced similar struggles with command early in his career, Ryan became a relatable figure for Johnson. He encouraged him to embrace the mental side of pitching, teaching him how to approach hitters with strategy rather than relying solely on overpowering them. "Don't let anyone put barriers on what you can do," Ryan reportedly told Johnson, instilling in him the confidence to trust the process and believe in his ability to overwhelm hitters. Johnson would later impart that same wisdom to a new phenom, Paul Skenes, years later.[1] The impact of House's and Ryan's mentorship became evident quickly.

By the mid-1990s, Johnson's walk totals were cut nearly in half, while his strikeout numbers soared to historic levels. In 1995, he led the Seattle Mariners to their first-ever playoff appearance, earning the

AL Cy Young Award in the process. The wildness that had plagued him early in his career was replaced by precision, making him an even scarier version of the pitcher hitters already dreaded facing.

This mentorship helped Johnson to become one of the greatest pitchers of all time. Over his twenty-two-year career, he collected five Cy Young Awards, threw two no-hitters (including a perfect game), and struck out 4,875 batters, second only to Ryan's all-time record. Johnson would later credit Ryan and House for helping him unlock his potential, saying their guidance gave him the tools he needed to refine his mechanics and harness his mind.

Johnson's transformation stood as a testament to House's methods and Ryan's hard-earned wisdom, proving that even the most raw, unpolished pitchers could be molded into legends with the right tools, preparation, and mindset. Johnson's rise to greatness reshaped power pitching and also established a blueprint for developing the next generation of unhittable arms .

♦ ♦ ♦

THE EVOLUTION OF pitching training didn't happen overnight. It was a slow, quiet revolution born out of necessity, curiosity, and a desire to answer questions no one had dared to ask. Baseball relied on tradition, gut instinct, and vague advice to shape pitchers. Coaches barked instructions like "throw strikes" and "use your legs," but the reasoning behind those phrases was rarely explored. Pitchers relied heavily on feel, and injuries were shrugged off as bad luck or the inevitable result of overuse.

That shift began in the mid-to-late twentieth century, as video analysis emerged and computers became more integrated into everyday life. A handful of forward-thinking pioneers began asking fundamental questions: What separates good pitchers from great ones? What keeps them healthy? And, most importantly, how can success be consistently replicated?

Hall of Fame pitchers Tom Seaver and Nolan Ryan pushed the

boundaries of what a pitcher could do through strength training and conditioning, laying the groundwork for the modern understanding of durability and performance. But while Seaver emphasized leg drive and Ryan turned weight lifting into a year-round commitment, there was still a gap in understanding the "why" behind their success. Were they just exceptions? Or was there something to the training they embraced? Mechanics, in particular, were a mystery. What made some deliveries efficient and others a fast track to the injured list? That's where a self-proclaimed "average pitcher" with an obsession for understanding the *whys* behind pitching and a knack for out-of-the-box thinking stepped in—and rewrote the playbook.

Tom House was born to fully dive into and uncover the *whys* behind pitching.

Tom House's scientific approach to baseball didn't come out of nowhere—it was rooted deeply in his upbringing. His parents weren't athletes or even particularly familiar with the intricacies of baseball, but they instilled in him the values of curiosity, critical thinking, and a relentless drive to improve. They weren't the type to simply celebrate a success without analyzing how it happened. When House threw a no-hitter as a young player, he expected his parents to shower him with praise.

Instead, his father, an engineer, posed a question that would shape House's mindset for the rest of his life: "Why did you succeed?"

House's father wanted him to think critically, to break down the process that led to success instead of just basking in the result. This emphasis on the "why" behind performance became a cornerstone of House's career. Whether he was dissecting pitching mechanics or delving into biomechanics, that engineer's mindset—always asking how and why—drove him.

House's mother, an Iowa farm girl with a no-nonsense attitude, reinforced this approach in a different way. She didn't care about his on-field achievements if they came at the expense of his education. "I don't care what you did on the field . . . Did you get an A in English today?" she would ask. No A, No Play was her motto. For House, this focus on intellectual growth planted the seeds of a lifelong pursuit of knowledge. He wasn't satisfied with simply playing the game; he needed to understand it, refine it, and share that knowledge with others.

The combination of his father's analytical mindset and his mother's emphasis on education turned House into more than just another pitcher. It made him a thinker, setting aside conventional wisdom to seek empirical answers where others saw tradition. This foundation allowed him to pioneer the use of biomechanics, motion analysis, and scientifically grounded training techniques in baseball, changing the game forever. House was the embodiment of a question-driven upbringing, always striving to figure out why something worked and how it could work better.

House has had a Zelig-like ability to be on the scene for some of the greatest moments in baseball. The guy was everywhere, somehow tied to some of the biggest names and moments in sports history. And while he wasn't a flame-throwing ace—heck, in House's own words, he wasn't even an above-average pitcher by MLB standards—House's journey is proof that you don't need a triple-digit fastball to leave a seismic impact on the game.

House's pitching story starts at USC, where he was teammates with Tom Seaver, one of the greatest pitchers to ever touch a mound. They weren't equals on the field—Seaver had the raw talent, the power, and the presence—but House soaked up every bit of knowledge he could, learning from Seaver and their legendary coach, Rod Dedeaux. Dedeaux was both a coach as well as a baseball philosopher who drilled fundamentals into his players with military precision. (His name will come up over and over in this book.) House credited Dedeaux for instilling the importance of preparation and attention to detail, lessons that would guide his coaching philosophy for decades.

While Tom Seaver went on to dominate MLB hitters as one of the greatest pitchers of all time, Tom House's playing career was far more journeyman than superstar. He bounced between teams and never had overwhelming stuff, though his curveball did earn high praise from none other than Sandy Koufax. For a pitcher like House, hearing Koufax compliment his curveball was like Beethoven telling you your piano playing wasn't half bad. Reflecting on the moment, House joked to me, "When Koufax said I had a good curveball, I thought, 'Well, at least I've got something.'"

Though House's career was far from Hall of Fame material, it paved the way for his eventual status as a pioneer in pitching mechanics. From 1971 to 1978, he played parts of eight seasons with the Atlanta Braves, Boston Red Sox, and Seattle Mariners. His numbers were solid but unremarkable—he posted a 3.79 ERA and a 29–23 record. But what set him apart was his unending curiosity and analytical mind. Even as a player, House was more focused on understanding the game than simply surviving in it.

House's most memorable moment as a player didn't come from a strikeout or a big win—it came from the outfield. On April 8, 1974, House was stationed in the Braves bullpen when Hank Aaron hit his 715th home run, breaking Babe Ruth's all-time record. House caught the historic ball and jogged it out to Aaron, handing over a piece of baseball history with a smile. "I knew my arm wasn't good enough to throw it back to the infield," House later quipped. It was a perfect snapshot of House's career: not in the spotlight, but always finding himself at the heart of baseball's most iconic moments.

House's unique path—USC with Seaver, catching Aaron's historic homer, getting advice from Koufax and later coaching Nolan Ryan, Randy Johnson, Drew Brees, and Tom Brady—reads like a sports highlight reel that somehow intertwines with a single person. But House never just watched greatness from the sidelines; he absorbed it, analyzed it, and turned it into teachable moments for the next generation. Whether it was Dedeaux's discipline, Seaver's work ethic, or Aaron's grace under pressure, House turned his encounters with legends into the foundation of his coaching legacy.

It's fitting to call Tom House baseball's Forrest Gump, but don't mistake him for a passive observer. Every step of the way, House was quietly reshaping the game.

♦ ♦ ♦

AFTER HIS PLAYING days ended, House took his passion for pitching to another level, earning a PhD in Sports Psychology from US International University (now Alliant International University). His doctorate explored the mental side of the game, focusing on how confidence, focus, and preparation could separate good pitchers from great ones. He combined these insights with biomechanics (the study of the mechanics of skeletal and muscular activity in throwing a baseball), creating a unique approach that merged the psychological and physical aspects of performance.

Tom House's relentless curiosity and determination to decode pitching mechanics extended far beyond his firsthand experience alongside MLB pitchers. He scoured every resource available in his quest to understand why some pitchers thrived while others struggled. In an era before accessible video analysis or advanced motion capture, House turned to resources like Getty Images and any early video footage he could find to decode the secrets of pitching mechanics. His process was raw and painstaking, but it paved the way for the biomechanics revolution that followed.

"I started with still pictures," House explained. "I'd find a picture, sometimes from Getty Images, and ask a buddy to flag any that showed pitchers at maximum leg lift." With these snapshots, House began piecing together the movements of the best pitchers, walking around with a collection of thirty-two photos that he would pin up on boards or stages to study frame by frame. This rudimentary method was his first step in understanding the key points of pitching motion before video analysis became more widely available.

House's early work with film footage was painstakingly slow, requiring reels of film to be manually slowed down frame by frame. "Our video analysis was so primitive," House recalled. "We had to take film and slow it down with our hands. If we took too long, the film would burn."

Despite the challenges, this hands-on process allowed House to spot details others missed. It wasn't easy, but it gave him a deeper understanding of pitching mechanics at a time when few were even looking.

What House learned through these early efforts set the stage for everything that came later. He used these insights to identify patterns in the most successful pitchers—details like optimal arm slots, stride lengths, and even how stepping across the body impacted command and velocity. The combination of still photos and film gave him an unparalleled understanding of what separated good pitchers from great ones, knowledge he would later refine with advanced motion capture and biomechanical tools.

These early efforts, while groundbreaking, were only the beginning. House's hunger pushed him to go beyond still images and manual film analysis. He knew that if he wanted to truly unlock the secrets of pitching, he needed to take his research to the next level. This realization led to his most ambitious project yet: building a biomechanics lab that would combine his observational insights with cutting-edge technology to transform how pitchers trained and performed.

Tom House's obsession with finding answers pushed him to risk nearly everything to unlock the secrets of pitching. He poured his savings into the effort, even mortgaging his home to build one of baseball's first *biomechanics* labs—long before most in the sport even knew what that word meant.

It wasn't flashy. It was raw, experimental, and way ahead of its time. To traditionalists, it was overkill—gimmicks that didn't belong in baseball. But to House, it was the key to answering the questions no one else dared to ask: Why do some pitchers dominate? Why do others break down?

The cost wasn't only financial. "It cost me fifteen thousand dollars and my marriage," House admitted. While he was consumed by his quest to revolutionize pitching, his first wife struggled to understand why he was pouring so much time and money into something that seemed so intangible. To House, though, the lab was more than an investment—it was a mission. He refused to be confined by tradition, relentlessly chasing understanding—even at the cost of stability in his personal life.

What did House learn from all of this? Everything.

House discovered that some of the "golden rules" of pitching, like "stay back" or "find your balance point," were actually working against what elite pitchers naturally did. By analyzing the sequencing and timing of movements, he found that the key wasn't rigid mechanics but functional, efficient motion. His work showed that pitchers could throw harder and with better control—not by working harder, but by moving smarter. And just as importantly, he felt that his findings led to injury prevention strategies that extended careers.

The lab became a proving ground for ideas that seemed crazy at the time but are now the foundation of modern pitching. House's analysis revealed that some of the best pitchers—guys like Nolan Ryan—employed "taboo" mechanics that coaches would have tried to fix. From dropping arm slots to unique timing patterns, House's research helped pitchers unlock their natural potential instead of conforming to one-size-fits-all coaching.

It was a bold, risky leap that challenged every traditionalist's idea of how the game should be played. He threw his savings, his time, and even his personal life into the lab, and in doing so, he forever changed how the game is played.

2

Nolan Ryan's journey to velocity stardom started in Alvin, Texas, where he spent his childhood throwing objects of all kinds. Ryan's rural upbringing forged his arm into one of the most powerful weapons the game had ever seen. Nolan Ryan's legendary arm strength wasn't built on the mound—it started on the ranch. As a ten- or eleven-year-old, Ryan showed his entrepreneurial spirit by leasing pastureland from the local American Legion, which owned the nearby rodeo grounds. With his parents' approval, he bought day-old dairy calves and raised them there, diving headfirst into the cattle business. The physical demands of ranch work—hauling feed, wrangling livestock, and managing chores—helped forge the raw strength that would later fuel his blazing fastball. Ryan himself laughed as he recalled this early introduction to the cattle business, but it's clear those formative years laid the foundation for his work ethic and physical durability.[1]

Nolan Ryan credited his legendary arm strength to his childhood days throwing newspapers with his father, Lynn. Together, they managed a massive paper route for *The Houston Post*, delivering 1,500 newspapers over a fifty-five-mile stretch. Day after day, Ryan honed his throwing mechanics by launching papers into driveways—a task he later said helped build the powerful arm that would overwhelm Major League hitters.

This repetitive motion not only strengthened his arm but also instilled the strong work ethic that defined his career. What began as a simple chore became the foundation for one of the most feared fastballs in baseball history. It probably struck fear into garages everywhere, too—imagine him unleashing a newspaper hard enough to punch straight through a garage door.[2] Who knows? The morning paper might have been the prototype for weighted balls!

By the time he debuted with the New York Mets in 1966, it was clear that his arm was almost mythical. Ryan's fastball rocketed out of his hand, earning him a reputation as a pitcher who could blow hitters away even when they knew what was coming.

Nolan Ryan's reputation as the king of velocity was cemented in 1974, and the numbers finally backed up the lore. At a time when baseball was just starting to dip its toes into speed measurement in game situations, Ryan's fastball became the perfect test subject for cutting-edge technology. On August 20, 1974, during a game against the Detroit Tigers, Ryan's heater was clocked at a blistering 100.9 mph in an experiment using an infrared laser device developed by Rockwell International, an aerospace and technology leader. This was different from some sterile reading on a radar gun in a lab—it was a calculated effort to measure the unmeasurable: the sheer terror of a Nolan Ryan fastball during a game. For the first time, baseball had proof that what hitters had been whispering about in dugouts for years—Ryan's ridiculous velocity—was no myth.

Later that same year, on September 7, at a promotional event in which fans were invited to guess Ryan's velocity, Rockwell International again set up their infrared laser device to measure Ryan's fastball with supposedly greater reliability, ironing out some kinks in the previous test. The "Ryan Express" became the benchmark for velocity.[3]

During the promotion, Ryan delivered, as always. He unleashed his signature heat, sending the ball screaming through the infrared laser beam. The outcome was a staggering 100.8 mph in the *ninth* inning of the game after well over one hundred pitches. But the setup required some creativity. Because there was concern that the laser technology could potentially harm Ryan's eyes if pointed directly at him, engineers positioned the system to measure the ball's speed approximately ten to fifteen feet in front of home plate. This ensured supposedly accurate readings without putting the Ryan Express and his eyes at risk.

In the movie *Fastball*,[4] experts estimated that if Ryan's in-game fastball had been measured at release like modern pitches, it would have been closer to 108 mph because pitches slow down several miles an hour on the way to the plate due to air resistance/drag. Is that even possible? For comparison, Statcast-era pitchers like Ben Joyce, Aroldis Chapman, and Jordan Hicks have been clocked at over 105 mph at release. That's either proof Nolan Ryan was far ahead of both his time and today's pitchers or, more likely, that the readings were somewhat flawed. After all, it was more publicity stunt than science experiment. Ryan undoubtedly threw flames, but the technology was new and not as reliable as today's battle-tested radar guns. The setup was also unclear, and nobody knew exactly where along the pitch the reading was taken, a detail that makes a huge difference in extrapolating how fast it really was. . . . We should remain somewhat skeptical of the accuracy of this test's results, as the readings from this early measurement technology were, frankly, all over the place—87.6 mph in the first inning; 91.3 mph in the sixth inning; and 94.1 mph in the eighth inning. This inconsistency highlights that the technology was still in its infancy and far from reliable. However, there's no doubt that Nolan Ryan threw flames, and this experiment marked another important step in baseball's growing fascination with velocity and the drive to measure it.

Regardless of any skepticism surrounding the technology, this moment solidified Ryan as the fastest thrower in baseball history. Bob Feller's unofficial 98.6 mph record (discussed later in this book) was now firmly in the rearview mirror, and Ryan became the new standard for velocity. Whether or not the exact numbers were perfect, the narrative was clear: Nolan Ryan threw harder than anyone before him, a fact that only deepened his legend and the aura of intimidation he carried to the mound. Breaking records was part of the story—it also signaled another cultural shift, fueling baseball's growing obsession with velocity, a fixation that still shapes pitching today.

Watching old games with modern radar analysis, I've personally seen

Ryan clock 99 mph at thirty-three years old—on his 105th pitch of a game, on just three days' rest![5]

Fans were witnessing the limits of human potential. Every time he took the mound, fans weren't just watching to see if he'd win—they were waiting to see if he'd unleash the fastest pitch ever recorded, potentially seeing something that no one had ever seen before.

Ryan's longevity as a pitcher was just as remarkable as his velocity. Over a career that spanned an incredible twenty-seven seasons, Ryan recorded 5,714 strikeouts—a record that may never be broken. Only three active pitchers have even crossed the halfway point: Justin Verlander, Max Scherzer, and Clayton Kershaw.

Ryan threw seven no-hitters, the most in MLB history, and routinely overpowered hitters well into his forties. While most power pitchers lose velocity as they age, Ryan seemed to defy time itself, still throwing flames late in his career.

Ryan's fastball was more than a pitch—it was a symbol. For hitters, it was an unrelenting trial; for fans, it was pure excitement; and for future pitchers, it was the gold standard. But perhaps most importantly, Ryan embraced the science of pitching in ways that advanced the game. His partnership with advanced technology showcased the potential for science and athletics to work hand in hand, paving the way for the data-driven era of baseball we see today.

The legacy of Nolan Ryan's fastball goes beyond numbers on a radar gun or laser. Today, when we marvel at 105 mph fastballs on Statcast or debate the greatest power pitchers of all time, it's impossible not to see Nolan Ryan's fingerprints all over the conversation. He threw gas, set standards for domination, and ignited the technology revolution in pitching.

◆ ◆ ◆

WHEN NOLAN RYAN joined the Rangers in 1989, he stood out as a rare exception to the prevailing old-school mentality. Ryan had long embraced strength training and functional conditioning, recognizing that physical preparation was crucial for both durability and performance.

His forward-thinking approach made him an ideal match for pitching coach Tom House's science-driven philosophy.

House and Ryan's collaboration was all about fine-tuning and amplifying what Ryan already did best, taking his training and performance to the next level. House used advanced video analysis to pinpoint inefficiencies in Ryan's mechanics, focusing on reducing arm stress while maintaining his trademark velocity. He also introduced new strength-building exercises tailored specifically for pitchers, such as explosive lower-body work and core stabilization, ensuring that every movement in the gym translated directly to the mound. Tom House didn't believe Nolan Ryan was the only one who could benefit from this training. He saw nothing unique about Ryan that made the methods work for him alone—if it could elevate Ryan, it could elevate others, too.

When Tom House first introduced his training methods with the Texas Rangers, many viewed him as the "Nutty Professor" for his seemingly outlandish ideas. Weight lifting for pitchers? Nearly unheard of, outside of a few pitchers who were still viewed by the baseball establishment as outliers. Skepticism ran deep among both coaches and players.

To combat this resistance, House enlisted the expertise of Dr. James Andrews, one of the most respected orthopedic surgeons in sports medicine. Andrews addressed the team, explaining that properly executed strength training was more than merely safe—it was essential for building functional strength, improving performance, and preventing injuries. His endorsement gave House's program instant credibility, helping to shift the mindset around weight lifting in baseball.

With Andrews's backing, House implemented a progressive strength program tailored to pitchers for everyone on the staff. This focused on developing functional strength and enhancing stability, endurance, and power in ways that directly supported pitching mechanics and arm health—rather than simply bulking up for its own sake.

As pitchers began to see tangible improvements, the Rangers became one of the first MLB teams to fully integrate weight training into their pitching development, setting a precedent that would alter the league's approach to conditioning for years to come.

At thirty-nine years old, Nolan Ryan was supposedly entering the twilight of his career—or so many thought.

House saw it differently.

Instead of decline, he saw an opportunity to extend and even enhance Ryan's dominance by combining his unrelenting drive with cutting-edge science and mechanics.

Ryan's open-mindedness made him the ideal subject for House's progressive methods. House used video technology to break down Ryan's delivery frame by frame, pinpointing inefficiencies that could cost him velocity or add unnecessary stress to his arm. For Ryan, the insights were a revelation.

"Tom helped me understand my mechanics in a way I never had before," Ryan said. "He gave me tools to stay on top of my game."

Ryan's trust in House's methods paid off, and their work together became one of the most successful pitcher-coach collaborations in history. Reflecting on their partnership during his Hall of Fame speech in 1999, Ryan credited House's relentless innovation.

"Tom is a coach that is always on the cutting edge," Ryan said. "And I really enjoyed our association together. He would always come up with new training techniques that we would try and see how they would work into my routine."

House's influence extended beyond mechanics. He introduced Ryan to revolutionary recovery techniques—long-toss programs, targeted rotator cuff exercises, and functional strength routines that were unheard of at the time. Ryan, always searching for ways to stay dominant, fully embraced the process.

The results were nothing short of extraordinary: a Hall of Fame career that lasted until age forty-six, a fastball that stayed elite into his forties, and a road map for future pitchers looking to defy time.

Ryan redefined what was possible for a pitcher his age. After turning forty, he threw two no-hitters, struck out 301 batters in a single season at age forty-two, and consistently hit triple digits on the radar gun when most pitchers his age were long retired. Together, House and Ryan shattered long-held misconceptions about weight training and arm care, proving that the right approach could both extend careers and also elevate performance.

Their partnership left a lasting legacy, reshaping how pitchers trained and recovered. The principles they championed—functional strength, advanced mechanics analysis, and recovery-focused routines—continue to influence modern pitching development. The team of House and Ryan set a new standard for what it means to dominate on the mound.

♦ ♦ ♦

IN 2000, TOM House launched the National Pitching Association (NPA), and it marked another significant development in the training of pitchers. This was more than a typical pitching camp or coaching job—House poured decades of experience working with elite pitchers into creating a blueprint for the next generation. The NPA became the ultimate hub for pitchers, blending biomechanics, strength training, mental skills, and injury prevention into one cohesive system. If you wanted to take your pitching to the next level—and stay healthy doing it—this was the place to be.

House had spent years in the trenches, breaking down mechanics with motion capture, studying arm health, and refining strength routines with guys like Nolan Ryan and Randy Johnson. The NPA was his way of bringing those big-league lessons to everyone, from youth players to pros.

What made it revolutionary? House looked at everything. Mechanics, functional strength, nutrition, sleep, recovery, mental focus—it was all part of the equation.

One of the most groundbreaking aspects of the NPA was its commitment to arm care and injury prevention. House had seen far too many talented pitchers lose their careers to preventable injuries, and he wasn't having it. He introduced concepts like pitch counts, structured recovery routines, and rotator cuff strengthening long before the rest of the baseball world caught on. His philosophy was about throwing harder, smarter, safer, and longer.

House didn't limit his focus to the physical side of pitching. He utilized his background in sports psychology to teach mental training techniques that helped pitchers stay focused, manage pressure, and recover from adversity.

Today, the NPA's influence is everywhere. From Little League fields to MLB bullpens, House's methods have shaped the way pitchers train, recover, and dominate. The NPA was more than a labor of love—it transformed Tom House's legacy into a framework for every pitcher striving to push their limits and stay on the mound longer.

♦ ♦ ♦

EVENTUALLY, TOM HOUSE'S reputation as a biomechanics guru transcended the sport entirely. His expertise found new life on the football field, but the seeds of that crossover were planted long before he started working with NFL quarterbacks. Nolan Ryan, one of House's greatest success stories, had incorporated footballs into his training regimen years earlier. For Ryan, throwing a football had become a calculated way to strengthen his arm, refine his mechanics, and develop the explosive power that defined his legendary fastball.

House strongly believes that throwing a football mimics many aspects of a pitcher's delivery. It requires proper sequencing between the upper and lower body while promoting shoulder stability. For Ryan, it was the perfect low-impact tool to fine-tune his mechanics and build functional strength. His use of the football went beyond a simple training method, showcasing his forward-thinking and unconventional approach to preparation. This innovative practice also became the basis for House's future work in football, demonstrating that the principles of throwing mechanics could seamlessly apply across multiple sports.

When House started working with NFL quarterbacks in the early 2000s, he brought those same principles to the gridiron, many of which were inspired by Ryan's success. House's philosophy—focused on efficiency, functional strength, and smart recovery—translated seamlessly from pitching to football. His journey into football began when a handful of quarterbacks, intrigued by his groundbreaking work in baseball, reached out to see if he could help improve their throwing efficiency, accuracy, and longevity. What started once again as a curiosity soon turned into a revolution.

One of House's first high-profile quarterback clients was Drew Brees, a future Hall of Famer whose meticulous work ethic aligned perfectly with House's approach. Brees was already one of the NFL's most accurate passers, but he saw House as a way to gain an edge. Using biomechanics and motion analysis, House helped Brees refine his throwing motion, ensuring it was as efficient and repeatable as possible. "Throwing is throwing," House often said, whether it involved a football or a baseball. The principles of sequencing, timing, and functional strength applied just as much on the gridiron as they did on the mound. Brees later credited House with extending his career and keeping him performing at an elite level.

House's work with Drew Brees soon caught the attention of Tom Brady, widely regarded as the greatest quarterback in NFL history. Already deep into his thirties, Brady was obsessed with sustaining his performance and extending his career. House applied his signature slow-motion video analysis to dissect Brady's mechanics, pinpointing subtle inefficiencies and refining his throwing motion for maximum efficiency.

Much like his work with Nolan Ryan years earlier, House also introduced Brady to advanced recovery techniques and functional strength training, ensuring his body could withstand the grind of an NFL season as he aged. For Brady, much like Ryan, the focus was on both outperforming and outlasting the competition. House's methods provided the blueprint to achieve exactly that.

House's work with quarterbacks like Brees and Brady was a holistic approach. He went far beyond fixing their throwing motions. House emphasized mental preparation, arm care, and recovery routines, just as he had with pitchers. By blending science with practical training, he turned two of the NFL's most iconic quarterbacks into even greater versions of themselves. His influence kept Brees and Brady at the top of their game and, more importantly, it fundamentally changed how quarterbacks think about training and preparation, cementing his legacy as a transformative figure across multiple sports.

3

For most of baseball's early years, pitching was an art, not a science. The game favored finesse—deception, movement, and command ruled the day. Velocity? It was an afterthought. There was no radar gun, no way to quantify how fast a pitch was traveling, only the reactions of stunned hitters and the occasional exaggerated newspaper report.

But as competition intensified, a shift began. Power arms started emerging—pitchers who didn't rely on movement or trickery but could flat-out overpower hitters. Batters who had once been comfortable tracking looping curves and well-placed fastballs suddenly found themselves overmatched by an entirely new force—pure speed.

Yet, without a way to measure it, velocity remained a mystery. How fast was a truly great fastball? Were certain pitchers throwing harder than others, or did it just seem that way? Baseball needed a way to measure speed, to put a number on the dominance hitters feared but couldn't quantify.

Walter Johnson, affectionately known as "the Big Train," was baseball's first true power pitcher. Standing six one and blessed with long limbs and a smooth, sidearm delivery, Johnson brought an effortless velocity that was almost mythical in his time. His supremacy on the mound made him the face of a new era, where sheer speed and power could overwhelm hitters in ways they had never experienced before.

Johnson's upbringing reflected the rugged, self-reliant spirit of the early twentieth century. Born in 1887 in Allen County near Humboldt, Kansas, he grew up on a farm, where daily chores built his strength. After drought drove the family off the land, they moved west in 1902 to Olinda, California, an oil boomtown where his father found work with the local oil company. It was there that Johnson first pitched for sandlot and company teams, and quickly gained attention for his blazing fastball. By the time he left for Weiser, Idaho, as a teenager to work at the local telephone company and play semipro ball, word had already begun to spread about his extraordinary talent. When the Washington Senators signed him in 1907, the legend of Walter Johnson was already in motion.[1] Hitters who faced Johnson often described his fastball in reverent tones. Hall of Fame outfielder Ty Cobb famously said, "The first time I faced him, I watched him take that easy windup—and then something went past me that made me flinch. I hardly saw the pitch, but I heard it. That was enough for me."[2]

Eyewitness accounts of Johnson's fastball likened it to a bullet, with the sound of the ball smacking into the catcher's mitt echoing like a gunshot. Even as far back as the early twentieth century, pitchers began to understand the power of velocity in getting hitters out, sparking a growing obsession with speed. That intrigue wasn't just anecdotal—it led to the first real efforts to put numbers behind the myth.

The fascination with Walter Johnson's fastball sparked one of baseball's earliest experiments with technology to measure velocity. Determined to quantify the speed of his heat, baseball turned to cutting-edge tools of the time, setting the stage for the radar guns and precision measurement systems that would reshape the sport decades later.

In 1912, baseball first tried to measure Johnson's legendary heat. At the Remington Arms factory in Bridgeport, Connecticut, Johnson threw his fastball through a two-by-two-foot wooden frame with a series of thin copper wires to trigger the start of a clock, and the clock was stopped fifteen feet later to measure velocity. It measured Walter Johnson's fastball at 122 feet/second, which equates to 83.2 mph. That number sounds low today, but then again this wasn't Statcast. The test measured the ball's velocity after it had slowed down, not at release like modern radar guns. Modern analyses, including those in the documentary *Fastball*, estimate his velocity at around 93.8 mph by extrapolating back to his release point—an impressive figure for an era without formal training, advanced mechanics, or modern conditioning methods.

Johnson's accomplishments were unparalleled. Over his twenty-one-year career with the Senators, he amassed 417 wins (second only to Cy Young), posted a career 2.17 ERA, and recorded an astonishing 110 shutouts—a record that still stands today and likely will never be approached. He led the American League in strikeouts twelve times and became a two-time MVP, cementing his legacy as one of the greatest pitchers in history.

But Johnson's influence went beyond the record books. He changed what a pitcher could be, proving that velocity could dominate a game. Until then, pitching had been more about finesse and placement, with deception as the primary weapon. Johnson upended the paradigm, introducing a new level of intimidation that forced hitters to adapt. His success paved the way for future power pitchers, setting the standard for what an overpowering arm could achieve. Most importantly, for our purposes, the Big Train helped usher scientific measurements into baseball.

♦ ♦ ♦

FOLLOWING IN WALTER Johnson's footsteps, but still well before radar guns and cutting-edge motion tracking, there was Bob Feller—a pitcher so fast he rewrote the way people thought about pitching. "Rapid Robert" was baseball's first true velocity icon, a phenomenon who turned speed into the game's ultimate weapon. His fastball intimidated batters—and ignited a cultural shift, making velocity the obsession it remains today.

Growing up on a farm in Van Meter, Iowa, Feller built his arm strength the old-fashioned way: by throwing. Whether it was hurling baseballs at a barn or "pitching hay," Feller developed the kind of raw power that would leave hitters shaking their heads in disbelief. By the time he debuted with the Cleveland Indians at just seventeen years old, his talents were mythic.

Of course, being the ultimate showman, Feller didn't rest on hitters' statements about his fastball velocity, he wanted to measure it. In 1940, he took his heat on the road—literally—by racing his fastball against a Cleveland police officer on a motorcycle. In a stunt straight out of a comic book, Feller faced off against a bike allegedly traveling 86 mph, as documented by video of the test. The twist? Feller showed up wearing dress shoes and pants, looking more like he was headed to a board meeting than a pitching duel.[3]

As the motorcycle roared alongside him, Feller wound up, rocking back with his trademark leg kick, and unleashed a fastball that reached home plate before the bike crossed the finish line. Some analysts extrapolated the pitch's speed as somewhere between 104 mph and 115 mph, though the test was very far from perfect. Watching the test on video, it's fairly intuitive that the motorcycle likely didn't maintain a constant 86 mph, since anyone riding a motorcycle would almost definitely slow down before driving straight into a target, even a paper one. Still, the spectacle was about the mystique instead of being about pinpoint measurement accuracy. Feller was throwing gas and building a legend.

Bob Feller didn't rest with the motorcycle test—he wanted more scientific proof. In 1946, Feller stepped into the national spotlight for another one of baseball's first attempts to measure velocity. Partnering with the U.S. Army (because, of course, his fastball deserved military-grade testing), he threw through a device known as a Lumiline Chronograph, which was designed to test the velocity of shells during World War II using photoelectric cells.[4] The verdict was a blistering 98.6 mph—a number that instantly became part of baseball lore.

But here's what's even more impressive: That velocity was measured as the ball crossed the plate, not at release like modern radar guns. By the time it reached home, the pitch had already lost several mph. Experts estimate that if measured at release, Feller's fastball might have clocked closer to 105 mph. Of course, the accuracy of the test is debatable—to me, it's more likely the pitch was in the mid-90s (based on comparisons of video of Feller's pitch side by side with video of today's hard-throwing pitchers with known radar gun velocity readings). Since this technology was designed for artillery and was untested as a baseball tool, no one really knows how accurately it was calibrated or how reliable the readings were when placed on a field to measure a pitch rather than a shell. But the result was a statement. Speed mattered, and Feller's fastball was totally changing the limits of what a pitcher could achieve.

♦ ♦ ♦

JOHNSON AND FELLER flipped the script, making speed the new gold standard and using the best technology of the day to test it. Suddenly, pitchers weren't there to set the table for the hitters—they were the main course. Johnson's and Feller's dominance set the template for what power pitching could be, inspiring generations of flamethrowers. Pitchers had the need for speed!

Of course, velocity alone isn't enough—a lesson made painfully clear by the story of Steve Dalkowski. While Johnson and Feller paired their velocity with command, Dalkowski became a cautionary tale of what happens when sheer power lacks even a shred of control. A lefty with an arm so electric it made hitters in the on-deck circle uneasy, Dalkowski's fastball is the stuff of legend. But when it came time to measure that legendary velocity, things went hilariously off the rails. In 1958, the Baltimore Orioles hauled him out to the Aberdeen Proving Ground, a military facility in Maryland, to clock his speed using cutting-edge radar tech.[5] Spoiler alert: the experiment didn't go quite as planned, but it only added to the myth.

First, let's talk about the conditions around the test. Dalkowski had pitched a full game the day before, so his arm was already toast. To make matters worse, they had him throw from flat ground instead of a mound—a setup that no pitcher would ever call ideal. And then there was the radar device itself, which required him to throw through a tiny target zone for the speed to register. For Dalkowski, one of the wildest arms in baseball history, this was like asking a tornado to follow a straight line. It reportedly took him forty minutes just to get enough pitches into the zone for the radar to even work.

When they finally got a reading, his fastball clocked in at 93.5 mph. Sounds solid, right? However, remember that number was measured at the plate, not at release, unlike modern radar guns. By today's standards, accounting for drag and distance, Dalkowski's fastball would have topped 100 mph, even with his arm already gassed. And if he'd been fresh, pitching off a mound, with modern tools measuring his velocity? The numbers might have melted radar screens. But yet again, since this was not modern radar gun technology and these tests were still not common to determine the velocity of pitches, you may need to take these numbers with a healthy grain of salt since there's little known about the accuracy of these tests. There's no doubt though, that Dalkowski likely threw flames, since in one season he struck out an impressive 17.6 batters per nine innings!

Hall of Famers who faced him didn't need technology to confirm what their eyes—and nerves—already knew. Ted Williams famously said Dalkowski's fastball "made my eyes water," and Cal Ripken Sr. called it "faster than anything we'd ever seen."[6] Hitters were both scared of the speed and terrified of where the ball might go! Dalkowski's lack of command was comically bad. During his minor league career, he once averaged an eye-popping 20.4 walks per nine innings in his worst season, and his best wasn't much better at 6.0. More than missing the strike zone; he often missed the catcher entirely.

Stories of Dalkowski's wildness are the stuff of baseball lore. In one game, he hit an umpire in the mask so hard it knocked the mask clean off and sent the ump stumbling backward. In another infamous incident, he hit a batter so hard it reportedly tore off the guy's earlobe. For hitters, stepping into the box against him was a gamble. You might strike out, you might walk, or you might get drilled. The only certainty? It was going to be a hair-raising experience.

Dalkowski's control issues kept him from ever making it to the majors, despite his once-in-a-lifetime arm. Coaches knew that if he ever figured out how to harness his heat, he'd be unhittable. But that day never came. His career ERA of 5.57 reflected how his walks often outnumbered his strikeouts, and his story became one of baseball's greatest what-ifs.

The Aberdeen velocity test, flawed as it may have been, never captured the full extent of Dalkowski's heat—but it didn't need to. His legend isn't about precise numbers; it's about the stories. It's about the guy who may have thrown harder than anyone, but couldn't always find the plate. It's about a pitch that blurred past hitters and a wildness that made every at-bat an adventure. Dalkowski threw gas, fear, chaos, and wonder, all in one motion. Even if the radar couldn't fully measure it, everyone who stepped into the box against him already knew: The "Steve Dalkowski Experience" was terrifying. Imagine the velocity numbers Dalkowski could have put up with today's radar guns, since it wouldn't require the "Wild Thing" to throw his pitches through a tiny target zone!

But in the end, his story is the ultimate reminder: Velocity without command might impress, but it won't last. To be truly unhittable, a pitcher needs more than just heat. He needs to know where it's going.

Growing up, Ben Brewster was an average baseball player until high school, when his lack of velocity and inconsistent mechanics became glaringly apparent against more advanced competition.

Determined to improve, Brewster embarked on a single-minded quest to develop his skills, relying largely on trial and error. Without access to formal instruction or advanced training programs, he immersed himself in niche forums like Let's Talk Pitching, where he learned from pioneers like Paul Nyman. At that time, the forum was the Wild West of pitching, where ideas were like gunslingers and only the best stayed standing.

This formative experience led Ben Brewster to create Tread Athletics, which he describes as "everything I wish I had at fifteen years old." To bring his vision to life, he partnered with Coan McAlpine, a like-minded former pitcher who had been training pitchers for over a decade. A high school All-American, McAlpine, like Brewster, battled adversity and injuries, fueling their shared belief that there had to be a better way to develop pitchers. They weren't interested in simply passing down what they had been taught. They wanted to push beyond it.

Brewster's and McAlpine's own experiences—marked by setbacks, relentless experimentation, and hard-earned breakthroughs—shaped their belief that the right guidance at the right time can change a player's career. Brewster himself is proof: Over the course of a decade, he added an astonishing 25 mph to his fastball, climbing from a high school pitcher barely touching 73 mph to a pro throwing in the mid-to-upper 90s.

Much of Brewster's development unfolded publicly on the Let's Talk Pitching message board, where he chronicled his progress and setbacks in a thread by Lanky Lefty (Ben's handle) titled "Till I Collapse." This public chronicle served as both an accountability tool and a proving ground for his ideas. He shared detailed accounts of mechanical changes, strength training routines, and pitching experiments, inviting feedback from a mix of contributors. The community, which included insights from data-driven innovators like Nyman and Driveline Baseball's Kyle Boddy, became a sounding board for refining his approach. This process of public experimentation resonates in Tread Athletics' philosophy today: demystifying the complexities of pitching and empowering athletes with tools Brewster wished he'd had during his own development.

On the Let's Talk Pitching message board, Paul Nyman frequently criticized Brewster's mechanics, insisting he would never become a hard thrower. But instead of discouraging him, the criticism became fuel. As Kyle Boddy recalls, "Paul Nyman was always quick to dismiss Ben Brewster, yet it was through that very criticism that Ben found his drive. Instead of being disheartened, he took it as a challenge, and look where it led him."

Rather than getting drawn into message board debates or letting detractors discourage him, Brewster stayed laser-focused, channeling his energy into an obsessive pursuit of improvement and the "truth" about pitching mechanics. In the end, arguing was pointless. Progress was what mattered.

The transparency of Brewster's journey also underscores the transformative power of social media in pitching development. Platforms like Let's Talk Pitching democratized information, enabling aspiring pitchers, coaches, and innovators to exchange ideas and debate techniques outside traditional coaching circles. Brewster's willingness to document his evolution inspired others and laid the groundwork for today's social media–driven training revolution, where platforms like

YouTube, Instagram, and Twitter/X amplify philosophies and connect players with industry leaders like Tread Athletics.

For countless pitchers, geography, cost, and time constraints made elite training feel out of reach. Those who didn't live near a major facility were often left with limited options, relying on local coaches who lacked access to the latest advancements in velocity training, biomechanics, and strength conditioning. Without motion analysis, data-driven programming, or customized mechanics adjustments, many pitchers hit a developmental ceiling; not because of talent, but because they simply didn't have access to the right resources.

That's where Tread Athletics stepped in.

♦ ♦ ♦

WITH JUST A handful of clients—most of them remote—Tread relied on personalized training plans and video analysis to deliver results.

Reflecting on those early days, Brewster recalls, "We were figuring out how to deliver value to athletes who didn't have access to the resources I wish I'd had growing up." Early successes, including players like my son Jack, who was one of their first remote clients, validated their approach and set the stage for Tread's rapid growth. Unlike many in the industry, they didn't even have their own facility at first, instead operating out of a borrowed space in Simpsonville, South Carolina.

In 2015, Tread Athletics published *Building the 95 MPH Body*, a step-by-step guide to one of modern baseball's ultimate milestones—overpowering velocity. It served as a blueprint to throw gas, blending biomechanics, strength training, and science-backed methods to help athletes maximize their potential and break the 95 mph barrier.

With a foreword by Kyle Boddy (Driveline Baseball) and acknowledgments to Eric Cressey and Paul Nyman, the book reflected the core principles of modern pitching development—many of which are explored throughout this book.

More importantly, the book reinforced that elite velocity comes from building a powerful body—not just perfecting mechanics. Most old-school pitching guides were cookbooks of scattered recipes, focused only on mechanics, grips, or strategy. *Building the 95 MPH Body* was the chef's manual, teaching pitchers how to stock the pantry, fire up the stove, and create a body capable of cooking with upper-90s gas.

It broke down the key components of physical development, covering the following:

Strength, Mobility & Conditioning: The foundation for sustainable velocity gains.

Rotational Power & Explosiveness: How to transfer raw strength into on-field performance.

Core Stability: A critical element in maximizing efficiency and repeatability.

Recognizing that no two pitchers are alike, the guide provided customizable programming based on body type, experience level, and specific needs. Whether an athlete needed to add muscle, improve mobility, or enhance explosiveness, *Building the 95 MPH Body* delivered targeted solutions.

The book backed up its theories with real-world data. Integrating speed-strength training, plyometrics, and progressive overload, it helped pitchers break through velocity plateaus. These principles were reinforced with case studies, player data, and Tread Athletics' experience working with hundreds of clients, making the guide both practical and effective.

Beyond being a playbook for developing the next generation of unhittable flamethrowers, the book also served as a bold introduction to Tread's philosophy—a way to showcase its training methods to the wider pitching world.

♦ ♦ ♦

AS DEMAND SURGED, Tread Athletics grew from a two-man operation focusing on remote training into a fully staffed enterprise, complete with specialized coaches, mobility experts, and performance analysts. Leveraging technology like motion capture, biomechanics analysis, and detailed data tracking, Tread scaled its remote coaching model without sacrificing its commitment to individualized development.

In the early days of their expansion, Brewster and McAlpine visited my home in Atlanta to discuss the possibility of opening a facility there. Sitting in my basement, we talked about their ambitious vision for the future of Tread and how they could better serve their growing client base. Their passion for revolutionizing pitching development was undeniable. I offered Brewster some advice, suggesting he might need to set aside his personal dream of pitching in the majors to focus fully on building Tread into the premier player development organization it had the potential to become. But at that moment, Brewster wasn't ready to let go of his dream. His competitive fire still burned brightly.

Ultimately, Tread Athletics didn't expand to Atlanta. Instead, Brewster and McAlpine established a small five-thousand-square-foot facility in Fort Mill, South Carolina, providing in-person training while scaling their operations. This move set the stage for their eventual transition to a state-of-the-art training center in Charlotte, North Carolina, in 2020. The Charlotte facility became the cornerstone of Tread's mission, equipped with the latest modern technology to deliver personalized coaching to athletes at every level.

Years of incessant effort took their toll on Brewster's body, forcing him to step away from his dream of pitching in the majors. After two elbow surgeries and three hip surgeries, he made the difficult decision to focus entirely on Tread Athletics. Yet, even now, Brewster will admit with a wry smile, "Somewhere in my heart, I'd still rather be pitching in the majors than running Tread Athletics."

This personal struggle became a driving force behind Tread's mission. Brewster often reflects, "While my own playing career has been defined by injuries, these struggles give me a crystal-clear perspective that this company isn't just about building superior athletes—it's about fighting toward a shared dream." For Brewster, that dream takes many forms: making a high school roster, earning a college scholarship, signing a pro contract, or debuting in the big leagues. His setbacks mirrored the challenges athletes face and strengthened his resolve to provide the guidance he never had.

Today, Tread Athletics operates out of a sprawling facility spanning tens of thousands of square feet, equipped with millions of dollars' worth of cutting-edge technology. Motion capture systems, force plates, and high-tech video analysis tools provide precise biomechanical assessments, while proprietary software and analytics platforms deliver hyper-personalized coaching for athletes at every level—from high school prospects to MLB stars.

Insights gained from in-person training have further refined Tread's remote coaching methods, creating a seamless integration between hands-on instruction and online development. It's a remarkable evolution from the borrowed facility in Simpsonville.

Despite its rapid growth and global clientele, Tread Athletics remains true to its founding principles: customization, individualization, and an unrelenting focus on unlocking each athlete's potential.

♦ ♦ ♦

COLE RAGANS'S REMARKABLE transformation with Tread Athletics exemplifies the impact of a tailored, science-driven approach to player development. His journey began with a full-body assessment conducted remotely by Tread, where their team analyzed video of his movements to identify inefficiencies.

Reflecting on the process, Ragans said, "They watched my outings from the season, they had me send over video. Then, they gave me all of these mobility assessments to identify the areas where I was inefficient." This deep analysis revealed key areas to address, setting the foundation for his improvement. "They saw how my body moves: hips, ankles, (thoracic) spine, all that kind of stuff. They broke it down and gave me all these exercises that would essentially loosen the things that needed to be loosened up and get things moving how they should be moving. My body is just moving better," Ragans explained.

The plan Tread Athletics created for Ragans focused on movement prep, targeted mobility exercises, and strength training customized to his unique needs. Ragans embraced the program wholeheartedly, saying, "They give me my movement prep, they give me my workouts, and from the moment I started doing it, I told myself, if I'm going to spend the money on this, I'm going to buy in completely with it. I'm going to do every little thing to a tee. And it's obviously helped out tremendously." This disciplined mindset highlighted his commitment to maximizing the program's benefits, a decision that paid off in remarkable ways.

This meticulous approach yielded extraordinary results. Ragans's fastball velocity surged from an average of 92 mph to 96.7 mph, with peaks reaching an electric 101 mph. Beyond velocity, Tread's program enhanced Ragans's efficiency and durability, giving him the tools to maximize his potential while maintaining his health. The transformation didn't go unnoticed, as Ragans earned a spot on the 2024 MLB All-Star Roster and solidified his status as one of the game's most exciting rising talents. Summing up the experience, Ragans shared, "I honestly don't know where I'd be if I hadn't signed up with Tread."

◆ ◆ ◆

CLAY HOLMES'S STEADY improvements with Tread Athletics shows the power of its personalized, data-driven training. When Holmes first reached out to Tread in 2020, he was struggling with a 5.91 career ERA and a -0.9 WAR (wins above replacement), as he was unable to find consistency in his performance. Despite his raw talent, Holmes needed a structured plan to unlock his potential and take his game to the next level.

Tread Athletics designed a comprehensive program tailored to Holmes's needs, focusing on refining his mechanics, improving his movement efficiency, and optimizing his pitch arsenal. Through biomechanical analysis, mobility work, and strength training, Holmes then began to fix inefficiencies in his delivery while improving his ability to generate consistent velocity and sharp movement on his pitches.

The results were outstanding. Holmes transitioned from a struggling pitcher to a two-time MLB All-Star with over +5 WAR since joining Tread. Holmes has since returned to a starting role with the New York Mets, adding a new weapon to his arsenal—a kick change, developed with input from Tread. This unique spiked changeup generates significant drop without relying on pronation (i.e., rotating the palm downward/twisting the hand toward the thumb), which is the primary mechanism behind a traditional circle changeup's arm-side movement and drop.

For pitchers like Holmes, who struggle with pronation—the way the forearm rotates inward at the end of the pitching motion—the kick change offers another way to create the desired movement. Instead of relying on wrist action, the pitch achieves negative vertical break (drop) through seam orientation at release, with the spiked grip (using one finger bent like on a knuckleball or knuckle curve) naturally positioning it for optimal movement.

Since his turbo sinker already had heavy downward movement, his changeup needed to create a distinct movement profile rather than blending into his existing arsenal. Brewster noted that the kick change's movement perfectly aligned with Holmes's strengths, giving him a true velocity differential and a deceptive look against hitters.

Early signs suggest the pitch is dropping sharply, making it a nightmare for hitters and a key weapon in Holmes's arsenal—this pitch had one of the lowest slugging percentages against it of any changeup in MLB in 2025. Like most successful innovations, the kick change is quickly spreading across the league, becoming a go-to pitch for those who struggle with pronation and an essential tool in modern pitch design.

Tread Athletics has firmly established itself as a powerhouse in modern baseball development, with a track record that speaks for itself. From transforming players like Cole Ragans, Clay Holmes, and Mitch Keller into MLB All-Stars to working with flame-throwing relievers like Josh Hader and Tanner Scott, as well as veterans like Jameson Taillon, Tread's impact spans every level of the game. With over 750 athletes guided to college baseball commitments, more than 250 players drafted or signed by MLB organizations, and twenty-five MLB debuts, Tread's influence is nearly unmatched. By combining cutting-edge science and individualized coaching, Tread Athletics continues to redefine what's possible for pitchers chasing greatness.

The rise of third-party facilities like Driveline Baseball (discussed in detail later) and Tread Athletics forever changed pitching development, equipping athletes with scientific tools, data, and techniques once unheard of in traditional baseball circles. These organizations reshaped how pitchers trained, proving that technology and biomechanical insights could create truly unhittable pitchers.

Now all they have to do is stay healthy.

5

In the beginning, baseball was without form. Its shape was chaos. The ball varied in size and weight, a creation of whim and happenstance. The game moved upon fields untamed by science, and there were no stats to measure its glory or numbers to quantify its truths.

One of my favorite early memories of baseball was a childhood trip to Cooperstown to visit the National Baseball Hall of Fame. Wandering through the exhibits, I was captivated by the old black-and-white videos and photographs of the game in its infancy. The players, dressed in baggy uniforms and stiff caps, seemed almost timeless. The game itself looked so simple, so pure—almost like the pickup games I played in my backyard.

Baseball in the mid-nineteenth century was a game of raw instinct, unstructured rules, and chaotic improvisation. Imagine stepping onto a baseball field in the 1860s: The ground is uneven, the bases staked roughly into dirt, and the "pitcher's mound" is nothing more than a flat strip of earth. The ball in the pitcher's hand is handmade, its seams uneven and weight inconsistent. Gloves are optional, little more than padded leather for those who choose to wear them.

This was baseball in its infancy—a game stripped to its simplest form. Pitchers lobbed the ball underhand, their goal was not to overpower hitters but to serve up a hittable pitch.

That's right: According to **Rule 9 of the Knickerbocker Rules**—the foundation of modern baseball—the ball was to be "pitched, not thrown, for the bat." In the earliest days of the game, pitchers were expected to be hittable.[1]

Overhand pitching? That wouldn't come for nearly forty years. Back then, hitters took pride in their ability to make contact and put the ball in play. It wasn't about strikeouts or launch angles; it was about skill, precision, and a sense of fair play that reflected the game's priorities. Pitchers were more like stagehands than stars, tossing pitches to set the stage for the action rather than stealing the spotlight.

The idea of blowing hitters away with blazing fastballs or deceptive movement would've been seen as unsportsmanlike, a violation of baseball's earliest spirit. Back then, pitchers weren't there to blow hitters away. They were there to play a supporting role, offering the hitters a chance to shine.

The players of this era embodied baseball's scrappy working-class roots. They were sons of blue-collar families, many with little formal education, who brought grit and toughness to the diamond rather than polished technique or refined strategy. For them, each game was a fight, a test of heart and willpower played out under the sun.

Training regimens were as rough and unstructured as the fields they played on. Talk of "scientific approaches" or measurable outcomes would've been laughed off, seen as distractions from the real work of competing. Adjustments? Those were made on instinct, not data. These players relied on what they could see, feel, and hear in the moment—the crack of the bat, the snap of the ball into a glove—playing with a rawness that defined the era.

Even in the early to mid-1900s, weight lifting was widely believed to make athletes "muscle-bound" and inflexible, leading coaches to discourage it.[2] This perspective was so prevalent that some coaches forbade their athletes from even touching weights, fearing it would hinder their performance.

Instead, emphasis was placed on "farm strength," a term that referred to the natural durability and toughness developed through manual labor and daily physical tasks. This approach valued the rugged, all-purpose strength seen in individuals with farming backgrounds, who often exhibited exceptional endurance and resilience.

Baseball's old-school mentality clung to the belief that raw natural strength was king, and structured training programs or scientific methods were distractions at best, harmful at worst. This philosophy shaped the game for decades. Take Walter Johnson, one of the greatest pitchers of all time—he didn't rely on fancy training regimens. His strength was forged on the farm, doing chores like pitching hay and chopping wood, and in the oil fields. Pure grit. Pure simplicity.

♦ ♦ ♦

AN EARLY ECCENTRIC pitcher who typified the time was Rube Waddell. Waddell was far more than a pitcher—he was a spectacle. In an era when pitchers were often raw, unpolished talents who relied more on brute force than strategy, Waddell stood out as the archetype of the early fireballer. He threw hard—really hard—and for a time, that was all he needed. With a fastball that overwhelmed hitters and a curveball that buckled knees, Waddell became one of baseball's first true stars. But for all his talent, Rube was just as famous for his quirks as he was for his strikeouts.

Waddell's eccentricities were the stuff of legend. He once reportedly left the mound mid-game to chase a fire truck barreling past the ballpark, leaving his manager and teammates dumbfounded. Stories about his short attention span were endless: Opposing teams were said to distract him by waving shiny objects or releasing puppies near the field. And it worked—Waddell would abandon his focus to play with the dogs or investigate whatever had caught his eye. It was this mix of brilliance and unpredictability that made him both a fan favorite and a manager's nightmare.[3]

On the field, Waddell was electrifying, leading the league in strikeouts for six straight seasons from 1902 to 1907. Off the field, he lived like a kid in a candy store, never taking the game—or life—too seriously. While his antics could be frustrating, they were also emblematic of the time. Pitchers like Waddell were celebrated for their natural gifts, with little emphasis placed on discipline, mechanics, or strategy. Baseball in those days was more about entertainment than precision, and Rube Waddell delivered plenty of both.

It's almost impossible to picture Rube Waddell sitting through a lecture on pitch design or diving into the finer points of optimal mechanics without bolting halfway through to pet a puppy or chase down a firetruck. The guy had an arm that could light up a radar gun—if radar guns existed back then—but the patience for science? Forget it.

Waddell's brilliance on the mound came from raw, untamed talent, not from studying spin rates or biomechanics. No one asked him about his workout routine.

He was the ultimate early era fireballer: pure chaos, unfiltered, and completely unpredictable. Waddell's natural gifts made him a star in his time, but in today's game, raw talent alone might not get you past Triple-A. The sport has evolved, and so have its pitchers—raw ability is no longer enough; precision, strategy, and science now rule the mound.

Even by the 1930s, Bob Feller carried this mindset forward. Growing up on a farm, Feller swore that "pitching hay" was what helped him "pitch baseballs." Sure, he dabbled in weight training, but heavy lifting? Nope. Like most players of his time, as discussed earlier, he feared becoming "muscle-bound" and losing the fluid motion needed to be at his best on the mound. Instead, Feller focused on light weights, chasing what he called "long, lean muscles" that kept his pitching mechanics smooth and explosive.[4]

This was the culture: grit over gadgets, instinct over innovation. It wasn't about data or cutting-edge training; it was about finding strength in what you had around you, whether it was a pile of hay or a stack of firewood. That mindset dominated baseball for decades, until a new generation began asking: What if there's a smarter way?

Obviously, even in this unstructured world, competition made change inevitable. While baseball in its early days lacked formalized training or scientific insights, creativity and curiosity thrived. The first great pitching revolution didn't emerge from labs or algorithms but from instinct, trial, and error—qualities that defined the spirit of the game.

This spirit came to life through moments of individual brilliance, like Hall of Famer Candy Cummings, a teenage boy on a Brooklyn beach experimenting with a way to make the ball curve mid-flight after seeing the way clamshells curved when he tossed them.

These trailblazers began to rewrite the trajectory of the game, turning a casual pastime into a game of strategy, precision, and endless innovation. While diving into the full roster of early pioneers behind data—technology, pitch design, and velocity would take a book of its own—it's impossible to tell the story of the modern game without tipping the cap to some of the legends who laid the foundation.

♦ ♦ ♦

BASEBALL, FOR MUCH of its early history, clung to its traditions with a white-knuckled grip, dismissing anything that felt too "academic" or removed from the game's gritty, instinct-driven roots. If Feller's and Ryan's fastballs were a window into the possibilities of measurement, the rest of the sport was still opposed to using technology to improve baseball, muttering, "We don't need all that math and science nonsense to make players better."

This aversion to science was practically institutional. Baseball stuck with its timeworn regimen: running poles—the near-universally-hated training method where coaches force pitchers to run foul pole to foul pole—along with throwing and shagging flies, was the extent of most pitchers' conditioning. The idea of a structured training program? That was practically sacrilegious.

Even as statistics like batting average and ERA gained acceptance, anything beyond those basic stats was met with skepticism. Managers and players often dismissed deeper data as "abstract nonsense." They believed that baseball was meant to be played and understood through gut instinct, not numbers. If you couldn't see it with your own eyes or feel it in your bones, it wasn't real.

Recognizing the lack of structure, Branch Rickey saw an opportunity to turn player development and the use of data into a competitive advantage.

Branch Rickey, baseball's ultimate maverick, saw the game's unstructured training environment as an opportunity to outsmart the competition. Best known for breaking the color barrier by signing Jackie Robinson, Rickey was also a trailblazer in baseball analytics. In the 1930s and '40s, while most of baseball was stuck in its old ways, Rickey was building what would become the blueprint for modern front offices. As the general manager for the St. Louis Cardinals and later the Brooklyn Dodgers, Rickey hired statisticians to track player performance. Long before anyone had heard of WAR or OPS+, Rickey was pioneering the use of on-base percentage to find hidden gems in the talent pool.[5]

Rickey's methods were a shock to baseball's system. Traditionalists scoffed at the idea that numbers could replace instinct. One old-school coach reportedly quipped, "A slide rule can't tell you if a kid has the guts to play in the big leagues."

But Rickey didn't care about the pushback. He knew that combining observation with data would give his teams a competitive edge. His work laid the foundation for the analytics revolution that would reshape baseball decades later, culminating in concepts later documented in Michael Lewis's *Moneyball* and the rise of sabermetrics.

Rickey proved that science and tradition didn't have to be enemies—they could coexist, even thrive, when balanced correctly. It took time for the rest of the sport to catch on, but Rickey's vision of merging intuition with analysis marked a turning point. The baseball world would never be the same.

So while Walter Johnson, Bob Feller, and Nolan Ryan showed the power of measurement, it was Branch Rickey who brought science into the dugout, proving that numbers could win games—even if it took the rest of baseball a while to believe it.

While most teams treated spring training as a time for players to shake off the rust, Rickey transformed it into a laboratory for teaching and refining skills, including for pitchers. One of his most innovative contributions was the introduction of command training, a concept that was ahead of its time. Recognizing that control was as important as velocity or movement, Rickey devised a simple yet effective technique to help pitchers improve their accuracy: hanging strings across the strike zone.

These strings, set at different heights to mimic the top and bottom edges of the strike zone, gave pitchers a visual target to aim for. Rickey encouraged his pitchers to focus on hitting specific spots, helping them develop pinpoint control. This was especially useful for younger or less experienced pitchers who struggled with consistency. The drills emphasized locating pitches in ways that would challenge hitters, setting the foundation for modern approaches to command training.[6]

Rickey didn't limit himself to strings. He viewed spring training as a time for rigorous evaluation and individualized instruction, tailoring drills to each pitcher's strengths and weaknesses. Under Rickey's direction, the Dodgers turned spring training into a high-intensity period of preparation, blending physical conditioning with strategic lessons on pitching statistics, game management, and mechanics. His emphasis on structured, purposeful training soon caught on, with other major league teams adopting similar methods to maximize the potential of their pitching staffs.

By emphasizing command, visualization, and preparation, Rickey reshaped how pitchers were developed and evaluated. His approach raised the bar for how the game was coached and prepared, leaving a legacy that continues to influence baseball training today.

Despite Branch Rickey's early innovations, pitcher training remained stuck in the past. Since baseball's inception, the old guard viewed strength training as a reckless gamble—one that could ruin a pitcher's career rather than extend it. The belief was simple: Lifting weights would make pitchers overly muscular, reduce flexibility, and throw off their mechanics. Instead of building strength, they were told to stick to light exercise, run, and simply "throw more" to build endurance.

♦ ♦ ♦

THIS OUTDATED MINDSET trapped pitchers in a cycle of limitations. Velocity wasn't something you could develop—it was something you were either born with or without. If a pitcher lacked elite velocity, he was expected to rely on deception, movement, or pinpoint command. Meanwhile, injuries piled up, yet few dared to challenge the idea that getting stronger could actually make a pitcher more durable.

Then came Tom Seaver and Nolan Ryan, determined to chip away at those myths and help pave the way for what would eventually spark a strength training revolution.

For Tom Seaver, dominance on the mound was more than using your natural talent—it was about finding a better way to sustain excellence over the long haul. The traditional belief was that pitchers should avoid strength training, fearing it could hurt their mechanics or lead to injury. But Seaver saw a flaw in that logic. If a pitcher's power came from their lower half, why wouldn't building leg strength make them better?

His answer? Drop-and-drive mechanics powered by explosive lower-body strength.

"I drive with my legs; that's the secret to my power," Seaver often said, making it clear that his workouts weren't just a supplement to his game—they were the foundation of it. Instead of avoiding weight training, Seaver leaned into it. He built a training routine focused on leg strength, core stability, and durability, challenging conventional wisdom at a time when most pitchers relied solely on running and long toss for conditioning.

"I knew a lot of people in the sport felt weight lifting hurt pitchers," Seaver once admitted. "But it seemed logical that it would help me, and it still does, so I did it."[7]

The results? Hall of Fame numbers and a level of durability few could match.

Over a twenty-year career, Seaver pitched in over six hundred games, and while others faded late in the season—or even late in games—he stayed sharp. His conditioning not only kept him healthy but allowed him to maintain velocity and command deep into games.

Seaver's success changed how other pitchers prepared. The weight lifting, strength-focused training programs you see pitchers grinding through today? They owe a lot to "Tom Terrific," the pitcher who proved that leg strength, work ethic, and a problem-solving mindset were just as important as a killer slider.

If Tom Seaver laid the foundation, Nolan Ryan built an entire skyscraper. Ryan, who was Seaver's teammate during their time with the New York Mets and looked up to Seaver, took strength training to another level. Early in his career, Ryan stumbled upon a weight room in Anaheim and decided to give it a try. The baseball world might've called him crazy, but Ryan trusted his instincts. "I started slipping in there and working out, being careful not to overdo it and letting my body tell me how it was responding," he later said.[8]

Ryan's approach to training was unorthodox, especially for pitchers in his era. He dedicated up to five hours a day, six days a week, to conditioning, even well into his forties. Rather than lifting weights aimlessly, he carefully structured a program that combined strength training, running, and stretching to enhance stamina and maintain precise mechanics—even when unleashing 100 mph fastballs late in games. His approach centered on two key goals: gaining an immediate edge on the mound and building long-term durability. Ryan conditioned his body to withstand the demands of a twenty-seven-year career, following a regimen designed for both longevity and sustained peak performance.

The payoff? Ryan did more than defy Father Time—he embarrassed him. His velocity famously didn't drop as games wore on; if anything, it seemed to increase in the later innings. Ryan himself credited his strength training for his durability and recovery. "There's no way I could have recovered quickly or been as durable without a firm base of strength from lifting," he said.[9]

Ryan's work ethic and results went beyond extending his own career; they set a new standard for the entire game. Alongside Seaver, he proved that the weight room could be an integral part of being a dominant pitcher. Today's flamethrowers grinding out dead lifts and med ball slams in the gym are standing on the shoulders of giants like Seaver and Ryan. These two reimagined what it meant to be a pitcher, showing that strength training wasn't a threat to the craft; it was its future.

Seaver and Ryan might've been ahead of their time, but let's be honest—their training wasn't exactly backed by science. It was all about feel, instinct, and straight-up trial and error. Seaver focused on building leg strength because he felt it would work for his explosive delivery, and Ryan hit the weights because he believed it would keep him throwing gas. They didn't have biomechanics labs or spreadsheets breaking down efficiency. They trusted what felt right and kept experimenting until they saw results. It came down to determination, relentless work, sharp logic, a refusal to follow tradition blindly, and an unyielding drive to improve.

What makes their methods even more impressive is that they were figuring this out on the fly. They proved that strength and conditioning could completely change the game for pitchers, even without scientific tools or analytics. But while they opened the door, their approaches weren't dialed in the way we see today.

Obviously, in pitching, the emphasis on velocity was undeniable. Harder-throwing pitchers gave hitters less time to react, tilting the balance of power firmly in favor of the pitcher. As velocity increased, so did effectiveness, pushing pitchers to unprecedented levels of "unhittability."

However, this newfound dominance came with an unfortunate cost. The endless pursuit of velocity led to a surge in pitching injuries, as pitchers "red-lined" their bodies striving to eke every last ounce of velocity out of themselves, raising concerns about the sustainability of these developments.

To protect their investments—players commanding multimillion-dollar contracts—teams began using biomechanics to identify and reduce injury risks. The result was a dual focus: making pitches tougher to hit while also ensuring that pitchers could stay healthy enough to contribute over the long term.

The Los Angeles Dodgers' commitment to progress has translated directly to success on the field, with the team capturing World Series titles in 2020 and 2024. Their ability to stay ahead of the competition stems from a forward-thinking approach that leverages biomechanics, advanced analytics, and cutting-edge technology to optimize player development. While many teams across Major League Baseball have made strides in these areas, the Dodgers stand out for their early adoption of these methods and their relentless pursuit of progress.

As one of the wealthiest franchises in Major League Baseball, the Dodgers have long been synonymous with innovation. From Branch Rickey's revolutionary farm system to breaking the color barrier with Jackie Robinson, the Dodgers have consistently sought ways to stay ahead of the competition. True to this legacy, the team has embraced biomechanics, advanced technology, and data-driven strategies to improve performance and minimize injury risks, ensuring their multimillion-dollar investments can deliver on the field for years to come.

Jimmy Buffi stepped into this rapidly evolving landscape through an unconventional yet highly relevant path. With a background in aerospace and mechanical engineering from Notre Dame and a PhD in biomechanics from Northwestern University, Buffi brought an interdisciplinary approach to pitching development. Initially focused on prosthetics and computational modeling of the human forearm, he had a breakthrough during his doctoral studies: He realized the simulation techniques he used for prosthetics could be applied to how forearm muscles protect the UCL (ulnar collateral ligament) during pitching. This insight set the stage for his entry into baseball.

Buffi's groundbreaking research caught the attention of Kyle Boddy, founder of Driveline Baseball. Writing for Driveline's blog, Buffi shared insights into how muscles influence elbow stress and gained visibility in the baseball world. This exposure eventually led to his recruitment by the Dodgers in 2015, where he joined an R&D team assembled by Andrew Friedman, the Dodgers' President of Baseball Operations, and Doug Fearing, Director of Research and Development. Friedman, known for his analytical and innovative approach, prioritized hiring experts from nontraditional baseball backgrounds. Fearing's vision for a collaborative "baseball think tank" created an environment where Buffi and his colleagues could integrate biomechanics and data seamlessly into player development.

At the Dodgers, Buffi's role evolved. While his initial focus was on injury prevention, he soon shifted toward optimizing pitching mechanics to improve efficiency and performance. This pivot was driven by the inherent challenges of injury analysis. "The injury data, even within pro teams, is not great," Buffi explained, highlighting the difficulty of drawing actionable conclusions. He elaborated on the challenge of balancing performance and injury prevention with an example: "Let's say someone like Kershaw in his prime pops out as having a 1 percent more risk of injury. Are you really going to have him pitch less because of that small increase?"

These limitations underscored why injury analysis remained an imprecise science, prompting Buffi to prioritize pitching mechanics efficiency. By focusing on aligning movements to optimize energy transfer, Buffi sought to enhance performance while indirectly reducing stress on vulnerable areas, offering a more practical approach to balancing risk and reward.

Buffi's work also delved into the theoretical limits of pitching velocity. Using simulations, he explored the maximum potential speed a pitcher could achieve with perfect mechanics and energy transfer, estimating a staggering 125 mph under ideal conditions. However, Buffi acknowledged that this number required several unrealistic assumptions, such as perfect muscle efficiency and the absence of physical limitations. "If we can get perfect energy transfer efficiency, which is super questionable, it just might be too much for actual human ligaments to withstand," he explained. Buffi tempered expectations by adding, "Do I think pitchers are going to throw 125 miles an hour? Probably not, probably not in my lifetime."

One of Buffi's most significant contributions was his efforts implementing motion capture systems like Kinatrax at Dodger Stadium. This technology allowed the team to analyze pitcher biomechanics with unprecedented precision. Although it took years to fully integrate, the system set the path for advancements in pitch design and workload management. In the interim, Buffi used his expertise in aerodynamics and spin dynamics to refine pitch strategies. "It was just awesome analyzing how pitchers were spinning the ball . . . and using that data to figure out what type of fastball or slider they should throw," he explained.

The Dodgers' collaborative environment further amplified Buffi's impact. He worked closely with progressive pitching coordinators like Chris Fetter—now the Detroit Tigers' pitching coach—who embraced Buffi's insights and integrated them into on-field training. Buffi described this era as unique, noting how "pitching coordinators and R&D people hung out and talked about data," fostering a culture of innovation that bridged the gap between analytics and coaching.

In addition to his work on biomechanics and spin dynamics, Buffi played a key role in implementing velocity development programs. Partnering with Driveline Baseball, these programs used weighted balls and targeted training regimens to safely and effectively increase velocity. Buffi cited examples of under-the-radar prospects, like Corey Copping and Andrew Istler, who were transformed into valuable assets through these methods. "They went from prospects that people weren't really thinking much of to legitimate pitchers," he noted, underscoring the program's success in bolstering the Dodgers' farm system and the value of these young pitchers in the trade market as well.

While Buffi initially focused on reducing injuries, the Dodgers' early adoption of biomechanics and their willingness to embrace interdisciplinary expertise helped redefine pitching development in MLB. By blending modern technology with a collaborative culture, they set a new standard for how teams approach performance optimization, cementing their status as one of baseball's most innovative organizations.

Buffi's work with the Dodgers underscores a fundamental challenge in addressing the persistent injury problem among MLB pitchers. While advancements in biomechanics and technology have significantly improved our understanding of pitching mechanics and performance optimization, the injury bug remains elusive. Buffi's insights into velocity limits and injury risks highlight the delicate balance teams face: pushing pitchers to maximize velocity and effectiveness without overloading their bodies to the point of breaking. The complexities of analyzing injury data, as Buffi noted, make it difficult to establish clear causal relationships or actionable strategies. This leaves teams navigating a gray area, where the pursuit of peak performance often comes at the expense of long-term health—a tension that continues to shape the modern game, as discussed below.

◆ ◆ ◆

BIOMECHANICS IS NO longer confined to high-level MLB think tanks; it has evolved into a hands-on approach implemented directly in the dugout. During his rise with the Detroit Tigers, Tarik Skubal made significant strides in improving his velocity, thanks to the expertise of Tigers pitching coaches Robin Lund and Chris Fetter. Their application of biomechanics played a pivotal role in refining Skubal's mechanics and approach, enabling him to unlock his full physical potential while minimizing unnecessary stress on his arm.

Robin Lund, the Tigers' assistant pitching coach and a biomechanics expert, was instrumental in identifying adjustments tailored to Skubal's unique movement patterns. Lund helped Skubal recognize his preference for external over internal hip rotation due to his body's natural structure. By adjusting his foot positioning on the pitching rubber—slightly moving his heel off the rubber—Skubal was able to make his mechanics more efficient. Skubal noted, "It allowed me to stabilize with my lead leg faster, transferring energy up to my arm and helping me create better hip-shoulder separation."

Chris Fetter, the Tigers' pitching coach, complemented Lund's biomechanical analysis with a focus on communication and tailored feedback. Fetter emphasized the importance of personalized approaches, explaining, "You have to be individualistic with each pitcher. Some guys may need extra tension and aggressiveness, while others, like Skubal, benefit from being a little looser." This philosophy fostered an open dialogue with Skubal, ensuring that adjustments felt natural and effective.

The integration of biomechanics into Skubal's training allowed him to make small but impactful changes that unlocked new levels of velocity. These changes were validated through data-driven tools like Hawk-Eye and motion capture systems, which helped the coaching staff analyze performance in real time. "With the proliferation of motion capture and Hawk-Eye systems, we're starting to create actionable teaching moments directly from what we see in games," Fetter explained. By incorporating this technology, the Tigers staff translated analytical insights into drills and adjustments that could be applied immediately.

One of the most visible results of this work was Skubal hitting 100 mph for the first time in his career. Reflecting on this milestone, Fetter remarked, "Once he touched 100, it became commonplace for him. It's about helping pitchers feel what it takes to reach their potential and repeat it consistently." Skubal's increased velocity and improved mechanics also bolstered his confidence. "Now I feel like I can just throw the ball as hard as I want to, and it's going to go over the plate," Skubal shared.

These efforts culminated in Skubal's stellar 2024 season, where his increased velocity and refined mechanics made him nearly unhittable. His ability to blend power with precision allowed him to overpower hitters consistently, leading the American League in strikeouts and posting career-best marks in ERA and WHIP, and earning him the 2024 AL Cy Young Award. Then, in a jaw-dropping moment on May 25, 2025, Skubal capped off a 13-strikeout complete game by firing a 102.6 mph fastball—the hardest pitch of his career—on his 94th pitch of the night.

Chris Fetter credited the collaborative environment with pitching coach Robin Lund and bullpen coach Juan Nieves as key to the team's success. "Our ability to work together, be ego-less, and deliver quality information, no matter who it's coming from, is what makes our group unique," Fetter said. For Skubal, the results speak for themselves: a Cy Young Award and a place among the best pitchers in baseball, powered by science, precision, and an incessant pursuit of perfection.

David Cone's reflection to me on the lack of biomechanics in his era underscores just how transformative these tools have become. "We didn't have the ability to see inefficiencies in mechanics like pitchers do today," Cone remarked. "Mel [Stottlemyre] was my pitching coach. He would just say . . . stay back a little bit more, hold your shoulder in a little bit more. I mean, it was the eye test and it happened so fast, there's no way you could tell . . . where your body was or where the inefficiencies were in your mechanics."

Cone believes biomechanical analysis could have significantly influenced his own career. "Imagine being able to see exactly how your body moves and where energy is lost," Cone mused. "It's incredible what pitchers today can do with that information."

Cone's acknowledgment underscores the divide between his generation and today's pitchers. While his era relied on intuition and observation, modern pitchers can blend raw talent with technology, ushering in a new age of performance and longevity. "It's a different world now," Cone reflected. "And it's one that's making pitchers better and healthier than ever before."

♦ ♦ ♦

AFTER HIS TIME with the Dodgers, Jimmy Buffi saw a problem that most teams didn't want to admit or probably didn't even know they had: They were drowning in motion capture data and had no clue how to use it. "You've got all these dots flying around in 3D space," Buffi told me, "but unless you've got a physics degree or a PhD in biomechanics, good luck turning that into something actionable."

So Buffi did what innovators do—he built the solution no one else had. He started Reboot Motion as a way to deliver biomechanics-as-a-service: a way for teams to outsource elite-level motion analysis without hiring an in-house biomechanics team. Whether it's identifying inefficiencies, breaking down a delivery frame by frame, or figuring out how to transfer more energy from the ground into the baseball, Reboot turned raw motion capture data into insights teams could actually use—offering it as a service they could "rent" instead of investing in a full-scale biomechanics department.

No proprietary black-box stuff. Just physics and knowledge applied to cleaned-up data, all the mountains of information decoded and clear feedback pitchers and coaches can use—without needing to be rocket scientists. As Buffi put it, "We built Reboot so teams wouldn't need someone like me on staff to use this tech. Now they can get the same kind of breakdowns the Dodgers had—without years of setup."

What was the impact of Buffi's work? A lot more pitchers, across a lot more teams at all levels, including colleges, are able to unlock the power of data, throw harder, move better, and hopefully stay healthier—because an enterprising biomechanical engineering "nerd" built a system to make biomechanics accessible to the masses.

Buffi was brought in to help reduce injuries, but like many before him, discovered that solving the injury puzzle was far harder than improving mechanics or boosting velocity. Developing efficient movement patterns and designing nastier pitches? Doable. Cracking the code on arm health? Still elusive.

No one can even agree on whether the solution is throwing more or throwing less.

Even as biomechanics and motion analysis have revolutionized how pitchers train and compete, injuries remain stubbornly common. Teams now have the tools to maximize velocity and spin like never before—but that same push for performance has come with a cost. UCL tears, rotator cuff damage, and other overuse injuries continue to rise, especially among young pitchers chasing triple-digit heat.

Buffi set out to solve the injury epidemic but found that the same tools helping pitchers move more efficiently were also pushing them past what the body could reliably handle. The result? A modern dilemma: The faster you throw, the greater the risk. And the question every pitcher has to face: Is the pursuit of greatness worth the price of breaking down?

That tension is clear in pitchers like Tarik Skubal, whose rise to dominance shows how biomechanics can unlock elite performance while helping manage the physical toll of pitching. But for every Skubal, there are countless arms sidelined—proof that even with smarter training, the velocity–durability trade-off is still very real.

As Buffi rhetorically asked: If an ace pitcher in his prime shows a slightly higher risk of injury, are you really going to have him pitch less because of that small increase? Or, as a team and a pitcher, do you take your chances because every athletic endeavor involves some risk?

Before diving back into the era of pitch design and data, it's worth briefly examining how baseball is trying to solve the injury equation—from motion capture and workload tracking to evolving philosophies around mechanics, recovery, and whether "safe" velocity is even possible in today's game.

Pitching injuries remain one of baseball's most frustrating unsolved problems. As velocity climbs and pitchers push their bodies to the limit, UCL tears, rotator cuff damage, and other arm issues have become disturbingly routine. Despite advances in biomechanics, training, and workload tracking, MLB still hasn't been able to meaningfully make a dent in the injury issue.

For the deep dive, Jeff Passan's *The Arm* is the definitive guide to the history and science of pitcher injuries.[1] But this section zooms in on where things stand now—the philosophies, tensions, and debates from the minds shaping modern pitching.

In December 2024, MLB released a 62-page report linking the rise in Tommy John surgeries to the sport's obsession with velocity and max-effort throwing. It laid bare what many already suspected: the pursuit of elite performance might be pushing pitchers past what their arms can handle.[2]

The challenge today isn't just throwing harder—it's figuring out how to survive it.

Eric Cressey, founder of Cressey Sports Performance (CSP), emphasized that injury prevention in pitching requires a multifaceted approach tailored to the individual athlete. He highlighted the importance of addressing structural and functional issues early in a player's development to create a foundation for durability. Cressey noted that, while technology and diagnostic tools have advanced significantly, prevention often comes down to managing workloads and focusing on early intervention. "The best solution is kind of prevention and to minimize," he explained, stressing the value of maintaining pitch count and workload guidelines, particularly for younger athletes.

Cressey also pointed out that the modern emphasis on velocity has increased injury risks. He cited research showing that for every 1 mph increase in average fastball velocity, there is a corresponding 15 percent increase in the likelihood of UCL injuries. This, combined with the pressure on athletes to perform at high levels from a young age, contributes to the epidemic of arm injuries. Cressey advocated for prioritizing comprehensive assessments to identify risk factors such as asymmetry and fatigue, using both advanced technology and an individualized approach to training and recovery.

Kyle Boddy, founder of Driveline Baseball, has been a vocal advocate for using data and technology to address pitcher injuries, but he remains realistic about it. "We have a lot of tools; I think we got it surrounded," Boddy said. While understanding the mechanics of pitching has improved significantly, he noted that effectively applying injury data remains a persistent challenge. "It's slow going," he admitted, reflecting the frustration of those working to keep pitchers healthy.

One area where Boddy's Driveline has led the way is in tracking and quantifying every throw a pitcher makes not just in games (which has long been done through pitch counts) but also in warm-ups and practice as well. They're not only counting these throws; they're also measuring the effort behind each one.

Rather than relying on vague terms like "70 percent effort," Driveline encourages pitchers to measure intent using tools like radar guns and the PULSE sensor. They view this as a critical missing piece in traditional baseball development. In their experience, two pitchers might have completely different interpretations of what a "low-effort" throw means—making it nearly impossible to accurately manage workload and stress.

Because the majority of a pitcher's throws happen when a pitcher is not on the mound—in flat grounds, warmups, and training—they believe monitoring and managing these throws is essential to making real progress in injury prevention.

Boddy also criticized what he sees as overprotective practices in the minor leagues. "As an industry, we are babying minor league pitchers far too much to the point of workload underexposure," he argued, explaining that this leads to breakdowns when pitchers face the natural stresses of throwing at max effort in MLB. Because velocity remains crucial— "Because it works"—Boddy rejected the idea that pitchers should intentionally throw with less effort. "The notion that pitchers should simply be worse at their jobs is not the answer," he asserted, highlighting the need to balance performance demands with smarter, evidence-based workload management.

Similarly, Alan Jaeger, a prominent advocate for arm care and long toss, emphasizes the importance of increasing arm conditioning through more frequent throwing. He argues that a strong foundation of arm fitness can be built by incorporating a higher volume of lower-intent throws, which prepare the arm for the rigors of high-intent throwing. Once this base fitness is established, Jaeger suggests shifting focus to high-intent throwing to fully develop strength and durability. In short, he believes that pitchers often attempt to throw hard before their arm is properly conditioned. His solution is more throwing, not less, to build the necessary strength and endurance.

Paul Nyman, founder of SetPro, stressed the importance of efficiency in movement patterns as a key to injury prevention. Nyman's work with weighted ball training and biomechanical analysis revealed that efficient mechanics could not only maximize velocity but also reduce stress on vulnerable areas like the elbow and shoulder. "By throwing something heavier, it forces the body to organize itself in a better way," he explained. For Nyman, the focus on momentum and kinetic chain efficiency offered a dual benefit of performance enhancement and injury mitigation.

Brent Strom, one of the most respected pitching coaches in MLB, echoed the importance of movement patterns but pointed out the challenges of implementing these insights at scale. "The problem is, you're dealing with athletes who have ingrained habits," Strom explained. He highlighted the difficulty of altering mechanics in pitchers who have been throwing a certain way for years without creating other unintended issues.

Ben Brewster, founder of Tread Athletics, brought another perspective, emphasizing the interconnectedness of factors beyond just mechanics. "It's way more challenging and way less predictable," he said, arguing that focusing solely on one area, like strength or nutrition, is insufficient because the interactions between various factors—mechanics, recovery, mental approach—are what ultimately determine outcomes.

Former Cy Young Winner Trevor Bauer told me that his approach to injury prevention was meticulous and data driven. By tracking over fifty metrics daily, including bloodwork and sleep patterns, he ensured his body remained in optimal condition. Advanced imaging techniques allowed him to monitor the health of his shoulder and elbow, while his focus on refining efficient mechanics minimized stress on vulnerable joints and enhanced durability.

His recovery routine was equally rigorous, utilizing tools like wearable technology and cold tub cycles to accelerate recovery and optimize performance. This unwavering attention to detail and innovative approach exemplified Bauer's commitment to balancing peak performance with long-term health, embodying the cutting edge of modern pitching science.

Tom House, widely regarded as a pioneer in biomechanics, emphasized that injury prevention in baseball, particularly for pitchers, requires a holistic approach that integrates multiple facets of athletic preparation. He highlighted four key factors to keeping a pitcher healthy: mechanical efficiency, functional strength, workload management, and the capacity to recover. House explained that improving mechanical efficiency reduces unnecessary stress on the body, while functional strength supports the physical demands of high-velocity pitching. He stressed that understanding and managing workloads is critical to avoid overuse injuries, and the capacity to recover is equally important, as improper recovery increases the risk of long-term damage.

Additionally, House discussed leveraging scientific tools like thermographic imaging to assess recovery noninvasively. "We can look at the hotspots in the body and, if we can get them to recover, that athlete has less chance to hurt and more chance to perform," he explained. This approach exemplifies House's belief in using science to guide injury prevention strategies. He also mentioned the idea of prehabilitation—essentially implementing return-to-throw programs before injuries occur—as a proactive way to maintain pitcher health and potentially reduce the frequency of Tommy John surgeries.

Brian Bannister, a former MLB pitcher and current coach, brought a creative lens to the discussion. He highlighted how the evolution of pitching into a "relay race," with an emphasis on velocity and shorter outings, has pushed pitchers into the "red line" of their physical capabilities. Bannister noted, "We've turned pitching into nine 100-meter dashes instead of one 400-meter race," emphasizing the high torque and stress this creates on pitchers' elbows and shoulders.

He proposed that rule changes, such as penalties for pulling starters too early or over-relying on bullpen games, might incentivize teams to manage pitcher workloads differently. He stated, "Unless we force pitchers to throw at slightly lower velocities by requiring them to pitch longer, this issue won't go away." His comments underline the paradoxical nature of modern pitching—teams are simultaneously investing in injury prevention while encouraging pitchers to throw harder, often exacerbating the problem.

Despite these diverse approaches, one common thread runs through all perspectives: Injury prevention is a complex, multifaceted challenge. While advances in technology and biomechanics have provided tools to address the issue, achieving a meaningful reduction in injuries will require collaboration and integration across disciplines, along with a recognition of the inherent limitations of the human body.

◆ ◆ ◆

ALEX FAST, NOW MLB Director of Content and Product Strategy, has been exploring innovative ways to mitigate pitcher injuries. One of Fast's novel contributions is his work on a tool that measures finger pressure on a baseball.

The device quantifies the grip force applied by pitchers, offering a unique lens into how grip strength affects not only pitch movement but also injury risk. Fast explained, "If you're gripping it too hard, you may be causing unnecessary stress on your arm, which could lead to injury. This tool allows pitchers to calibrate their grip to find the sweet spot where they can maintain effectiveness without overstraining." Fast envisions this technology as both a diagnostic and preventative tool, giving pitchers actionable data to optimize their performance while minimizing stress on the arm.

Fast also emphasized the importance of educating pitchers on how to internalize these metrics to make them part of their pitching routine. He believes that understanding the nuances of grip pressure can empower pitchers to make real-time adjustments, potentially catching inefficiencies that could lead to fatigue or injury before they escalate. "The goal is to give pitchers another tool in their arsenal to understand what's happening with their body and make adjustments before it's too late," he added.

Fast also believes that the tool measuring finger pressure on a baseball could also serve as a critical asset in pitch design. By quantifying the grip force applied by pitchers, the device provides a new avenue for refining pitch movement. Fast elaborated, "If I told a pitcher to ease up on their grip to 80 percent, that doesn't mean much without a tool to quantify what 80 percent actually feels like. This device creates a framework where pitchers can learn how grip strength impacts pitch profiles, such as spin and movement." He emphasized how the ability to measure and adjust finger pressure could allow pitchers to fine-tune grips to achieve optimal pitch movement while maintaining repeatability.

Fast sees this as a complementary tool to the existing metrics used in pitch design, allowing pitchers to better understand and replicate the physical cues that produce their most effective pitches.

"Imagine being able to tell a pitcher not only how to grip the ball but exactly how hard to grip it to create specific break or spin," Fast mused.

8

MLB's quiet introduction of pitch-tracking technology in every ballpark in 2008 represented a monumental leap forward in understanding how pitchers dominated hitters. Suddenly, everything could be measured: velocity, spin rate, movement profiles, release points. It was the kind of data that could reshape the sport. Technology-forward thinkers around baseball like Brent Strom and Brian Bannister recognized its potential, using it to refine mechanics, sharpen arsenals, and gain a competitive edge.

But there was one problem.

For most, this treasure trove of information might as well have been buried under lock and key. The aggregated data—rich, detailed, and potentially game-changing—was kept behind closed doors, accessible only to teams. Fans, independent coaches, and aspiring players? Completely shut out.

Even MLB players themselves weren't guaranteed access. Many had to rely on whatever selective insights their coaches or analysts chose to share.

And often, teams deliberately withheld the data. Some feared that too much information would overwhelm players, leading to mechanical overcorrections or mental paralysis on the mound. Others saw it as a power move—keeping players reliant on coaching staffs rather than allowing them to take ownership of their own development.

If a pitcher wanted to know why his slider wasn't fooling hitters—or how it compared to Clayton Kershaw's—he couldn't just look it up. He had to trust whatever feedback he was given. And if the team decided that knowledge wasn't in their best interest to share? Tough luck.

For years, this was how baseball operated—the sport's most valuable insights hidden away, reserved for the decision-makers, while the fans and players themselves remained in the dark.

That didn't sit right with Daren Willman, a former college outfielder and little-known software architect working for the Harris County District Attorney's Office in Houston. A lifelong baseball fanatic with a knack for numbers, he immediately saw the potential of this information and decided to do something MLB hadn't: Make it public.

In the process, Willman accidentally ignited a revolution—reshaping how baseball analyzed and shared information and, in turn, playing a key role in making pitchers unhittable.

By day, Willman specialized in untangling massive amounts of law enforcement data, streamlining criminal case records, mugshots, and offense reports into a single, user-friendly system. His job was all about finding patterns, connecting the dots, and making complex information accessible—skills that would later prove invaluable in the world of baseball analytics.

"I was basically doing Criminal History Savant," Willman joked, drawing a parallel between his work and what he would soon create for baseball.

But no matter how deep he was in case files and databases, baseball was always on his mind. A former D3 ballplayer at Texas Lutheran, Willman was the kind of person who needed to know *why* things happened on the field, doggedly digging into the numbers behind them. That curiosity set him on a path that would change baseball forever.

In 2008, during his downtime at his day job, Willman stumbled upon MLB's PITCHf/x data while watching a spring training game. What most people saw as just another flood of on-screen stats that appeared on the MLB app, he saw as a goldmine of untapped information. The data tracked every pitch—velocity, movement, release points—but there was a problem: It was scattered, raw, and nearly impossible for anyone outside of MLB to decipher.

So, he did what any relentlessly curious baseball mind with solid programming skills would do. He built something better.

Willman wrote scripts to scrape, clean, and organize the data, reorganizing it from an overwhelming mess of numbers into a powerful, user-friendly system. What started as a side project became an obsession. He was converting raw numbers into a language fans and players could actually use—turning complex pitching metrics into digestible, intuitive, and visually engaging insights.

Most importantly, rather than keeping this data to himself, Willman took the data he was scraping and started sharing it publicly on the Web.

"I didn't have an endgame," Willman said. "I was just doing it for fun."

The result of Willman's efforts? Baseball Savant—a website that quietly changed the way baseball minds analyzed and understood the game. His creation became a vital resource, empowering a new generation of players, coaches, and fans to embrace analytics as part of the game's evolution.

For the first time, fans could break down a pitcher's arsenal with the same depth as a front office. Broadcasters could go to the website, study the data, and add layers of insight to their calls. And MLB pitchers? Even those with little technical know-how could easily access the data behind their pitches and see exactly what made their stuff elite or why hitters weren't biting, whether or not their team chose to share it with them.

Willman had unlocked MLB's walled-off data, and in doing so, he changed baseball forever.

What started as a side project quickly became the go-to platform for exploring pitch data, spin rates, and player performance, unlocking a new depth of understanding for players, coaches, analysts, and fans alike.

♦ ♦ ♦

BASEBALL SAVANT OPENED the data floodgates. Suddenly, pitchers no longer had to wait for a coach to explain why their pitches weren't getting swings and misses—they could pull up the numbers themselves.

Was their slider breaking like a Frisbee—or just spinning in place? Now, they could line it up next to Max Scherzer's, studying the exact horizontal and vertical movement, tweaking their grip until their pitch bent and dove just like his.

Was their curveball getting hammered instead of buckling hitters' knees? Baseball Savant laid everything bare—raw spin rates, active spin percentages, seam orientation—turning a once-mystifying problem into something pitchers could diagnose and fix on their own, no need to wait for a team analyst's interpretation.

For a fringe prospect clawing for a roster spot or a veteran desperate to stay relevant, Baseball Savant was a lifeline, a direct line to the same advanced metrics front offices used to judge their worth. Instead of relying on sometimes vague or one-size-fits-all cues from coaches or hoping their team was open enough to share the right data, pitchers could now see the numbers for themselves and take control of their careers.

Baseball Savant grew from a resource for major league pitchers and coaches into a vital tool for player development at every level. Minor leaguers, independent league players, and even college arms could now break down their performances with the same precision once reserved for front offices and elite aces, gaining insights that were previously out of reach.

A college pitcher eyeing the draft could analyze how his slider's break compares to Corbin Burnes's and tweak his grip accordingly.

A journeyman in the independent leagues could diagnose why his fastball wasn't generating swings and adjust his approach to earn another shot with an affiliated team.

A Double-A pitcher fighting for a call-up could pinpoint why hitters weren't chasing his curveball and refine its shape until it became a true weapon.

Even Little League pitchers could see how their fastballs stacked up against Jacob deGrom's, fueling their dreams with real data instead of guesswork.

For the first time, pitchers at all levels had the power to take control of their development and make adjustments based on hard numbers rather than vague coaching cues or subjective scouting reports. Access to this data also changed coaching at every level, reshaping how baseball was taught and developed. High school and travel ball coaches began using its tools to refine their players' pitch shapes and build customized arsenals based on what worked for the game's elite. College programs could now provide players with real, actionable insights, breaking down how MLB pitchers attacked hitters and helping them apply those strategies to their own game.

By tearing down the barriers to baseball's most valuable information, Willman's work gave elite pitchers an edge while also empowering an entire generation. With access to the same tools as the pros, aspiring players could study, emulate, and refine their game like never before. Baseball Savant opened doors and reshaped the path to the big leagues.

Soon, access to Baseball Savant became so widespread that MLB players began incorporating its data into everyday conversations and interviews. This led to a surreal moment for Willman. "I remember hearing Joey Votto say he checked his page, and I thought, 'Wow, this is real,'" Willman recalled. This personal hobby started by a curious fan grew into a beloved resource for fans, analysts, and players, becoming the go-to site for exploring advanced metrics. Its intuitive design and vast database quickly gained traction. As media outlets like Fangraphs and high-profile analysts such as Brian Kenny began referencing it regularly, Baseball Savant's influence skyrocketed, cementing its place as an essential tool in the modern baseball landscape.

♦ ♦ ♦

AS BASEBALL SAVANT gained traction, MLB recognized its potential and made a decisive move to bring Willman into the fold. They offered him the opportunity to work remotely, grow the platform, and expand its capabilities with the full backing of MLB. "I didn't want to move or give up the site," Willman told me. "But MLB made it clear they just wanted me to keep doing what I was doing—only bigger."

MLB often takes heat for being out of touch with fans, but the expansion of Baseball Savant proved they understood what fans craved, before fans even knew it themselves. By making advanced stats like exit velocity, pitch movement, and spin rates accessible to everyone, MLB went above and beyond catering to hardcore baseball nerds, redefining how the game is enjoyed and understood. Suddenly, fans could dive deeper into the game than ever before, analyzing the same data that teams use to evaluate players. The impact went beyond numbers, elevating the experience and turning every at-bat and pitch into a chance to discover something new. In an era where younger audiences demand more interactive and immersive experiences, Baseball Savant showed that MLB could evolve, giving fans a way to engage with the sport on an entirely new level.

To ensure Baseball Savant reached its full potential, MLB assembled an all-star writing team that included Tom Tango, David Adler, Sarah Langs, and Mike Petriello. Each brought unique strengths to the platform, collectively making Baseball Savant a cornerstone of modern baseball analysis.

Mike Petriello, who joined MLB.com full-time in 2016 as a senior analyst, contributed his knack for making advanced metrics relatable and engaging. A Boston University graduate and former writer for ESPN and Fangraphs, Petriello blended extensive analytical knowledge with accessible storytelling. "I manage the Baseball Savant team, work with broadcasters, and get on air myself," Petriello explained to me. "It's a lot of jobs in one, but that's what makes it fun. Every day is different." Together with Tango's statistical genius, Adler's insightful articles incorporating the latest analytics and 3D tracking tools, and Langs's unmatched passion for baseball, storytelling, and statistics, the team made Baseball Savant an essential resource for fans, players, and professionals.

Petriello became a leading voice for Statcast on game broadcasts, translating complex analytics into practical insights for fans, players, and broadcasters alike. Under his leadership, the Baseball Savant team introduced new tools and leaderboards, offering fans a deeper connection to the game. "When we come up with these new tools, it's about more than just stats," Petriello said. "It's about creating a tangible connection to the game—why did a pitcher dominate? What's behind a breakout season? The numbers tell those stories."

♦ ♦ ♦

WHILE THE CONTRIBUTORS behind Baseball Savant fueled its growth and expanded its impact, MLB's substantial investments in tracking technology were equally vital, enhancing the accuracy and depth of its data. The evolution of tracking technology in baseball, from PITCHf/x to Trackman to Hawk-Eye, significantly enhanced the quality and depth of data available on Baseball Savant. These innovations reshaped how the game is analyzed and understood by front offices, coaches, players, and fans.

Each new system brought improvements in accuracy and expanded the scope of metrics, making it possible to explore the game with unprecedented precision. This growth wouldn't have been possible without MLB's commitment to investing in advanced tracking systems.

PITCHf/x, introduced in 2006, was the first widely used pitch-tracking system, designed to measure pitch speed, location, and movement. It changed how fans and analysts evaluated pitching, giving them a new lens to understand the game. However, PITCHf/x had limitations, particularly in its inability to capture batted-ball metrics like exit velocity and launch angle. These gaps became evident as baseball analytics advanced, prompting the introduction of more sophisticated systems.

Trackman, implemented in MLB stadiums in 2015, took data collection to the next level. Using Doppler radar, Trackman tracked pitches with greater accuracy and also measured critical batted-ball data, such as exit velocity and launch angle, which were pivotal for understanding hitter performance. This added a new dimension to Baseball Savant, enabling users to analyze both pitching and hitting with deeper insights. Despite its state-of-the-art capabilities, Trackman had its limitations in fielding and baserunning data, areas that required even more advanced tracking.

In 2020, Hawk-Eye vastly improved baseball tracking by replacing radar with high-speed cameras, dramatically enhancing the granularity and reliability of data. This system provided unparalleled accuracy in measuring defensive positioning, outfield jumps, and baserunning efficiency. Hawk-Eye also elevated pitch-tracking capabilities, capturing release points, spin axis, and spin efficiency with remarkable detail, making it the most comprehensive tracking system to date. Additionally, Hawk-Eye introduced bat-path tracking, analyzing swing speed and length to determine whether a hitter was fooled or aggressive on a pitch, offering insights previously unavailable in the game and giving pitchers and coaches more information about the effectiveness of their arsenals.

Importantly, Hawk-Eye can also track every movement of a pitcher's body in real time, capturing joint angles, stride lengths, and rotational speeds with unparalleled precision. This effectively turns a ballpark into a biomechanics lab, providing teams with the tools to analyze and refine pitching mechanics by looking at in-game movements without the need for specialized labs or wearable sensors. The implications for injury prevention, pitch optimization, and career longevity are immense. Pitching coaches and analysts now have data on how mechanics evolve over time, enabling them to make targeted adjustments before issues arise or even determining whether a pitcher is tiring, without the need to ask them.

◆ ◆ ◆

WHAT BEGAN AS a side project for Daren Willman has become an indispensable tool for the baseball world. Baseball Savant is now the premier platform for advanced analytics, offering data and visualizations that have reshaped how fans, players, and analysts experience the game.

Fans now expect to hear Baseball Savant data referenced during broadcasts, and it's become a cornerstone of game analysis on social media. Terms like "barrel rate" and "expected batting average" have entered the mainstream lexicon, thanks to the platform's accessible and intuitive design. "You can't watch a game now without hearing a stat from Baseball Savant," Mike Petriello said, reflecting on how the platform has altered the way people interact with the game.

Historically, hearing players talk about data was as rare as hearing a catcher say he loved catching knuckleballs. But today, MLB players are more data-savvy than ever, and it's now common to hear them break down spin rates, pitch shapes, and expected stats in interviews or conversations with coaches. Baseball Savant has become an essential tool in their development, giving them direct access to the same advanced metrics that front offices and analysts use to evaluate performance.

In just over a decade, Baseball Savant has evolved from a side project by an enterprising fan into an indispensable part of baseball's ecosystem. Its influence is so profound that fans and players alike often say they can't imagine baseball without it. By making advanced metrics accessible, it has reshaped how the game is analyzed while also deepening fans' love and understanding of baseball. Crossing the chasm between front offices and the bleachers, Baseball Savant has seamlessly integrated analytics into the game's fabric, changing the way players prepare, fans engage, and teams strategize.

Greg Maddux, an eight-time All-Star and four-time Cy Young Award winner, is often regarded as one of the greatest pitchers in baseball history. Known for his pinpoint control and masterful ability to outthink hitters, Maddux retired with 355 career wins—the eighth-most in MLB history—along with 3,371 strikeouts and a career ERA of 3.16. He also holds the distinction of being the first pitcher in history to win the Cy Young Award in four consecutive seasons (1992–95). Despite never lighting up radar guns with high velocity, Maddux's historic career stemmed from his intelligence, precision, and ability to exploit a hitter's weaknesses.

Maddux relayed to me how modern tools, such as spin rate data and advanced heat maps, could have elevated his game even further. While his playing days relied heavily on video analysis and conversations with teammates and hitters, he acknowledged the advantage of today's detailed metrics. "I would have used it to my advantage," Maddux told me, envisioning how he could have employed information such as a hitter's tendencies against certain pitches to refine his pitch selection.

For example, Maddux cited his late-career use of tools like Inside Edge to uncover insights, such as Dante Bichette's struggles with changeups before two strikes but his superior performance against them afterward. This information shaped Maddux's approach to pitch sequencing, helping him avoid situations that would play into a hitter's strengths. "You can use it to your advantage to help with pitch selection," he explained, emphasizing the importance of eliminating the one pitch a hitter could punish in any given count.

Maddux's hallmark was his ability to think pitch-to-pitch and read swings, a skill that allowed him to adjust in real time based on the hitter's response. Even with a repertoire of four or five pitches, Maddux ensured each decision was based on both the hitter's tendencies and his comfort in executing the pitch. Modern tools would have provided him with even greater precision in formulating his strategy. Considering Maddux's cerebral nature, which earned him the nickname "the Professor," it's intriguing to imagine how today's data-driven insights could have further enhanced his mastery of the craft.

Some MLB pitchers in today's game have told me they've become addicted to the type of data that Baseball Savant readily provides. Michael King, a star pitcher for the San Diego Padres, is one of many modern players who've fully embraced analytics in their approach to pitching. During games, King uses both his iPad and the scoreboard to track real-time pitch movement—a practice that has become integral to his pitching strategy. "I love the stadiums that have the horizontal and vertical movement after every pitch," King explained, noting how looking back at the scoreboard for this data gives him a clear picture of how his pitches are behaving.

He also regularly checks the metrics after each inning on an iPad, focusing on things like the horizontal movement on his sinker. "If I see that I threw a sinker with twenty horizontal and one vertical, I know it's working that day," he said. King's 2024 performance spoke volumes to the power of pitch movement data: a 2.95 ERA, 201 strikeouts, and a 1.19 WHIP in 173.2 innings. His ability to harness modern technology is a key factor in his achievement of these impressive numbers, as he continually refines his technique and confidence on the mound.

As one of MLB's most electric pitchers, Spencer Strider's evolution of his slider showcases how modern pitchers leverage Baseball Savant's advanced metrics to sharpen their arsenals. Strider focused on creating a slider that complemented his flaming fastball, studying metrics like spin axis, velocity, and movement profiles to ensure the pitches paired effectively. Reflecting on his process, Strider explained to me, "I worked on trying to get it in the velocity range where I felt like it was an effective complement to my fastball and making sure it had enough vertical depth." To refine his approach, Strider turned to looking at Statcast pitch metrics in Baseball Savant, where he analyzed Jacob deGrom's slider. "I looked at Jacob deGrom's slider, how it paired with his fastball, and tried to replicate those principles," he said. By blending natural talent with pitch metrics from deGrom's slider, Strider fine-tuned his slider's shape and speed, turning it into a devastating secondary weapon.

◆ ◆ ◆

LANCE BROZDOWSKI, A player development analyst for Marquee Sports Network and widely read pitching analyst, emphasized the importance of making data accessible to the public, particularly through platforms like Baseball Savant. He argued that public access to advanced information serves as a catalyst for both driving interest in the sport and fostering innovation. "I think it's really important to have good public information and analysis in order to both drive interest in the sport and also make advancements in research," Brozdowski explained. This openness encourages broader participation in the development of new ideas, bridging gaps between fans, analysts, and professionals.

Brozdowski also highlighted the concept of "cross-pollination"—the exchange of ideas between organizations and individuals—as a critical driver of progress in baseball. He noted that many of the sport's brightest minds, such as Max Bay, and Connor Kurcon, began their careers in public research spaces. Their work, shaped in the open forum of public analysis, now influences major league teams.

"When you have more really smart people on the internet thinking about these things," Brozdowski remarked, "you almost progress the game a bit quicker."

♦ ♦ ♦

AFTER FIVE SEASONS with MLB, Daren Willman got an offer from the Texas Rangers that he couldn't ignore: a chance to bring his expertise directly to a team. "I loved my job at MLB," he admitted. "I was serving all thirty teams, and honestly, I never thought about leaving." But the opportunity to compete for a championship tipped the scales. As the Rangers' Senior Director of Research and Development, Willman was tasked with building a state-of-the-art data infrastructure to give the organization a competitive edge. His role expanded beyond analytics, involving collaboration with coaching staff, scouting departments, and player development to integrate insights seamlessly into decision-making processes.

Willman spearheaded projects that utilized state-of-the-art technology, including custom tools to evaluate player performance and optimize in-game strategy. His systems allowed coaches to access real-time data more effectively and enabled the Rangers' front office to make more informed decisions on roster construction, trades, and free agent signings. By embedding analytics deeply into the organization, Willman ensured that the Rangers operated at the forefront of modern baseball innovation.

By 2023, the gamble paid off in the biggest way possible. Willman's work helped propel the Rangers to their first-ever World Series title, a historic achievement for a franchise long in search of postseason glory.

"I still pinch myself," he said. "From D3 baseball to a World Series ring? What timeline is this?" Willman joked, but his journey was no accident. It's a tribute to the sport's embrace of data-driven insights and the potential for MLB outsiders to change the game's future. Willman's story serves as a reminder that innovation takes more than technology. It takes passion, persistence, and the belief that baseball's best days are yet to come.

The paradigm shift sparked by MLB outsiders like Daren Willman stretched far beyond analytics, paving the way for a new wave of innovators who reimagined pitcher development from the ground up. Many of these trailblazers had no professional playing experience, yet they spotted opportunities others overlooked—leveraging data, biomechanics, and cutting-edge optimization techniques to challenge conventional wisdom and fundamentally change how pitchers are trained.

Working outside the rigid structures of MLB organizations, they also built high-tech pitching facilities and developed groundbreaking training methods that refined mechanics, increased velocity, and pushed pitching performance to new heights. Their relentless pursuit of optimization transformed pitchers into nearly unhittable forces, reshaping the modern game and the limits of what's possible on the mound.

9

Since the advent of pitcher training in MLB, development had been solely controlled by the teams. If a player wanted to refine his mechanics, increase velocity, or add a new pitch, he had to rely on the resources provided by his organization. The idea of seeking outside training was practically unheard of. In MLB, teams dictated a pitcher's progress, and players were expected to trust the process, even when that process was outdated, ineffective, or didn't align with their individual needs.

The problem was clear: one-size-fits-all coaching wasn't working for everyone. Teams relied on traditional models, emphasizing workload management and feel-based instruction rather than individualized training methods designed to unlock a pitcher's full potential. If a player wanted to improve, his options were severely limited—tinker on his own, hope for a coach's approval, or risk stagnation (or worse, alienation from his organization).

But what if there was a better way? What if pitchers could take control of their own development, learning from experts outside the MLB system who weren't bound by outdated methods or long-standing traditions?

That's the world that strength training guru Eric Cressey stepped into.

Eric Cressey's journey to becoming one of the most influential figures in baseball strength and conditioning is remarkable not just for what he achieved but also for how he got there. Unlike many strength coaches at the time who played baseball professionally or competed at a high level, Cressey's athletic foundation came from an entirely different sport: high school tennis. "I was actually a better tennis player," he admitted. "Baseball and tennis were the same season, so my baseball career kind of finished off in eighth grade unless you count rec league softball and just playing catch with the guys."

Far from being a liability, this unconventional background became one of Cressey's greatest assets. Unencumbered by the entrenched traditions and misconceptions that often shaped baseball training, Cressey approached the sport with fresh eyes. He leveraged his academic expertise in kinesiology and exercise science, earned during his undergraduate studies at the University of New England and graduate studies at the University of Connecticut, and applied it to the specific demands of baseball. "I wasn't a guy who played in the big leagues," Cressey acknowledged, "but that allowed me to approach the game differently—without the preconceived notions that sometimes hold people back."

As detailed earlier, baseball's relationship with strength training has long been fraught with skepticism. For decades, conventional wisdom warned against lifting weights. It was a strange contradiction: a sport that glorified farm-boy strength from tossing hay bales or chopping wood often dismissed the idea of deliberately building that same strength in a weight room with carefully structured and targeted workouts. Even into the early 2000s, when weight training gained some degree of acceptance, many strength programs for baseball players were either adapted from football's brute-force mentality or overly cautious rehab routines that failed to meet the sport's specific demands.

David Cone recounted a story that perfectly encapsulates the old-school attitude toward strength and conditioning in baseball. "I walked into the weight room at Candlestick Park in the '80s," Cone recalled, "and there's Rick Reuschel sitting on a stationary bike. He's got a cup of coffee in one hand and a cigarette in the other. That was our strength and conditioning program back then." Despite the casual approach, Reuschel pitched seven shutout innings the next day, leaving Cone both amused and amazed. "It just showed how different the mindset was back then," Cone added. "There was this idea that strength training wasn't necessary—or even that it could mess you up."

Amid this landscape of outdated practices, Eric Cressey founded Cressey Sports Performance in 2007 with a mission to bridge the gap between scientific research and the unique physical requirements of baseball players. Recognizing that strength and conditioning was key not only to keeping pitchers healthy but also to elevating their performance, Cressey reshaped what training for baseball excellence could look like.

"There wasn't really a middle ground where you could push athletes while keeping in mind the unique demands and injury risks of baseball," Cressey explained. He recognized that players, especially at the high school level, were ignored by training programs that either overemphasized raw strength or avoided any form of progressive overload. His mission was clear: to create baseball-specific training that addressed critical areas like shoulder health, rotational strength, and mobility—needs often overlooked by generic programs.

Cressey's work began with high school athletes, a group he described as "super underserved." His approach emphasized individualized programming tailored to the demands of baseball. "I wanted to make sure athletes had a place to train that respected the complexities of their sport and didn't treat them like they were just football players with balls and gloves," he said. His early efforts yielded immediate success: One of his first athletes earned Massachusetts State Player of the Year honors and led his team to a state championship.

Word spread. "It started with just a few kids who were willing to try something new, but once they saw the results, they brought their teammates, and then their teammates brought others," Cressey recalled. This organic growth established Cressey Performance as a hub for baseball talent, with players progressing from high school to college and eventually professional baseball.

♦ ♦ ♦

CRESSEY'S UNIQUE PERSPECTIVE was bolstered by his impressive background as a competitive powerlifter. Specializing in the bench press, squat, and deadlift, Cressey achieved remarkable numbers, including a six-hundred-pound deadlift. His powerlifting career provided him with firsthand experience in the principles of strength development, recovery, and injury prevention, which he later applied to baseball athletes. "Competing in powerlifting taught me not just the science but the psychology of pushing limits," Cressey said.

While powerlifting and baseball might seem like vastly different worlds, Cressey saw key parallels. The emphasis on progressive overload, proper movement patterns, and explosive power aligned with the needs of baseball players. However, he also recognized the limitations of traditional powerlifting for the sport. "What works for a powerlifter won't work for a pitcher," Cressey explained. "You can't just train for brute strength—you have to think about mobility, joint health, and how strength translates to sport-specific movements."

This ability to provide a connection between disciplines, combined with his outsider perspective and rigorous scientific approach, enabled Cressey to redefine strength training for baseball. It also paved the way for the revolutionary methods that would transform how players trained, making him a trailblazer in blending biomechanics, sport-specific training, and groundbreaking science to unlock athletic potential.

To Cressey, advanced technology plays a pivotal role in optimizing training programs and ensuring athletes perform at their peak. In the early days of baseball, training was often simplistic, focused solely on lifting heavy weights with little regard for biomechanics or sport-specific needs. But as the game evolved, so did its approach to player development. Cressey has embraced these advancements, integrating modern tools to analyze and enhance performance. "Our goal is to meet athletes where they are and give them the tools to get better," Cressey has said, underscoring the importance of leveraging technology to maximize potential.

One important tool in Cressey's arsenal is Proteus Motion, a state-of-the-art system that employs patented 3D resistance to assess and develop strength and power across a variety of movement patterns. Unlike traditional resistance machines that operate in fixed planes, Proteus uses electromagnetic brakes to provide constant resistance in all directions, closely mimicking the demands of rotational sports like baseball. According to Cressey, the only other place on Earth where an individual can experience this type of 3D resistance is in water. In fact, the machine was named after Proteus, a son of Poseidon in Greek mythology, symbolizing its fluid, unrestricted movement patterns. This unique quality allows athletes to train explosively through natural movement pathways, just as they would on the field.

Cressey utilizes this system to conduct the Cressey Power Test, which evaluates power, acceleration, and movement efficiency through multiple exercises performed in under five minutes. The test generates detailed performance metrics on force production, speed, and coordination, pinpointing strengths and identifying inefficiencies in an athlete's kinetic chain. This data enables Cressey to create highly targeted training plans, monitor progress over time, and adjust strategies to ensure continuous development.

The real advantage of Proteus Motion lies in its ability to provide instant, personalized feedback. Because the system offers resistance in every direction, athletes can move fluidly through any exercise, just as they would in water. By analyzing an athlete's force production in real time, Cressey can refine mechanics, improve efficiency, and enhance sport-specific power, ensuring pitchers and hitters can maximize their athletic potential.

Another cornerstone of Cressey's approach is his use of Hawkins Dynamics force plates, which capture precise, actionable data on biomechanics and movement efficiency. These plates measure ground reaction forces during dynamic movements, providing insights into strength, power, balance, and asymmetries between limbs. For baseball players, whose success often hinges on explosive lower-body power, such detailed analysis is invaluable. These force plates can measure how well a pitcher is using his lower half to develop velocity to ensure that the crucial part of a pitcher's delivery is creating the requisite power.

They're like the launch pad readings for a rocket, showing how much thrust a pitcher's legs are producing before liftoff.

Force plates allow Cressey to uncover inefficiencies or imbalances that might not be apparent through observation alone. They make the unseen parts of performance measurable and, therefore, coachable. For instance, jump tests or loaded squat assessments can reveal disparities between the left and right limbs, which may signal an increased injury risk or an area that requires targeted development. This data informs training decisions, such as incorporating plyometric exercises to enhance explosive power or prescribing corrective movements to address asymmetries and improve overall performance.

◆ ◆ ◆

ONE OF THE defining early public successes for Cressey Sports Performance came with the rise of Tim Collins. Standing at just five seven, Collins defied traditional scouting expectations with his high-effort delivery and explosive velocity. When Collins debuted with the Kansas City Royals in 2011 as the shortest player in MLB, his story became a sensation. "Timmy was special," Cressey said. "That 2011 year really put us on the map. Everyone was talking about this undersized pitcher dominating, and it brought a lot of attention to what we were doing."

Cressey worked closely with Collins to develop a strength and conditioning program that maximized his athletic potential while addressing the unique demands of his pitching style. Collins's success wasn't just a win for him—it was a turning point for Cressey Performance. "Timmy's rise showed that we could take athletes from all backgrounds and help them succeed at the highest level," Cressey noted.

Collins credits Eric Cressey and Cressey Sports Performance for transforming his career. Collins went from a 130-pound high school athlete to a 172-pound professional pitcher, thanks to the personalized training regimen designed by Cressey. Reflecting on his journey, Collins shared, "I don't know where I might be right now. I might be working at a construction site. It's unbelievable. I can't stress enough how much he's meant to my career."[7] Collins's dramatic transformation underscores the power of individualized strength and conditioning programs in helping athletes overcome physical limitations and achieve success.

Another pivotal figure in Cressey's growth was Steve Cishek, a tall, side-arming reliever who went on to enjoy a remarkable thirteen-year MLB career, posting a 2.98 ERA across more than seven hundred appearances. Cishek began training with Cressey long before reaching the majors, validating Cressey's unconventional approach to baseball-specific training. "Steve Cishek was a huge part of my growth," Cressey said. "He trusted what we were doing and became a vocal advocate, which helped bring in more professional players."

Cishek's trust and eventual success provided a real-world testament to Cressey's methods, particularly his focus on biomechanics, arm care, and rotational power. Reflecting on his time with Cressey Sports Performance, Cishek stated, "After twelve-plus years with Cressey Sports Performance and their unparalleled expertise, I can say without hesitation that this is a game-changer for athletes."

As Cishek's career progressed, he referred teammates and coaches to Cressey Sports Performance, opening doors to new clients and solidifying its reputation as a hub for baseball excellence. His endorsement, both in word and action, played a crucial role in expanding Cressey's influence, further establishing his facility as a destination for pitchers seeking to elevate their performance and sustain their careers.

♦ ♦ ♦

COREY KLUBER, A two-time Cy Young Award winner, epitomized meticulous preparation and focus during his time working with Cressey. Known for his stoic demeanor on the mound, Kluber stood out not just for his almost unfair pitch arsenal but for his disciplined approach to training. "Every single throw was just a crazy precise experience," Cressey said, highlighting Kluber's ability to eliminate distractions and focus entirely on execution. This unrelenting attention to detail translated to Kluber's consistent success, as evidenced by his 2017 Cy Young season, during which he led the league with a 2.25 ERA, a 0.869 WHIP, and 265 strikeouts.

Kluber credits Cressey for helping him establish and refine his process-oriented approach to pitching, emphasizing attention to detail in every aspect of his preparation. Speaking on a CSP podcast, Kluber described his training philosophy, stating, "I've always liked to be coached and work on things, not really one of those guys that wants to be left alone and figure it out on my own."

Kluber highlighted how his work at CSP allowed him to focus on routine and consistency. "I think the biggest thing is learning that patience to do [the work] properly," he said, referring to his commitment to detailed preparation, from movement routines to pregame bullpens. This meticulous approach has been central to Kluber's durability and ability to maintain high-end performance.

Kluber's work with CSP extended to refining his in-season training. He emphasized the importance of consistency, explaining, "I want to feel the same every time it's my day to pitch. I'd rather give up a little bit on that day so that I feel great in order to avoid those days I'm dragging." This mindset shaped how Cressey and Kluber structured his program, prioritizing recovery and sustainability throughout the season.

Max Scherzer, another three-time Cy Young Award recipient, embodies a fierce competitive spirit that Cressey believes is unparalleled. "Max has the 'compete' gene," Cressey said, likening Scherzer's mentality to Michael Jordan's infamous ability to create personal rivalries to fuel his drive. This mindset, paired with Scherzer's superior physical conditioning, has enabled him to maintain his overwhelming stuff well into his thirties. In 2021, Scherzer delivered a stellar campaign with a 2.46 ERA, 236 strikeouts, and a 0.864 WHIP across thirty starts, cementing his status as one of baseball's premier pitchers.

Max Scherzer's collaboration with Cressey highlights his dedication to maintaining peak physical condition and adapting his training as his career progresses. Following a microdiscectomy to repair a herniated disc in his lower back in December 2023, Scherzer turned to Eric Cressey to guide his rehabilitation.

Scherzer, who has worked with Cressey for years, benefited from an individualized approach, which allowed him to focus on exercises tailored to his recovery. Reflecting on his rehabilitation process, Scherzer emphasized the importance of patience and gradual progression, noting that stepping away from the high-pressure environment of the clubhouse was crucial.

"I needed to be in my own environment where I'm doing my own thing, my own rehab, and just gradually take it a step at a time and respect the process," Scherzer said.[2]

Scherzer's reliance on Cressey exemplifies how the best athletes use specialized facilities to address their evolving physical needs, enabling them to extend their careers and maintain high levels of performance. By trusting experts like Eric Cressey, Scherzer continued to adapt and excel.

Cressey has also worked with another multiple Cy Young winner, Justin Verlander, to help him keep pitching at a high level when some were beginning to think he was "washed up." He characterized Verlander as one of those guys who would "turn over every rock to try to get better."

Despite their differences in style and personality, Cressey told me that Kluber, Verlander, and Scherzer shared the traits of having an unwavering commitment to excellence and an openness to using data-driven approaches to refine their performance. Cressey's ability to tailor his methods to each athlete's unique strengths and needs has helped pitchers sustain their success and pushed the boundaries of what top pitchers can achieve.

Over the years, he has worked with a wide array of pitchers, from rising stars to seasoned veterans, each benefiting from his meticulous approach to biomechanics and individualized training.

Among the standout names is Lance Lynn, known for his durability and bulldog mentality on the mound. Cressey highlighted Lynn's ability to maintain his performance deep into games, a skill that's become increasingly rare in the modern era. With Cressey's help, Lynn has been able to refine his physical conditioning, contributing to his league-leading eighty-four innings pitched in the shortened 2020 season and his 2.69 ERA that same year.

Cressey has also worked with rising stars Josiah Gray and Jesús Luzardo, two of baseball's most promising young arms. These pitchers represent the next generation of players embracing the integration of data, biomechanics, and traditional pitching wisdom.

Blake Treinen's journey from minor leaguer to 2024 World Series hero highlights the transformative power of Eric Cressey's individualized data-driven training. Known for his devastating sinker-slider combo, Treinen began working with Cressey in 2012, moving to Massachusetts to fully commit to Cressey Sports Performance. Their work helped Treinen sustain velocity and movement while minimizing injury risk. This foundation propelled him to a brilliant 2018 season with the A's, posting a 0.78 ERA, thirty-eight saves, and one hundred strikeouts.

By 2024, Treinen's hard work shined on baseball's biggest stage. As a key bullpen piece, his lethal pitches baffled hitters, and his composure under pressure secured a World Series title. "Blake's work ethic and attention to detail have always been off the charts," Cressey remarked. "Seeing him excel at this level is incredibly rewarding."

Eric Cressey's expertise in baseball-specific strength and conditioning reached new heights in 2020 when he joined the New York Yankees as their Director of Player Health and Performance. The move was another significant milestone in Cressey's career, bringing his innovative approach to one of the most storied franchises in baseball. "The Yankees are a forward-thinking organization," Cressey noted at the time. "They've made a real commitment to player health, and I'm excited to bring what we've built at Cressey Sports Performance into a larger-scale environment." His role with the Yankees involved overseeing the team's entire health and performance program, integrating strength and conditioning with injury prevention and recovery strategies tailored to each player's unique needs.

The Yankees' hiring of Cressey marked a broader trend of MLB organizations embracing external expertise and data-driven methods to gain a competitive edge. Cressey's proven track record of working with the top players in baseball, including multiple Cy Young winners, made him a natural fit for a franchise looking to combine tradition with innovation.

♦ ♦ ♦

AS ERIC CRESSEY'S reputation grew, so did the influence of his training philosophies within Major League Baseball. One of the most notable milestones came when Matt Blake, a former pitching coach at Cressey Sports Performance, was hired as the Yankees' pitching coach. Blake, a key architect of Cressey Sports Performance's pitching program, had established himself as one of the brightest minds in pitching analytics and player development. His work at the facility reflected Cressey's philosophy of blending biomechanics, data, and individualized coaching to optimize performance.

Blake's transition from CSP to the Yankees underscored the growing impact of independent training facilities in shaping MLB coaching staffs. His approach, cultivated at Cressey's facility, aligned seamlessly with the Yankees' focus on modernizing their pitching development strategies. Reflecting on the move, Cressey remarked, "Matt is one of the smartest and most dedicated pitching coaches I've ever worked with. His ability to communicate complex ideas in simple, actionable ways serves the Yankees incredibly well."

Matt Blake credited his time at Cressey Sports Performance—as well as the rise of social media and coaching conferences—as key factors in his path to the MLB coaching ranks, helping him bridge the gap between private-sector expertise and professional baseball.

Blake explained that platforms like Twitter (now X) allowed him to share insights and educational content from his work at Cressey, giving him visibility among MLB teams.

"Social media gave me a platform to be seen, and it allowed me to showcase both the work I was doing with athletes and my understanding of the game," Blake noted.

That exposure opened doors to speaking at major coaching conferences like ABCA and Pitch-a-Palooza, further building his credibility and positioning him as one of the brightest minds in pitching development.

However, Blake acknowledged that transitioning from a private-sector role at Cressey Sports Performance to professional baseball wasn't without its challenges. As one of the first hires from outside the traditional player-coach pipeline, he faced skepticism from some who questioned his qualifications. "There was pushback initially," Blake said. "The first year, I had to work hard to prove that my approach could complement the traditional methods." He emphasized the importance of collaboration and mutual respect, stating, "I wasn't there to take anyone's job; I was there to help us all grow."

The pipeline of talent from Cressey Sports Performance to MLB continued in November 2024, when the Arizona Diamondbacks appointed Brian Kaplan as their pitching coach, succeeding Brent Strom. Kaplan, who co-founded Cressey Sports Performance's Florida facility, brought with him a wealth of knowledge rooted in Cressey's methodologies. His hire further cemented the influence of independent development programs on MLB teams seeking innovative approaches to player optimization.

The hirings of Cressey, Blake, and Kaplan symbolize the increasing integration of modern training methodologies into MLB's traditional framework. These moves represent a bridge between the private development world and the major leagues, highlighting how lessons learned at independent facilities are reshaping even the most established teams.

10

Even as velocity training, biomechanics, and data-driven pitch design were reshaping pitcher development outside the traditional system, MLB pitchers were still bound by the very organizations that expected them to improve. Teams held onto conservative methods, resistant to new-school approaches that challenged long-held beliefs about workload, mechanics, and arm care.

MLB pitching coaches, often former players who had risen through the ranks, perpetuated the same methods they had learned, a cycle of tradition with little room for variation. Open-mindedness was rare, and players who questioned the status quo risked being labeled difficult or uncoachable. Some pitchers sought outside training, but often in secret, aware that these methods were to be kept out of the clubhouse. What happened in those outside facilities stayed there, and revealing it could invite the wrath of their coaches.

For pitchers hoping to maximize their potential—or simply understand the rationale behind their MLB training—the frustration was inevitable. They were expected to improve but were often denied access to the very tools that could help them succeed. Their choices were limited: Comply with the system and hope for the best, or challenge it and risk being ostracized. The cruelest part? If they didn't improve, *their* careers were on the line, not the team's.

Few pitchers embodied this conflict more than Trevor Bauer. So he took matters into his own hands.

A relentless student of the game, Bauer refused to accept the status quo. But when he tried to apply those same methods within an MLB clubhouse, he ran into roadblocks, skepticism, and resistance.

Trevor Bauer, one of modern baseball's most polarizing figures, was the first pitcher to prominently integrate technology and advanced pitch design into MLB preparation and served as a catalyst for the widespread adoption of Driveline's methods in MLB. Through techniques like extreme long toss, weighted ball drills, and rigorous data analysis, Bauer refined his mechanics and elevated his performance. His dogged pursuit of perfection culminated in his crowning achievement: the 2020 National League Cy Young Award, where he showcased the impact of his groundbreaking approach on the sport's biggest stage.

While Trevor Bauer's career has been marked by controversy—both on and off the field—his impact on modern pitching development is undeniable. His divisive personality and outspoken nature led to heated social media battles and public criticism of MLB policies (including the league's handling of foreign substances). He was also handed a 194-game suspension for violating MLB's domestic violence and sexual assault policy. (Authorities reviewed the evidence and did not bring criminal charges.)

This section focuses on Bauer's on-field impact because, like him or not, he changed how pitchers train. Pretending otherwise might avoid drama, but it wouldn't be honest. Coaches, trainers, and players I interviewed repeatedly credited him with reshaping everything from pitch design and biomechanics to analytics and daily routines. His prickly demeanor and off-field controversies remain divisive, and while it may be tempting to overlook his contributions due to these controversies, his influence on the tech-driven evolution of pitching is impossible to deny. Any book on this subject would be incomplete without discussing him.

♦ ♦ ♦

TREVOR BAUER'S BASEBALL career began with an unconventional yet highly influential dynamic between him and his father, Warren. Bauer credits his father, a chemical engineer trained at the Colorado School of Mines, for instilling in him a systematic, scientific approach to learning and problem-solving. This engineering mindset became the foundation of Bauer's development as a pitcher. His father's philosophy emphasized three key engineering principles: understanding where you are, knowing where you want to be, and designing a process to bridge the gap. Through years of trial, error, and iteration, this framework has both shaped Bauer's pitching mechanics and also his willingness to embrace failure as a stepping stone for growth.

Despite not having a background in baseball, Warren applied his engineering expertise to help Trevor learn the game. Together, they analyzed techniques, dissected problems, and sought innovative solutions, creating a unique father-son bond rooted in discovery. Reflecting on this experience, Bauer described it as "a father and son trying to learn baseball together," with his father's structured problem-solving process ultimately becoming Bauer's own. This rigorous, experimental approach became instrumental in shaping Bauer's signature methods and his ability to challenge traditional norms in the sport.

Trevor Bauer's journey from a young player to the major leagues was defined by powerful drive, methodical precision, and the early influence of his father. Initially, Bauer didn't view baseball as a professional goal until high school, when facing tougher competition sparked his determination to improve.

◆ ◆ ◆

IN HIGH SCHOOL, Bauer immersed himself in the science of baseball, starting in an unexpected place—his ninth-grade physics class. His teacher, Martin Kirby, introduced him to the fundamental principles of physics, sparking a passion that would profoundly shape Bauer's approach to pitching. Reflecting on Kirby's impact, Bauer explained, "I took a class that I really loved, and I was like, wow, there's a way to describe what's going on around me and understand the physics of stuff."

This newfound understanding of physics opened Bauer's eyes to how he could apply scientific concepts to baseball. "Why does the ball bounce? How high is it going to bounce? Why does the ball move through the air? Oh, wait—torque, momentum—how do I apply this to baseball?" Bauer recounted to me. Kirby's lessons on forces, motion, and mechanics gave Bauer the tools to analyze and refine his pitching. "That class was probably still my favorite class that I've ever taken at any level of school," Bauer shared.

Kirby's unconventional teaching methods and personality also left a lasting impression. Bauer fondly remembered the British teacher as a quirky character with a sense of humor. "He had a picture on his wall of him smiling with two packs of cigarettes in his mouth. He decided to quit smoking cold turkey, so he lit them all at once, got super sick, and never smoked again," Bauer recounted with a laugh. This personal anecdote highlighted the unique dynamic Kirby brought to the classroom, making learning both engaging and memorable.

Bauer's exposure to physics through Kirby deepened his intellectual curiosity and gave him a framework to approach pitching scientifically. This foundation would later drive Bauer to dissect pitching mechanics using concepts like torque and momentum, eventually making him one of the most analytically minded players in Major League Baseball. Kirby's influence was the first step in a path that bridged the gap between science and sport, setting the stage for Bauer's important contributions to pitching.

Trevor Bauer's endless pursuit of improvement, with an engineering slant, led him to obsessively study the mechanics of Tim Lincecum, a pitcher known for generating exceptional velocity despite his smaller stature. Using video analysis, Bauer meticulously attempted to replicate Lincecum's delivery, believing it could help him unlock his own potential. "At the time that I had started going to [Ron Wolforth's Texas Baseball Ranch], they were talking about momentum and all this stuff,"

Bauer explained. "I was like, well, here's a guy who's my size—maybe a little bit smaller than I am—throwing a hundred, so I'm just going to copy what he does exactly."

While this approach was ambitious, it ultimately proved to be the wrong path for Bauer. "Of course, his body's different than mine," Bauer reflected, recognizing that biomechanics are unique to each individual. Nevertheless, the process was not without value. "It got me a lot of the principles that I needed to then be able to fine-tune later on. Had I not tried to copy his mechanics, I probably wouldn't have been as comfortable flying down the mound as fast as I could," he said. This experimentation provided Bauer with foundational insights, including the importance of linear momentum in his delivery, even though the exact mechanics didn't suit his body.

The attempt to mimic Lincecum's mechanics, combined with teachings from the Texas Baseball Ranch, led to several challenges for Bauer. He explained, "I have limited internal rotation in my back hip, so that caused me not to be able to drop into my back leg." This biomechanical limitation disrupted his delivery, leading to issues like an uneven pelvic load, a long stride, and an inability to properly rotate his hips. "My hips weren't level . . . I had to dump my torso off toward the first-base side so I could clear my arm, and then I had my head shifting and all this different stuff going on," Bauer detailed.

The consequences of these mechanical flaws were significant. In 2012, during his first year in professional baseball, Bauer suffered a strained right groin, which persisted throughout the season. This initial injury set off a chain reaction of other problems, including biceps tendon strain and issues with his elbow. "I ended up with bicep tendon issues, back of the elbow, [and] olecranon tip issues," Bauer recalled. Recognizing the unsustainability of this approach, he made the decision to adjust his mechanics and tailor his delivery to his own biomechanical strengths.

♦ ♦ ♦

TREVOR BAUER'S ADOPTION of extreme long toss in his teenage years, a practice championed by throwing guru Alan Jaeger, became one of his most defining and controversial methods. Long toss, which involves throwing a baseball at maximum effort over extended distances, is designed to build arm strength, improve throwing mechanics, and enhance endurance. Bauer took this practice to new extremes, often throwing distances that many coaches and players deemed excessive. Critics, including some coaches and players within Major League Baseball, questioned the utility and safety of such a rigorous practice, labeling it as unnecessary or potentially harmful. Some dubbed him a "showoff" as they watched him fire baseballs from foul line to foul line before his start. Despite this, Bauer remained steadfast in his commitment to the method.

Trevor Bauer also began using weighted baseballs early in his pitching career; he was intrigued by their potential to enhance arm strength, increase velocity, and refine mechanics. They look simple, just baseballs of different weights, but when used correctly, they trick the arm into moving faster and cleaner, unlocking velocity that traditional training couldn't reach. At a time when this training method was unconventional and often dismissed by traditionalists, Bauer embraced it with his systematic and analytical approach, making it a cornerstone of his development.

Bauer's implementation of weighted balls was precise, rooted in biomechanical insights and tailored drills designed to address specific weaknesses in his throwing motion. By focusing on efficiency, durability, and strength, he transformed what was once considered a fringe practice into a validated training tool. However, critics initially questioned the safety and effectiveness of weighted ball training, fearing it could cause arm injuries or disrupt traditional pitching mechanics. Reflecting on this resistance, Bauer shared, "They didn't know what they're talking about, throwing weighted balls... but they wanted to criticize because it was different and challenging what they knew about baseball, and you're the new guy."

Bauer's success—marked by increased velocity and maintained arm health—helped dispel these concerns and demonstrated the utility of weighted ball training when applied correctly. Over time, his advocacy significantly contributed to their broader acceptance in baseball training programs, including those championed by Driveline Baseball.

One of Trevor Bauer's defining traits was his ability to set bold, ambitious goals—but what set him apart was his methodical approach to achieving them. He did more than dream big; he engineered a step-by-step road map using an analytical, process-driven mindset.

As a young pitcher, Bauer's goals were nothing short of extreme: make the high school varsity team, break UCLA's strikeout record, win the Golden Spikes Award, and eventually capture three Cy Young Awards in the major leagues. These aspirations reflected both his unwavering determination and his willingness to challenge baseball's traditional development paths.

At UCLA, Bauer's goal-oriented mindset propelled him to greatness. He not only broke the school's all-time strikeout record but also won the Golden Spikes Award in 2011, recognizing him as the nation's top amateur baseball player. Reflecting on his approach, Bauer explained: "You have to evaluate exactly where you are and where you want to be. Then you design a process to get there and iterate through it as much as possible."

His relentless pursuit of his Cy Young ambitions fueled his obsession with measurable progress. Bauer himself admitted, "I was like, I'm gonna go win three Cy Youngs . . . for the next ten years, that was the goal. At that point, I didn't care about anything else. That was the thing."

Though he didn't win three, he did capture the 2020 National League Cy Young Award, cementing his reputation as one of baseball's most innovative and technically advanced pitchers.

Bauer's unyielding commitment to his goals—even in the face of skepticism and criticism—pushed him to embrace data, analytics, and nontraditional training methods. By blending his competitive drive with scientific precision, he placed himself at the forefront of baseball's modern pitching revolution. His travels—from a driven young pitcher with lofty ambitions to a Cy Young winner at the cutting edge of the game—underscores the power of setting extreme goals and fully committing to the process of achieving them.

◆ ◆ ◆

TREVOR BAUER'S PATH to the Majors was marked by his achievements on the mound and also by the challenges he faced off it, including in Bauer's words "persistent bullying." From a young age, Bauer's unconventional approach to the game and refusal to conform made him a target. "I was made fun of a lot. I was bullied a lot by my teammates, by people at school, by my coaches," Bauer recalled to me. His high school coach, in particular, frequently threatened to kick him off the team despite Bauer insisting he had done "absolutely nothing wrong." Meanwhile, to Bauer, peers engaging in overtly problematic behaviors—like drinking or fighting—faced no such consequences. This toxic environment ultimately pushed Bauer to graduate early, deciding he could no longer remain part of the program.

Bauer attributes much of this mistreatment to his individuality and unique methods. According to Bauer, his intelligence, combined with his dual identity as both an athlete and an academic, set him apart. "I was kind of the odd bird," he admitted, balancing Advanced Placement classes with an undying passion for baseball. His unorthodox training routines also drew attention; he could often be seen lugging a five-foot shoulder tube around school or practicing his delivery at a local pool before sunrise. Bauer's simple wardrobe of sweats and T-shirts further reflected his indifference to fitting in socially. "I was just an easy target for a lot of people," Bauer said, acknowledging how deeply this treatment affected him during his formative years.

Halfway through high school, Bauer reached a turning point. After an early morning workout, he looked in the mirror and questioned why people disliked him. "I decided I like what I see in the mirror. I do well in school. I do well in baseball. I have ambition. I treat people well," he reflected. From that moment on, he resolved to stop caring about others' opinions, embracing his identity with newfound confidence. While this mindset allowed Bauer to weather challenges and build resilience, it also led him, by his own admission, to adopt an overly defensive posture. This confidence became both a shield against criticism and a catalyst for his determination to redefine pitching norms.

This constant perceived adversity fueled Bauer's self-declared drive to "fight back," both on and off the field. "After that, anytime someone said something to me, I just fired back," he admitted to me, describing how the need to assert his worth and defend his unconventional methods shaped his personality. This fighting spirit followed him into his professional career, where his innovative techniques and outspoken nature often clashed with traditional baseball culture. While Bauer's resilience and boundary-pushing highlighted his transformative impact on the game, they sometimes alienated those around him. Whether this early bullying contributed to Bauer later exhibiting similar behavior toward others remains a question for debate.

Bauer himself acknowledged that his desire to "fight back" sometimes went too far, leading to behavior that wasn't acceptable for a public personality. Reflecting on his past, he admitted, "I've been a jerk to a lot of people because I've felt like I've been mistreated my entire life." He recognized the consequences of this approach, telling me, "There are a lot of times I probably should've just shut up." This self-awareness underscores a critical duality in Bauer's character: His fighting spirit drove both his success and his interpersonal struggles, shaping the complexities of his legacy.

Trevor Bauer also admitted to me that his disregard for managing his public persona played a significant role in his professional challenges and eventual exile from Major League Baseball. "I don't give a shit about my image . . . scripting my image in a certain way so that people think this about me or that about me just doesn't do anything for me," he confessed. While this mindset enabled him to focus singularly on his craft, it ultimately became a double-edged sword. Bauer described this undisciplined approach as "a massive failure," one that cost him the opportunity to continue doing what he loved most: pitching at the highest level.

Reflecting on his career, Bauer acknowledged the disconnect between his meticulous attention to baseball and his disregard for personal branding. "Now I don't have a job in baseball because I've been extremely undisciplined in that area of my life," he admitted, expressing regret over how his choices outside the game impacted his goals. Having dedicated decades to perfecting his craft, Bauer lamented, "I had just gotten to the point where I was like, okay, I've invested thirty years of my life in this . . . and now I can't do the thing I've done for thirty years."

Trevor Bauer's odyssey highlights the challenges faced by individuals who consistently push against the grain. His determination to rage against the machine and swim against the tide made him a trailblazer in the world of baseball, but it also cemented his polarizing reputation. For someone driven by an overpowering need to challenge norms and prove doubters wrong, knowing when to step back—or simply remain silent—can be an immense struggle. This inability to "shut it off" often led to unnecessary conflict, further fueling the negative image that came to define him among many around the sport.

Bauer's story provides a valuable lens into the complexities of modern sports and the demands placed on athletes. In an era where exceptional talent must coexist with personal branding and public scrutiny, his journey reveals the cost of constant rebellion. The same qualities that made him an innovator—his defiance and refusal to conform—often alienated those around him. Striking a balance between pushing boundaries and knowing when to yield is a delicate act, and Bauer's experience underscores just how elusive that balance can be. His career serves as both a cautionary tale and an illustration of the double-edged nature of unyielding defiance in the pursuit of greatness.

♦ ♦ ♦

TREVOR BAUER'S IMPACT on Major League Baseball extends far beyond his performance on the mound; he played a transformative role in integrating data and technology into pitching at the sport's highest level. Bauer brought advanced methodologies once confined to third-party facilities such as Driveline Baseball and the Texas Baseball Ranch into MLB clubhouses.

His pioneering work in pitch design, command training, and questioning the movement of baseballs due to "seam effects" (the origin of the scientific exploration of Seam-Shifted Wake effects, discussed later in this book) established new standards for modern pitching. Through constant innovation and a willingness to share insights publicly, Bauer reshaped his own career and also democratized access to modern pitching techniques, providing the missing link between independent research and mainstream baseball.

Trevor Bauer epitomizes the modern concept of a "made" pitcher—a player whose success stems from unflagging effort, intellectual curiosity, and a willingness to experiment, rather than innate talent alone. Unlike many pitchers throughout the history of the game who relied on natural athleticism, Bauer systematically engineered his abilities. Influenced by his father's background in engineering, Bauer approached pitching as both a science and an art.

Bauer's ascent wasn't marked by the natural gift of a blazing fastball or effortless mechanics from the outset. Instead, it was the result of grueling work and unwavering focus. From early mornings perfecting mechanics at a local pool to lugging unconventional training tools like a five-foot shoulder tube to school for arm care, Bauer embraced a meticulous, experimental process. By leveraging technology like high-speed cameras and motion analysis, he optimized every aspect of his performance, proving that excellence could be achieved through precision, persistence, and a nonstop commitment to improvement.

Trevor Bauer's tenure with the Arizona Diamondbacks as a rookie was marked by clashes with then-manager Kirk Gibson, highlighting the challenges of integrating his unconventional methods into MLB's traditional culture. Gibson, known for his old-school, hard-nosed approach, reportedly struggled with Bauer's insistence on following his own data-driven routines, including weighted ball training and extensive warm-ups.

The friction between Bauer's forward-thinking methods and Gibson's traditional philosophies peaked in 2012 during Bauer's rookie season. After several starts, Gibson publicly criticized Bauer's performance, pointing out his failure to adhere to coaching staff game plans. "He has a lot to learn about pitching at the Major League level," Gibson remarked, a thinly veiled critique of Bauer's independent approach.

This disconnect ultimately led to Bauer being traded to the Cleveland Indians after just four MLB starts. The trade signified the Diamondbacks' unwillingness to accommodate Bauer's style, despite his immense potential. This conflict became emblematic of the resistance Bauer faced as a trailblazer.

Bauer's desire to execute his own game plan also led to tension with veteran catcher Miguel Montero during his rookie season. The friction stemmed from a miscommunication surrounding a planned meeting to align Bauer's pitching preferences with the team, including Montero. Bauer explained the situation:

"My pitching coach came to me during BP and said, 'After BP, I want to have a meeting with you, Montero, Henry Blanco, Gibby, and the coaching staff just to get on the same page about pitches.' I just assumed everyone had been told. After BP, I'm at my locker, and the media crowds around me asking, 'What are you going to do about getting on the same page?' I said, 'We're going to have a meeting, and it shouldn't be an issue.' Then they went to Miguel's locker, and he said, 'If he wants to have a meeting with me, he knows where my locker is. Who am I? I've only caught Hall of Famers.' The pitching coach hadn't told Miguel about the meeting. That's where the tension started."

Bauer acknowledges his occasional immaturity during this time, admitting that some of his actions contributed to the narrative. Reflecting on the 2012 season, he recalled, "I got super pissed in the last game of the season when I got taken out one out before qualifying for the win—like it matters."

These moments, combined with his outspoken nature, solidified a divisive reputation that followed him long after his rookie season, despite his efforts within the game.

Trevor Bauer's innovative use of technology fundamentally altered how pitchers analyze and refine their craft. By integrating Edgertronic high-speed cameras with Rapsodo pitch-tracking devices, Bauer pioneered a data-driven approach to pitch design that has become a cornerstone of modern baseball.

In pitching, an Edgertronic high-speed camera and a Rapsodo pitch-tracking device work together like a buddy-cop duo. The Edgertronic is the detail-obsessed detective, breaking down the release in ultra-slow motion—every finger position, wrist angle, and seam under the magnifying glass. The Rapsodo is the big-picture partner, charting spin, movement, and where the ball crosses the plate. When they work together, every pitch can be engineered and every mystery solved. Bauer was one of the first players to adopt Edgertronic cameras, using them to gain insights into pitch movement, spin rate, and grip. "I was the guy who brought Edgertronic cameras and married them to Rapsodo, being able to do pitch design and figure out how pitches moved the way they did," Bauer explained.

Eric Jagers, then at Driveline Baseball, described the significance of Bauer's work: "Trevor was using Edgertronic and Rapsodo together, counting revolutions by frames and pairing the data to understand exactly how the ball was coming out of his hand. At that time, he was really the only person in the world doing that on a day-in, day-out basis.

That's where it all started—it set the stage for pitch design to become what it is today."

The Rapsodo device provided Bauer with real-time feedback, allowing him to refine his pitches with unmatched precision. He spent countless hours experimenting to develop new breaking pitches. "I spent hours with the Rapsodo, tweaking grips and arm angles, trying to understand how to generate the desired break or spin," Bauer recalled.

By combining Edgertronic video analysis with Rapsodo data, Bauer unlocked a deeper understanding of what made certain pitches effective and how to replicate them consistently. A scattered puzzle snapped together, and the picture was finally clear. His efforts elevated his performance, while also paving the way for the mainstream adoption of these technologies across MLB. Today, nearly every MLB Spring Training facility utilizes Edgertronic cameras and Rapsodo devices, proof of Bauer's lasting influence on the sport.

Moreover, Bauer didn't keep his findings to himself. He shared insights with teammates and younger pitchers, helping popularize data-driven training throughout the baseball community. His groundbreaking work bridged the gap between independent innovation and widespread MLB adoption, proving that technology can transform performance and strategy on the mound.

During Bauer's time in Cleveland, Matt Blake, then a pitching coordinator with Cleveland and now the New York Yankees pitching coach, observed firsthand how Bauer introduced Edgertronic cameras and Rapsodo technology to refine and advance pitch design. Blake credited Bauer with introducing these tools into Cleveland's professional environment, where his methodical approach and constant experimentation initially met with hesitation. "Trevor was the first person to take the Edgertronic and set it up in our pro environment," Blake explained. "He would break down the video, count revolutions, and analyze spin axis, essentially acting like a professor to teach others how to use the tools."

Bauer's impact extended beyond his own performance, as he often mentored teammates like Mike Clevinger and Shane Bieber, showing them how to refine their pitches using state-of-the-art technology. Blake highlighted Bauer's unique role in Cleveland's player development system, noting, "He was integral in upskilling our players and coaches, helping us understand and implement these advanced methods effectively."

In fact, Bauer's former teammate with the Dodgers, Blake Treinen, told me that Bauer played a key role in helping him develop and understand his slider grip. Bauer showed him how subtle adjustments to his thumb position could alter the speed and shape of the pitch—an insight that became a turning point in the evolution of Treinen's slider, now considered one of the filthiest pitches in baseball.

Bauer himself embraced this role, famously calling himself "the highest-paid player development coach in baseball." He took pride in sharing his findings and connecting the dots for his teammates and coaches, leaving a lasting legacy in the evolution of the sport.

One of Bauer's primary inspirations in his quest to become a better pitcher was Corey Kluber, his teammate and a two-time Cy Young Award winner, renowned for his exceptional command and devastating breaking ball, now commonly referred to as the Sweeper.

Kluber's ability to manipulate pitch movement with precision made him one of the top pitchers of his era, and his breaking ball became a benchmark for excellence. Determined to unlock the secrets behind Kluber's success, Bauer turned to advanced technology to analyze the mechanics and metrics of his teammate's devastating pitch.

"I just took a slow-motion camera and filmed his hand," Bauer recalled. "I still have the footage on my computer somewhere. I was like, 'Okay, great. Now I can see exactly what's going on.'" Through meticulous comparisons, Bauer discovered a key difference: Kluber's arm tilt was slightly lower than his own—a critical insight into replicating the pitch. He expanded his analysis to other pitchers like Marcus Stroman and Mike Clevinger, matching arm angles and grips to uncover what made their breaking balls so effective.

Matt Blake explained how Bauer approached Kluber's abilities from a scientific perspective, reasoning, "It's the same baseball whether I'm throwing it or he's throwing it. I've got to be able to make it move like he does." This philosophy drove Bauer to investigate spin axis and seam orientation in depth. Blake added, "Trevor got to the point of saying, 'I can make it sweep.'"

Bauer adhered to the principle of "Imitate before you iterate," layering video footage of himself alongside footage of Kluber and others to isolate the nuances of their deliveries. "What are the similarities? What's the grip? Oh, it happens to be the exact same grip," Bauer explained. These insights became the foundation for integrating refined elements of their breaking balls into his own arsenal.

Bauer devoted entire offseasons to throwing and analyzing thousands of sliders, using Edgertronic cameras to capture minute details and Rapsodo devices to measure spin rates and pitch break. His tireless pursuit of precision not only elevated his own performance but also demystified the mechanics behind MLB's best pitches.

♦ ♦ ♦

TREVOR BAUER'S COMMAND training was also rooted in the engineering process, focusing on three fundamental principles: consistent delivery, repeatable ball trajectory, and precise targeting. He emphasized the importance of consistency in his mechanics, stating, "The first thing you need to do is be consistent at projecting the object through space. If you have a different launch mechanism every time, of course, you can't have consistency of trajectory or location." Bauer meticulously refined his delivery to ensure it was repeatable, which was a key for him in improving his command.

One unique aspect of Bauer's mechanical work was inspired by nature, specifically, the way birds stabilize their heads while flying. He likened his approach to keeping his head still during a pitch to how a bird maintains focus and alignment mid-flight. This attention to head stability minimized unnecessary movement, ensuring his eyes stayed locked on the target. "When your head moves, your eyes move, and when your eyes move, your target moves. You can't hit a moving target consistently," Bauer explained.

"Targeting" was another critical aspect of Bauer's command training. While his mechanics and pitch movements were consistent, he identified his eyesight and focus as areas needing improvement. To address this, Bauer trained himself to lock onto specific, small targets, even simulating game-like conditions during practice. He broke down every component of targeting, from aligning both eyes on the target to maintaining focus throughout his delivery. "I just went to work on that, and about three months after I started my command training program, I went from walking four per nine-ish in 2019 to walking two per nine in 2020 and winning the Cy Young."

Trevor Bauer also employed an extensive and data-driven approach to monitor and maintain his health, obsessively relying on a variety of methods to optimize performance and prevent injury. One of his most notable practices was collecting over fifty metrics daily, which included drawing blood, tracking hydration, and monitoring sleep. Bauer emphasized the importance of consistent tracking, stating, "When I was trying to compete at the absolute highest degree, I drew blood every day." By analyzing these metrics, Bauer identified patterns in his health and performance, enabling him to address potential issues proactively.

A significant element of Bauer's health regimen involved advanced imaging techniques to assess the health of his shoulder and elbow. He also meticulously analyzed the movement and stress on these joints, aiming to balance mechanical efficiency with durability. "The elbow is supposed to function like this dart throw," Bauer noted, explaining his efforts to refine mechanics in ways that minimized stress while preserving high-velocity performance. He viewed these adjustments as essential, saying, "How close to that can we get while still being able to throw the velocities necessary to compete?" Bauer's methods sought to build tissue quality that exceeded the stress his body endured, focusing on joint stability and strength.

Additionally, Bauer utilized wearable technology, such as the Oura Ring, and conducted regular at-home sleep studies to monitor recovery. These insights guided his personalized recovery routines, including cold tub cycles to enhance hormone levels and lock in skill acquisition after high-intensity training sessions. Bauer explained, "The quicker you get back to a parasympathetic nervous system state after working out, the more effective the workout."

Bauer's holistic approach combined data, imaging, and biomechanical insights to prevent injuries and enhance his performance. "I'm terrified of getting to a point in my career and saying, 'I wish I knew this when I played,'" he reflected.

◆ ◆ ◆

TREVOR BAUER'S IMPACT extended beyond his training methods; it was also his unprecedented use of social media to share his journey, influencing both the way pitchers train and how they connect with fans and the baseball community.

Before Bauer, it was rare—if not unheard of—for Major League pitchers to openly share the details of their regimens and techniques with the public. Traditionally, such knowledge was closely guarded, treated as proprietary information that provided a competitive edge. Bauer disrupted this norm by turning social media into a platform for education and transparency, bringing fans and aspiring pitchers into the world of professional pitching like never before.

Bauer's influence on social media, particularly his early efforts to share in-depth details of his pitching methods, marked a significant cultural shift in baseball. His initiatives, such as launching a YouTube channel and creating series like Tips with Trev, aimed to educate fans, aspiring pitchers, and even fellow professionals. These efforts demystified advanced pitching techniques and brought transparency to his process. "That's when you saw me try to start giving more information via YouTube and . . . stuff like that because I'm in a place now where . . . I've mastered so much that it's time to start making it better for other players," Bauer explained.

Using platforms like YouTube, Twitter, and Instagram, Bauer documented his training, discussed the nuances of pitch design, and analyzed pitching mechanics. His videos offered behind-the-scenes insights into his use of tools like Rapsodo and Edgertronic cameras, demonstrating how he refined his pitches. Bauer's belief in the transformative potential of social media went beyond self-promotion. He envisioned a future where his efforts would normalize a culture of transparency and sharing within baseball. "In ten years, when baseball has a thriving YouTube landscape and social landscape, perhaps someone will have the same conversation with me for taking all the arrows in the back for starting a vlog and filming in the clubhouse," he stated.

Bauer's social media presence cultivated his reputation as both a trailblazer and a mentor among his online fans. His YouTube channel became a go-to resource for pitchers at all levels, featuring in-depth discussions on mechanics, pitch grips, and recovery techniques. On Twitter/X, he actively engaged with fans and players, answering questions and sparking conversations about baseball's evolving landscape. By normalizing open discussions about advanced methods, Bauer helped usher in a new era of transparency and collaboration in the sport. Reflecting on the broader impact of his efforts, he remarked: "Rookies are making an extra two or three hundred grand on their YouTube channels, and the fans have better information and access."

However, Bauer's openness received mixed reactions. Critics argued that sharing detailed insights into his methods risked eroding his competitive edge, potentially giving opponents an advantage. Traditionalists in baseball saw his transparency as unorthodox and viewed it as a violation of the sport's unwritten rules of professional secrecy, as if a magician had stepped onstage and explained how every illusion worked. Additionally, some of his combative interactions with fans on social media drew significant criticism, further fueling debates about the appropriateness of his approach.

Bauer explained that he didn't feel disclosing his methods would allow others to surpass him because of his unique combination of traits: his ability to learn faster, iterate per repetition more effectively, and his self-described "unmatched work ethic." He stated, "I learn faster per rep than anybody else. I get incrementally, a tiny fraction of a percent better every single rep than everybody else. I'm willing to work longer than everybody else. I'm curious, I search things out, and I'm innovating more than anybody else player-wise."

For Bauer, surpassing him would require others to not only match but exceed his dedication, curiosity, and capacity for rapid learning—traits he believed most players lacked. He remarked, "In order to beat me, you will have to work longer than I do, learn faster than I do, and experiment more than I do, and there's just no one that's going to do that."

This mindset, combined with his belief in the importance of understanding the underlying principles of pitching and the iterative learning process, assured him that sharing his knowledge would not jeopardize his competitive edge.

◆ ◆ ◆

IN 2019, TREVOR Bauer launched Momentum, a groundbreaking player-led media company that made waves in the baseball world. Recognizing the disconnect between players and fans, Bauer sought to give outside audiences unprecedented access to the lives, personalities, and processes of professional athletes. Unlike traditional media, which often controlled the narrative, Momentum was designed to empower players to tell their own stories directly to the fans.

What set Momentum apart was its status as the first-ever player-led media company to receive official credentials from Major League Baseball. This milestone allowed the company to film behind-the-scenes content, providing fans with an insider's view of the sport. From documenting players' training programs and game-day routines to exploring their off-field interests and opinions, Momentum showcased the human side of baseball players, fostering a deeper connection between players and fans.

The platform also reflected Bauer's entrepreneurial and innovative spirit, extending his reputation as a disruptor in the game. Just as he pushed the boundaries of pitching with data and technology, he challenged the traditional ways baseball stories were told, opening the door for athletes to take control of their narratives in an era where media and fan engagement were evolving rapidly. Momentum served as a natural progression of Bauer's social media initiatives, seamlessly connecting his personal efforts to a larger vision of empowering players to take control of their narratives and engage directly with fans.

Despite the initial skepticism of some around the game, Bauer's approach resonated with a growing audience of players and fans who appreciated his willingness to pull back the curtain on the sport. His transparency challenged entrenched norms and helped normalize the idea of athletes leveraging their platforms to educate and engage. By embracing social media as a tool for connection and learning, Bauer changed how they communicate with the world, leaving an indelible mark on the culture of baseball.

♦ ♦ ♦

BAUER'S INFLUENCE ON modern pitching is undeniable, blending brilliance with controversy to position him as a critical figure in baseball's evolution. Brent Strom, one of baseball's most respected pitching minds, recalls first meeting Bauer at the Texas Baseball Ranch when he was just fourteen years old. "He and his father were among the first to embrace concepts like effective velocity and pitch shape," Strom remarked, highlighting Bauer's precocious understanding of the game. "Brilliant young man. He can do a lot of different things with the baseball."

Strom credits Bauer with pushing boundaries that many in the baseball establishment were reluctant to challenge. "Every team I've been with, I've asked them to sign him," Strom admitted, lamenting the resistance from organizations despite Bauer's clear talent. Describing Bauer as "a throwback," for advocating for an old school four man rotation and wanting to throw 130 pitches a game, Strom praised his willingness to challenge norms, while also pointing out that he's avoided significant arm injuries. "He knows something we don't know," Strom observed. Beyond MLB, Bauer's global impact is equally significant, with his YouTube channel and clinics introducing advanced techniques to players worldwide. "The one good thing is he's taking his information worldwide and doing it in a way that others can't," Strom noted.

Kyle Boddy, founder of Driveline Baseball, echoed Strom's sentiments, framing Bauer as a pivotal figure in integrating advanced tools like Edgertronic cameras and Rapsodo units into MLB-level preparation. "He is the pitcher who took a lot of this stuff to the next level," Boddy said, emphasizing Bauer's role as a link between independent innovation and professional baseball. Despite Bauer's polarizing personality, Boddy pointed out that within the game, he was highly respected. "Trevor is loved in the game and as a teammate . . . one of the greatest teammates you can have," Boddy noted, referencing players like Sonny Gray and Mookie Betts who appreciated Bauer's dedication and camaraderie.

Ben Brewster of Tread Athletics further underscored Bauer's impact to me: "I think he's integral . . . he's been a trailblazer in a lot of ways. As controversial as he is, I think he has to be a part of the book." Brewster highlighted how Bauer brought advanced pitch design, weighted ball drills, and modern technology into the mainstream. "He proved these methods could succeed on the biggest stage," Brewster said, pointing to Bauer's 2020 National League Cy Young Award as the culmination of his approach.

Bauer's integration of modern technology and training regimens such as extreme long-toss training, originally taught to him by long toss guru Alan Jaeger, elevated his performance—culminating in a Cy Young Award—and also demonstrated the transformative power of technology when applied at the highest level. Bauer's legacy serves as an example of how embracing data and technology can change what's possible in the sport, solidifying his place as an indispensable figure in this era of technology.

12

Throughout baseball history a pitcher could stand on the mound, throw two fastballs with identical effort, and get two completely different results—one exploding through the zone, the other getting hammered. Coaches and hitters could see the difference, but they couldn't explain it.

Why did one pitch work while the other failed? Why did some curveballs dive, while others floated or swerved? No one truly knew—at least not in a way that could be measured.

By the mid-2000s, that was beginning to change.

The introduction of PITCHf/x gave baseball its first real glimpse under the hood of what made pitches effective. Suddenly, teams had access to real-time data on velocity, spin rate, movement, and release points, offering a level of insight the game had never seen before.

But data alone wasn't enough. Baseball was at a crossroads—the numbers were there, but who would make sense of them? Who would take raw data and turn it into something pitchers could actually use?

Brian Bannister saw the game differently. Where most viewed analytics as just a way to explain "what happened," Bannister saw a tool that could also reshape how pitchers approached their craft.

Unlike most of his peers, Bannister was determined to understand the game. The son of All-Star pitcher and former number 1 overall draft pick Floyd Bannister, he grew up immersed in baseball's inner workings, watching firsthand what it took to succeed. But as technology began reshaping how pitching was analyzed, he saw an opportunity:

What if pitchers could create their own success?

That question would drive Bannister to become one of baseball's earliest pioneers in analytics-driven pitching development—fusing old-school wisdom with a new, data-fueled way to optimize performance.

At USC, Bannister was coached by Mike Gillespie—who played for Rod Dedeaux and later succeeded him as head coach. Dedeaux, long after his 1986 retirement, remained deeply embedded in the program as director of baseball, advising coaches, working with administration, and guiding USC's development. Bannister recalled Dedeaux's presence vividly and remembered him walking the grounds with a baseball bat cane. Dedeaux instilled in the program—and passed down to Gillespie—the belief that success lived in the little things, done right and done often. Bannister carried those lessons forward from USC, blending them with wisdom from his father and his own career to forge an analytics-driven approach that redefined how pitchers think about their craft. Like Tom House before him, Brian Bannister wasn't blowing hitters away with velocity—he was outthinking them. With a fastball that sat in the mid-80s, he didn't have the raw power typically tied to MLB success. But instead of trying to throw harder, he leaned into the art of deception.

Bannister, a seventh-round pick by the Mets in 2003, made his MLB debut in 2006 and became one of the smartest pitchers in the game. In 2007, he finished third in AL Rookie of the Year voting with a 12–9 record and a 3.87 ERA—not bad for a guy who didn't light up the radar gun. He dove deep into advanced metrics long before it was cool, studying spin rates, pitch efficiency, and vertical break to develop an arsenal that messed with hitters' expectations.

Bannister was basically a walking mathematics lab. He openly embraced sabermetrics, citing research from Voros McCracken and Tom Tango (two influential baseball statisticians and sabermetrics pioneers) while still an active player. That obsession with pitching analytics did more than help Bannister carve out an MLB career—it set him up for his second act as one of the game's most forward-thinking minds, helping develop the next wave of pitchers chart their way to nearly unhittable stuff.

For a pitcher like Bannister, whose success depended on precision over power, the advent of PITCHf/x in 2006 couldn't have come at a better time. Installed in every MLB stadium, the system provided a treasure trove of data that was previously impossible to quantify. PITCHf/x not only tracked what happened after the ball left a pitcher's hand—it told the story of how the pitch got there, offering insights into mechanics, effectiveness, and even deception. For the first time, pitchers, analysts, and coaches had the ability to measure the fine details that separated a good pitch from a great one. However, despite its groundbreaking potential, most players and teams were slow to embrace the data in its early years, viewing it as an unnecessary distraction or too complex to integrate into their routines.

Brian Bannister was one of the first pitchers to use PITCHf/x as a personal cheat code—analyzing spin rate, release points, and pitch movement in real time, even between innings. While many players ignored the data, Bannister embraced it, knowing he needed every possible edge to succeed without overpowering velocity. He broke down the metrics pitch by pitch, using them to refine his sequencing and locations, keeping hitters off balance. This approach both kept him in the league and also positioned him as an early pioneer of analytics in pitching.

Bannister turned to PITCHf/x to experiment with grips, pitch types, and release points. He kept detailed notes on specific pitches to review after games, studying movement patterns and effectiveness to identify what worked. This relentless self-evaluation led to one of his biggest transformations: realizing his traditional fastball wasn't effective, he replaced it with a cutter, which he threw nearly 50 percent of the time by 2009.

Here was a pitcher without top-tier velocity choosing to throw even slower. Only science could convince a pitcher to try that strategy.

He built an arsenal suited to his strengths, moving away from the traditional reliance on a dominant fastball to establish off-speed pitches.

Bannister studied the game's best, comparing his PITCHf/x data to elite pitchers. One thing he focused on was pitch tunneling. This is the way pitchers work to replicate, for instance, their fastball's release point and motion for their curveball, so that it travels through the same "tunnel" as the two pitches approach the plate. It gives hitters even less time to decide what kind of pitch they're about to swing at.

He mimicked All-Star pitchers' movement profiles, perfected tunneling effects, and found ways to make his pitches play up despite lacking top-tier velocity. Bannister's approach was more than a personal breakthrough—it marked a shift in how pitchers could develop and succeed. He proved that velocity wasn't the only path to dominance—sometimes, the smartest pitcher on the mound had the real advantage. His embrace of analytics helped pave the way for today's data-driven revolution in pitching.

♦ ♦ ♦

THE SAME ANALYTICAL mindset that extended and improved Brian Bannister's playing career made him an ideal partner for Zack Greinke, his teammate and one of the most cerebral and physically gifted pitchers of his generation. Bannister described discussing analytics with Greinke as akin to fine-tuning a race car: "Zack was the high-performance vehicle, and I was the pit crew making sure every piece worked at its best."

Greinke, known for his unique personality and razor-sharp baseball IQ, had a knack for keeping things both competitive and entertaining. Bannister once shared a story that perfectly captured Greinke's blend of humor, competitiveness, and analytical curiosity. "He sat down next to me out of nowhere, looked me straight in the eye, and asked, 'If you threw one hundred fastballs to me, how many home runs do you think

I'd hit off you?'" Taken aback but amused, Bannister would throw out a cautious guess, like, "Maybe eleven?" Greinke, without hesitation, would counter with, "forty-seven," delivering it with complete deadpan confidence before walking away as if it were a settled fact.

While Greinke often made these absurdly bold claims for laughs—he also backed them up. With Silver Sluggers and home runs to his name, his confidence wasn't totally misplaced. The exchange was emblematic of Greinke's unstoppable curiosity about the game and his knack for exploring every angle to gain an edge, even as a hitter.

This dynamic led to countless conversations between Greinke and Bannister about creating the nastiest pitch sequences imaginable. Bannister brought data-driven insights, while Greinke's arsenal of pitches and elite command made him the ideal test bed for experimentation. Reflecting on their time together, Bannister said, "The mental game with Zack was like a chess match. He had the physical ability to execute anything, but what made him special was his ability to think a step ahead of hitters."

Using their knowledge of in-game pitch analytics and sequencing, Brian Bannister and Zack Greinke crafted pitch sequences that became the stuff of legend, blending creativity and data in ways that left hitters baffled. Bannister highlighted one particularly iconic sequence from Greinke's 2009 Cy Young-winning season. "Zack would start with a sixty-mile-per-hour curveball for a first-pitch strike—something hitters couldn't bring themselves to swing at," Bannister recalled. "Then he'd come back with a ninety-seven-mile-per-hour fastball at the top of the zone, creating a nearly forty-mile-per-hour velocity gap. Finally, he'd finish them off with a ninety-two-mile-per-hour wipeout slider in the dirt. That sequence was our favorite, and it worked all year long."

These calculated pitch sequences showcased Greinke's enormous physical talent and highlighted his commitment to maximizing every advantage analytics offered. Bannister and Greinke's collaboration proved that even in a game as old as baseball, there's always room for new ways to defeat hitters.

We can see when a pitcher or a hitter is getting unlucky. A series of broken bat bloopers, accidental bunts, and balls lost in the sun can run up a pitcher's ERA without saying much about how well he actually pitched. Without the right stats, bad luck can be mistaken for bad skill. But how do you quantify luck?

Fielding Independent Pitching (FIP), developed by sabermetrician Tom Tango and building on the work of Voros McCracken, transformed how pitchers evaluate their performance. Unlike ERA, which is influenced by factors outside a pitcher's control—like defensive quality and batted-ball luck—FIP focuses solely on what a pitcher can control: strikeouts (K), walks (BB), hit batters (HBP), and home runs (HR). FIP is calculated: ((HR x 13) + (3 x (BB + HBP)) - (2 x K)) / IP + FIP constant where the "FIP constant" puts FIP onto the same scale as the entire league's ERA.[1]

McCracken's research challenged the traditional belief that pitchers could simply "pitch to contact" and rely on their defense. He showed that the outcomes of balls in play are far more dependent on defensive positioning, fielding ability, and luck than on a pitcher's skill.

How do we know FIP is better than ERA? It serves as a better predictor of future ERA than ERA itself. A pitcher who puts together a few seasons with an ERA all over the place usually has a more stable FIP. For Brian Bannister and Zack Greinke, FIP became a guiding principle. They embraced its insights to refine their approach, focusing on limiting walks and home runs while maximizing strikeouts. For these analytically inclined pitchers, FIP was a road map to success, emphasizing the importance of controlling what truly matters on the mound.

Bannister, in particular, saw the value of FIP in cutting through the noise to reveal a pitcher's true ability. Relying more on precision than raw power, Bannister used FIP to refine his craft. By understanding how walks and home runs inflated his FIP, he adjusted his strategy to limit free passes and induce weak contact, maximizing his effectiveness without overpowering stuff. FIP offered him clarity on where to improve and a framework to measure success on his terms.

Teaming with Bannister, Greinke took FIP to the next level, incorporating it into his pitch-to-pitch strategy. Known for his intellectual approach to the game, Greinke made FIP central to his decision-making on the mound. "That's pretty much how I pitch, to try to keep my FIP as low as possible," Greinke said, revealing how deeply the metric influenced his style.[2] His strategy prioritized limiting walks and home runs while racking up strikeouts—core components of a low FIP.

During his 2009 Cy Young season, Greinke's mastery of FIP was on full display. While his ERA was an elite 2.16, his 2.33 FIP proved that his success went beyond luck or stellar defense—it was his ability to dominate the elements he controlled. By blending FIP principles with his unique pitch mix—high-velocity fastballs paired with slow, looping curveballs—Greinke consistently kept hitters off-balance and minimized damage.

Both Bannister and Greinke exemplified how understanding FIP can transform a pitcher's mindset. For Bannister, it was a formula to maximize his strengths; for Greinke, it was a guiding principle that influenced every decision on the mound. Together, they demonstrated that FIP was a blueprint for pitching smarter, not harder.

◆ ◆ ◆

AFTER RETIRING AS a player, Brian Bannister transitioned into a front-office role, establishing himself as a leader in analytics-driven pitching development. In 2015, he joined the Boston Red Sox as the Director of Pitching Analysis and Development, a role that perfectly merged his on-field experience with advanced tools like Statcast and Trackman. Bannister described his approach to me as combining traditional baseball knowledge with science and math, emphasizing, "We've raised the floor of the industry . . . analytics were my steroids."

At Boston, Bannister fostered a data-driven culture among the pitching staff, helping optimize player performance, refine pitch usage, and adopt training methods grounded in advanced metrics. His efforts contributed significantly to the team's 2018 World Series championship. Reflecting on his time with the Red Sox, Bannister highlighted how analytics allowed teams to quantify concepts that older generations of players could only sense intuitively: "We've finally been able to measure things—like spin or seam effects—that players always knew mattered but couldn't define."

Building on his success in Boston, Bannister brought his expertise to the Chicago White Sox as the Senior Pitching Advisor. Here, he continued to provide a connection between data and practical coaching, refining individual pitchers while influencing the organization's broader pitching philosophy. Bannister championed the use of high-speed cameras, motion capture systems, and biomechanical analysis to dissect and enhance pitching mechanics, making advanced concepts accessible and actionable for both players and coaches.

Across every role, Bannister has worked to pull his colleagues into the next era of pitching, and every year it gets easier to convince them.

13

Today's pitchers, armed with data from systems like Hawk-Eye, owe much to Brian Bannister's early work with PITCHf/x, which proved that intelligence and innovation could reshape success on the mound. As Bannister established himself as a pioneer in analytics-driven pitching development, another influential figure was emerging—a former pitcher turned MLB pitching coach who found a way to merge traditional on-field wisdom with cutting-edge technology.

Instead of rejecting the old-school approach or blindly following analytics, he became the bridge between baseball's past and future—a grizzled former big leaguer with a sharp eye for coaching, who helped tear down entrenched traditions and enable pitchers to optimize their arsenals and do the most with what they have.

Brent Strom's introduction to baseball can be traced back to his childhood, when he was deeply influenced by his parents' encouragement and his early exposure to the sport. Strom fondly recalls his father taking him to Lane Field in San Diego, the home of the Padres' Triple-A team. The smell of the grass, the crack of the bat, and the atmosphere of the wooden stadium sparked a fascination that would define his life. "My dad loved baseball and passed that love down to me," Strom said, reflecting on those formative moments. "He took me to games, taught me to appreciate the little things about the sport, and it stuck with me forever."

His father's influence extended beyond those cherished trips to the ballpark. Strom shared a story about receiving a train set for Christmas, only to abandon it almost immediately in favor of a makeshift pitching setup in his backyard. "I remember drawing a strike zone on the garage door and pretending I was Whitey Ford," Strom recalled. "That garage door became my Yankee Stadium, my Wrigley Field. It was where I started to fall in love with pitching."

Strom's mother also played a role in nurturing his passion. "She didn't always understand the game, but she understood how much it meant to me," Strom said. Her encouragement helped reinforce the idea that baseball was something worth pursuing with dedication. Together, his parents provided a supportive environment where Strom's curiosity about the game could flourish.

This blend of familial encouragement, vivid imagination, and experimentation ignited Strom's lifelong curiosity about the game's nuances—a curiosity that would later fuel his groundbreaking coaching career. "I was lucky to have parents who believed in me, even when I was just a kid throwing balls at a garage door," he said. "They gave me the freedom to explore, to dream, and to fail, which is where all great learning begins."

Like House and Bannister, Brent Strom's path was shaped by his time at the University of Southern California, where he played under legendary coach Rod Dedeaux. This connection to Dedeaux created a lineage of forward-thinking baseball minds who sought to push the boundaries of pitching development.

Strom's MLB career, though relatively brief, offered invaluable lessons. The left-handed pitcher played five seasons between 1972 and 1977 with the New York Mets, Cleveland Indians, and San Diego Padres, compiling a 22–39 win-loss record and a 3.95 ERA over one hundred games. While his performance didn't place him among the game's best, the experience of sharing clubhouses with icons like Tom Seaver, Gaylord Perry, and others profoundly shaped his understanding of pitching.

Strom's time with Seaver stood out. The Hall of Famer's meticulous preparation and pioneering use of strength training made a lasting impression. "Tom was ahead of his time. Watching him carry a barbell to stay durable opened my eyes to how preparation could give you an edge,"

Strom recalled. This insight gathered from Seaver helped focus Strom's future emphasis on conditioning and mechanics.

Strom also credited Gaylord Perry, famed for his strategic cunning (and an occasional spitball), with teaching him the mental chess match of pitching. "Gaylord taught me to think a pitch ahead, to keep hitters guessing," Strom shared. These lessons, combined with observations of other Hall of Famers like Nolan Ryan and Sandy Koufax, gave Strom a deep well of knowledge he would later draw upon as a coach.

Brent Strom's playing career didn't hinge on overwhelming stuff; instead, he honed a reputation for seeking every possible advantage to succeed. His velocity was never overpowering, but his endless curiosity set him apart.

Strom reflected on this with me, saying, "I wasn't going to dominate anyone with sheer stuff, so I had to find ways to outthink and outprepare hitters."

◆ ◆ ◆

AFTER HIS PLAYING days, Strom transitioned into coaching—a journey marked by resistance to his forward-thinking ideas. He often found himself at odds with traditionalists who dismissed his innovative approach to pitching and pitching mechanics. Strom acknowledged the challenges, saying, "I don't think you don't like me; I think you may not like the message I present." Despite being let go from multiple coaching roles, Strom remained committed to challenging conventional wisdom.

Brent Strom's time with the Cardinals as minor league pitching instructor illustrated this clash of baseball philosophies. On one side stood Cardinals Manager Tony La Russa and Pitching Coach Dave Duncan, staunch advocates of the old-school approach: pitching to contact with sinkers, inducing ground balls, and relying on the defense. On the other side was Strom, championing the modern art of missing bats with rising four-seam fastballs and strikeouts, arguing that pitchers should avoid contact altogether. Strom emphasized that pitchers have little control over the outcome of balls in play, making whiffs far more reliable than pitching to contact. Unsurprisingly, the dynamic was tense. "If it was up to them, I would've been fired after a year," Strom admitted. Instead, he was sidelined, restricted to working with Low-A and Dominican Republic players, far removed from the Cardinals' Major League operation.

But Strom didn't exactly keep his mouth shut. In one meeting, Duncan, trying to encourage his pitchers to throw sinkers to get ground balls, rattled off stats highlighting batting averages on certain types of pitches, stating that ground balls went for a .233 average while fly balls were around .407. Strom, not one to back down, fired back: "Is a line drive considered a fly ball? A line drive [often the result of a sinker] has a batting average of around .700. An actual fly ball is more like .233, while a ground ball is .231." *Boom*. Mic drop. The room wasn't ready for that level of heat, and neither were La Russa and Duncan, who weren't about to give Strom any real say in the Cardinals' pitching philosophy.

In another heated exchange, he posed a provocative question to highlight his approach: "If I get a seventeen-year-old Dwight Gooden, a seventeen-year-old Bob Feller, and a seventeen-year-old Sandy Koufax, do you want me to teach them sinkers? It's ludicrous not to take someone's strengths and ride them." Again, this mindset didn't win Strom many fans among the St. Louis coaching staff. Even years later, Strom reflected on how young fireballers like Trevor Rosenthal and Lance Lynn were pushed to throw sinkers despite their ability to beat hitters with 98 mph four-seam fastballs elevated in the zone. "That's why the Cardinals pitched okay, but they didn't strike people out," Strom observed to me, underscoring the tension between his forward-thinking approach and the organization's traditional philosophy.

Enter Jeff Luhnow. Then a Cardinals executive, Luhnow saw something in Strom's approach and gave him a shot—albeit only with the minor league guys. But when Luhnow jumped ship to the Astros in 2011, everything changed. As Houston's GM, Luhnow leaned fully into analytics, creating the ultimate lab for Strom's pitching experiments. When he hired Strom as the Astros' pitching coach in 2014, it was game on. The Astros embraced data like no one else, and Strom finally got to unleash his "screw contact" philosophy on the big stage. The results? The Astros turned into a pitching powerhouse, proof that Strom's strikeout-heavy approach was inevitably the future of the game.

Strom's coaching career reached its inflection point in 2014. His partnership with Luhnow proved transformative, as Luhnow's analytics-forward philosophy perfectly aligned with Strom's openness to experimentation. Together, they turned the Astros' pitching program into a model of modern development.

Brent Strom taught pitchers how to weaponize their stuff, incorporating creative, nontraditional methods. One of his most trailblazing concepts was effective velocity, a term coined by pitching innovator Perry Husband. Husband theorized that "velocity" to hitters is more than the actual radar gun speed of a pitch; the location of the pitch can make hitters feel like the ball is coming in hotter than it actually is. "It's not just about throwing hard—it's about making 93 mph feel like 98 mph by changing where you throw it," Strom explained. Effective velocity exploits how location impacts a hitter's perception of speed: an inside fastball appears several miles per hour faster than the same pitch on the outside corner. For Strom, mastering this concept was like unlocking a cheat code for a pitcher's arsenal.

But Strom didn't rest there. He became a strong advocate for pitch tunneling, a concept that turns deception into an art form. The idea is simple yet incredibly effective: make different pitches look identical as they travel toward the plate, only for them to diverge at the last possible moment. Hitters have mere milliseconds to decide whether to swing, and if two pitches—like a high fastball and a 12-6 curveball—share the same initial "tunnel," they're forced to commit before they can even identify the pitch. By the time they realize the fastball is out of reach or the curveball is dropping out of the zone, it's too late. And the faster the fastball, the less time a hitter has to distinguish between the pitches. Think of two cars that are speeding down the road, parallel to each other and indistinguishable—until one veers onto an off-ramp, and you're left chasing the wrong one.

Strom loved combining these two concepts—effective velocity and pitch tunneling—especially with pitchers who threw gas. High velocity amplifies the impact of tunneling, as hitters are already pressed for time to react. Pairing a 98 mph fastball with a tunneling curveball that ends up two feet lower in the zone? That's a recipe for a swing-and-miss clinic.

◆ ◆ ◆

TWO OF BRENT Strom's greatest success stories with the Astros were Justin Verlander and Gerrit Cole, both of whom became nearly unstoppable forces under his guidance. Verlander, who had been struggling with inconsistency and injuries before joining Houston, credited Strom with helping him regain his form. Strom urged Verlander to abandon the sinker-heavy approach he had relied on in the past and instead focus on elevated four-seam fastballs that exploited his high velocity and top-notch spin rate. "Sandy [Koufax] once told me, 'You know who throws sinkers, Brent? Guys who can't throw fastballs,'" Strom said, illustrating his preference for attacking hitters with high-velocity heaters over inducing weak contact. The adjustment allowed Verlander to maximize the effectiveness of his devastating slider and curveball, leading to a Cy Young Award in 2019 and a World Series title in 2017.

For Gerrit Cole, Strom's impact was equally transformative. In Pittsburgh, Cole had been encouraged to pitch to contact, which limited the effectiveness of his electric fastball. Strom immediately saw the untapped potential in Cole's arsenal. "When we got Gerrit Cole in Houston, we completely revamped his pitch mix," Strom said, describing how they turned Cole into a strikeout machine by ditching his sinker, while emphasizing his high-spin four-seam fastballs and perfectly tunneled breaking balls. The results were historic: Cole posted a 20–5 record, a 2.50 ERA, and an MLB-leading 326 strikeouts in 2019, cementing his place among the league's best.

Not all of Strom's successes came from working with stars. Collin McHugh, a journeyman with an 8.94 ERA before joining the Astros, became one of Strom's most remarkable transformation stories. Strom recognized potential in McHugh's high-spin curveball and convinced him to ditch his ineffective sinker in favor of an elevated fastball-curveball combination. "McHugh got called up as an emergency starter and was warming up throwing sinkers and sliders," Strom recalled. I told him, "Colin, I think your best bet is four-seamers up and curveballs down. He struck out eleven that night and never saw the minors again." McHugh went on to post a 2.73 ERA with 157 strikeouts in 2014 and later played a key role in the Astros' 2017 World Series championship.

◆ ◆ ◆

AFTER AN INCREDIBLY successful stint in Houston, Brent Strom took his pitching expertise to the Arizona Diamondbacks in 2022, where he helped transform a young pitching staff into one of the league's most formidable units. His guidance played a pivotal role in the Diamondbacks' unexpected run to the 2023 World Series, with standout performances from pitchers like Zac Gallen, Merrill Kelly, and rookie Brandon Pfaadt.

Strom had particularly high praise for Zac Gallen, calling him an "extremely talented, cerebral pitcher" and ranking Gallen's curveball among the best he's ever coached—alongside Charlie Morton's. Strom admired Gallen's ability to command his fastball, pair it with a devastating changeup, and stick to a meticulously constructed game plan. "He's the best at self-scouting opposing hitters," Strom said. "He refuses to give in and sticks to what he knows works. He's extremely confident in his stuff and his plan."

In the 2024 offseason, Brent Strom joined the Pittsburgh Pirates as an assistant pitching coach, bringing decades of expertise to a team focused on developing its next generation of pitching stars. Among his new pupils is Paul Skenes, the reigning National League Rookie of the Year and one of the game's most promising young talents, who is discussed in detail later in this book. With Strom's unparalleled baseball knowledge and Skenes's generational talent, this pairing has the potential to be an electrifying combination.

14

For most of MLB history, game-planning against hitters was more art than science. Pitchers relied on a mix of visual observation, intuition, and anecdotal scouting reports to develop their strategies. Without advanced analytics, they had to rely on their eyes, instincts, and the collective wisdom of teammates and coaches.

Scouting reports were often built on firsthand accounts and memory, with coaches and scouts noting tendencies like a hitter's bat path, swing mechanics, or struggles against certain pitches. Dugout conversations were filled with verbal cues like "he'll chase sliders away" or "don't let him extend his arms." Hall of Famers like Pedro Martinez and Greg Maddux mastered this observational approach, using their keen baseball intellect to pick apart hitters based on subtle tells and in-game adjustments.

Pedro, for example, used a hitter's bat waggle as a guidebook to their power zones, picking up on subtle movements that revealed where they wanted the ball. He identified that elite sluggers like Barry Bonds and Mark McGwire had specific areas they unconsciously favored—both preferred to attack pitches low and middle-in, while Edgar Martinez subtly signaled his preference for pitches over the middle of the plate. Their bat waggles as they stepped into the box would actually show where they wanted the pitch.

By recognizing these patterns, Pedro could strategically avoid their hot zones, forcing hitters to chase pitches in spots where they were less comfortable and less dangerous. This observational approach, taught to him by Felipe Alou, gave Pedro a unique strategic edge.

"Even those little things you have to analyze as a pitcher," Pedro noted. "They're showing you the path where they want the ball to be."

By paying attention to details that most pitchers overlooked, Pedro was able to outthink hitters, dictating at-bats before the ball even left his hand. His ability to turn observation into execution made him one of the most cerebral pitchers of his era—a master of both the mental and physical aspects of the game.

Maddux, on the other hand, approached scouting with relentless precision, meticulously studying video, stance adjustments, and swing reactions to anticipate how a hitter would respond to certain pitches. He didn't solely rely on pregame scouting reports—he adjusted in real time, reading swings pitch by pitch and staying one step ahead of the hitter's thinking.

This level of deep, instinctual scouting set Pedro and Maddux apart, but for most pitchers, it wasn't something that could be easily replicated. Their mastery was as much art as science, honed over years of experience and an unmatched ability to process information mid-game.

That was the challenge.

For pitchers without their uncanny instincts or generational feel for the game, traditional scouting had limits. Reports were subjective, memory-based, and lacked precision. Without real-time access to heat maps, pitch-tracking data, or advanced analytics, many pitchers entered games at a disadvantage—relying on guesswork rather than concrete insights.

That's where Codify made its lasting impact on the game.

♦ ♦ ♦

CODIFY REVOLUTIONIZED PITCHER scouting, transforming the way pitchers prepare for hitters. By providing customized heat maps and advanced pitch data, Codify allowed pitchers to eliminate the guesswork, giving them clear, objective information about where a hitter thrives—and where they're most vulnerable. Instead of relying solely on instinct or anecdotal scouting, pitchers could now see the data for themselves and craft game plans with surgical precision.

What Maddux and Pedro did instinctively, Codify made accessible to every pitcher, turning scouting into a science.

Codify heat maps provide pitchers with a customized plan to target hitters' weaknesses. By combining the science of pitch movement with the art of precision placement, tools like Codify are taking the unhittable pitcher to the next level, turning innovation into domination one pitch at a time.

The brainchild of Michael Fisher, Codify is part of the revolution in how pitchers prepare and strategize in Major League Baseball by leveraging the vast database of insights from Baseball Savant, among other pitch information. By transforming complex analytics into hyper-customized heat maps and data visualizations tailored to each pitcher's strengths and opposing hitters' tendencies, Codify provides players with the ultimate pitching plan of attack. Their heat maps break down intricate statistics into actionable insights, enabling pitchers to exploit even the smallest weaknesses in a hitter's approach. With its seamless integration of Baseball Savant data and practical application, Codify epitomizes the modern marriage of technology and strategy, redefining how pitchers approach each batter—and making them, quite literally, unhittable.

Like many of the other innovators discussed above, Michael Fisher's background reflects an unconventional path to baseball analytics. Fisher began his career in banking analytics, where he identified inefficiencies in data measurement and process optimization. His knack for streamlining systems led to measurable improvements in performance and cost savings. As Fisher described, "I just started applying Codify-esque stuff to the bank," emphasizing how his mindset reshaped operations even in a field as rigid as banking.

Fisher's transition into baseball was serendipitous, sparked by an unexpected connection at a family barbecue in 2010. There, he learned that his uncle's stepson, Dan Straily, was pitching for the Kane County

Cougars, a minor league affiliate of the Oakland Athletics. As a lifelong Oakland A's fan and a data enthusiast, Fisher was intrigued and saw an opportunity to apply his skills to a new domain. "At first, it was just me sharing some Pitchf/x data I found online," Fisher recounted. "Dan was curious, and I was eager to help in any way I could."

Their partnership became more serious by 2015, when Straily was navigating struggles in his career and needed a fresh perspective to regain his form. Fisher, relying on his background in analytics, began developing rudimentary heat maps to provide Straily with actionable insights on pitch locations and patterns. "Dan would tell me about a game, and I'd run some numbers to find ways he could make adjustments," Fisher explained. The early success of their collaboration cemented their relationship and inspired Fisher to refine his tools further. Straily later reflected, "Michael's work gave me clarity I didn't have before. It wasn't just numbers; it was a way to approach the game differently."

As Fisher's insights began translating into tangible results on the field, he realized the potential to expand his efforts. Codify evolved from a hobby into a robust platform, offering tailored heat maps and analytics to help pitchers identify optimal pitch locations and strategies. "I never set out to create a business," Fisher said, "but the more I worked with Dan, the more I saw how this could help other pitchers."

♦ ♦ ♦

AFTER HIS INITIAL success working with Dan Straily, Michael Fisher's reputation as a data-driven pitching strategist began to grow. Straily's improved command and ability to locate pitches effectively demonstrated the potential of Fisher's heat map system, catching the attention of others in professional baseball. It wasn't long before Fisher's unique approach to optimizing pitch strategy was sought out by agents and players looking for an edge.

This momentum led to a pivotal connection in 2017 when Blake Treinen's agent approached Fisher. Treinen, a talented but inconsistent reliever, was searching for answers to unlock his full potential. The agent saw an opportunity for Fisher to replicate the success he had achieved with Straily and transform Treinen into an unstoppable force on the mound. What followed was a partnership that reignited Treinen's career and cemented Fisher's status as a key figure in the world of pitching analytics.

Fisher's insights into pitch movement and location helped Treinen refine his approach, especially with his devastating sinker-slider combination. The shift was immediate—Treinen rose from an underperforming reliever to one of the most impressive bullpen arms in MLB, highlighted by his historic 2018 season with the Athletics, where he posted a 0.78 ERA.

♦ ♦ ♦

MICHAEL FISHER CREATES Codify's heat maps by combining advanced analytics, customized visualization, and an understanding of individual pitchers' needs. The process begins with data from sources like Baseball Savant, which offers detailed information about pitch movement, velocity, spin rates, and hitter tendencies. Fisher's methodology involves using this data to identify patterns and optimal pitch locations, but tailored to each pitcher.

He ensures the maps account for each pitcher's unique strengths, arsenal, and target outcomes. "It's not just about where the ball should go," Fisher explained. "It's about understanding the pitcher's capabilities and the batter's tendencies in ways that can be executed consistently and effectively." By focusing on factors like the pitcher's preferred pitch types, velocity bands, and historical performance against specific hitters, Codify generates a playbook designed to exploit vulnerabilities in opposing lineups.

Fisher also incorporates feedback from the pitchers themselves, ensuring that the heat maps align with their comfort zones and strategic preferences. This collaborative process results in tools that provide actionable insights while boosting the confidence of the athletes using them. As Fisher puts it, "The maps aren't just about data—they're about transforming that data into something the pitcher can trust and use on the field. The confidence of having a clear plan of attack, rather than relying on generic advice, can make all the difference." This hands-on, iterative approach has made Codify an essential resource for pitchers throughout Major League Baseball.

Even as MLB teams continue to expand their analytics capabilities, Codify remains indispensable. Fisher's focus on individual players ensured that Codify became a trusted partner. Pitchers and catchers study Codify's maps at home, in the clubhouse before a game, and I've even seen them in the bullpen prior to a reliever entering the game, focusing on the first three hitters they would face.

Due to this approach, Codify has grown exponentially, evolving from a personal hobby into a transformative force in Major League Baseball. Originally created as a tool to help a single pitcher refine his game, Codify now has worked with over 250 MLB pitchers. Fisher's hyper-customized heat maps, tailored to each pitcher's unique arsenal and the tendencies of opposing hitters, have deeply resonated across the league.

Fisher attributes this rapid growth to Codify's tangible impact on pitchers' careers. "I realized this wasn't about selling a product," Fisher explained. "These guys are making more money, having longer careers, and being more effective on the mound. It's about providing real value to their careers." Word-of-mouth endorsements from high-profile clients like Blake Treinen and Liam Hendriks have played a pivotal role in Codify's expansion, with many pitchers crediting Fisher's insights as a key to their success.

Even as MLB teams continue to expand their analytics departments, Codify has maintained its competitive edge through Fisher's personalized approach. By offering direct communication with pitchers and tailored insights, Codify ensures its data is practical, actionable, and seamlessly integrated into a pitcher's routine. This player-centric model has cemented Codify as a trusted resource for those aiming to elevate their performance. As baseball technology and data continue to evolve, Fisher's system remains a disruptive and indispensable tool in the sport.

Houston Astros All-Star Lance McCullers is one of many pitchers who have praised Codify's heat maps for providing an extra layer of preparation and confidence. While the Astros have long been at the forefront of pitching analytics under legendary coach Brent Strom, McCullers sought even more precision. He likened Codify to "studying for a test and then asking the smartest kid in the class to help you study too." For McCullers, the heat maps served as a safety net, complementing his own research and video analysis to catch anything he might have overlooked. "Codify helps me get there before I show up to the ballpark," he explained. It allowed him to take the mound with a clear strategy tailored to his strengths and the weaknesses of opposing hitters.

Logan Webb, Kevin Gausman, and Liam Hendriks provide further compelling examples of how Codify empowers pitchers to optimize their game.

Logan Webb, a cornerstone of the San Francisco Giants' rotation, has leaned on Codify to refine his arsenal, particularly his devastating sinker. As Michael Fisher explained, Webb uses the maps to target specific weaknesses in hitters' swings, ensuring his pitches exploit their blind spots. This data-driven approach, combined with Webb's ability to manipulate pitch movement, has helped him consistently dominate on the mound and evolve into one of baseball's most effective ground-ball pitchers.

Kevin Gausman, known for his incredible splitter, credits Codify with simplifying his preparation. He described how the heat maps align with his instincts while providing an added layer of precision. "Sometimes we'd run into a hitter and the map would say something different than what I thought," Gausman noted, "but then I'd try it, and it would work."

Liam Hendriks, a flame-throwing closer renowned for his fiery competitiveness and pinpoint control, described Codify's heat maps as transformative. Hendriks likened the system to eliminating guesswork, saying, "The heat maps take the pressure off; I don't second-guess my pitch selection anymore." This level of confidence has directly translated into Hendriks's ability to thrive in high-pressure situations, solidifying his place as one of the game's most reliable bullpen arms.

Houston Astros reliever Tayler Scott offers yet another example of Codify's impact. Curious about Codify for years, Scott finally decided to dive in fully for the 2024 season. "I had seen Codify for years and always been interested," Scott said. "This year, I wanted to go all in and see what it was about." The results were undeniable: Scott's improved pitch mix and execution were due to his use of Codify's heat maps. Fisher described Scott as an ideal client, calling him "a thinker" with an open mind. "Once we had a discussion and convinced him something was better, he went all in with conviction," Fisher recalled.

Scott acknowledged Codify's transformative effect on his career: "I don't think it's a coincidence that I had the year I had, and we started working together." By seamlessly integrating Codify's insights into his game plan, Scott became one of the Astros' most effective bullpen arms.

Together, these pitchers highlight how Codify's personalized heat maps enable players to leverage data in ways that complement their natural abilities and maximize their effectiveness on the field.

♦ ♦ ♦

THE PSYCHOLOGICAL IMPACT of Codify's heat maps on pitchers cannot be overlooked. Fisher openly acknowledged the placebo effect as a significant benefit of the system. "Pitching is about confidence, and if you can confidently throw something somewhere, it makes all the difference," Fisher explained. He emphasized that even the "wrong pitch confidently thrown is better than the right pitch with no confidence." This sentiment highlights the dual role of Codify: It not only provides data-driven insights but also reinforces a pitcher's belief in their strategy, which can be just as important as the strategy itself.

The placebo effect does not diminish the scientific rigor of Codify; rather, it enhances its value by empowering pitchers to approach their craft with conviction. As Fisher put it, "If I were only as good as the team stuff, I wouldn't exist." Codify's strength lies in its ability to merge analytical precision with a psychological edge, offering pitchers a complete package for success on the mound.

The relationship between Codify and MLB organizations underscores a delicate balance between external innovation and the in-house capabilities of team analytics departments. While both aim to optimize player performance, their methods often diverge, creating a nuanced coexistence with occasional friction. Codify offers a highly personalized, player-centric approach that focuses on individual strengths and needs—a stark contrast to the broader, often generalized systems employed by MLB teams.

Brian Bannister highlighted this distinction: "Teams often have one-size-fits-all approaches because they're catering to the entire roster. What Michael does is hyper-focused, and that makes a huge difference." Codify's tailored heat maps and direct collaboration with players resonate in ways that team-issued reports sometimes fail to match, giving Codify a competitive edge even as MLB organizations invest heavily in their own analytics capabilities.

Fisher recognizes this dynamic and positions Codify as a complementary resource rather than a competitor. "It's not about competing with teams; it's about filling a gap. We're focused on individual pitchers and their specific challenges, while teams have to manage analytics for an entire roster," he explained. Thus Codify has thrived as an external specialist, offering unique insights that often supplement and enhance team strategies.

At the heart of Codify's success is Fisher's belief in empowering players to take charge of their careers. While MLB teams often define roles based on immediate roster needs, Fisher encourages players to think beyond these constraints. "Teams might have a predetermined role for you—like being the seventh-inning lefty guy—but you might know that if you made a few adjustments, you could get righties out too," Fisher noted.

This perspective is particularly valuable in an industry where players can feel limited by team strategies or analytics that prioritize short-term wins over long-term development. Fisher emphasized, "You're paying me to look out for you and your career, not just the next game. That's what teams can't always do." By focusing on individualized plans, Codify enables pitchers to unlock new potential, refine their craft, and position themselves for expanded roles or future opportunities. Codify can even generate heat maps for potential new pitches in a pitcher's arsenal, providing insights into how the pitch might perform in game situations—all before the pitcher ever faces a single hitter.

This tailored approach is transformative for players who might otherwise feel pigeonholed. Whether it's helping a pitcher refine their arsenal or reimagine their role on the mound, Codify's philosophy encourages athletes to see beyond their current assignments and take control of their professional trajectories. The result is a system that complements team analytics and empowers players to achieve more than they might have thought possible.

The transition from Trackman to Hawk-Eye technology has greatly expanded the breadth of data available for Codify's heat maps, promising even richer insights in the future. As Hawk-Eye measures pitch trajectories in three dimensions from hand release to plate crossing—and even beyond—it captures subtleties that were previously overlooked. This improvement is complemented by the integration of advanced metrics into Baseball Savant, such as bat speed and swing path data, which have enormous potential for refining heat maps.

Fisher highlighted the impact of these advancements, saying, "We're only as good as the data we get, and with every new layer of information—like swing behavior or bat positioning—our maps can become exponentially more precise." For example, the inclusion of swing data enables Codify to assess not just where a hitter struggles to make contact but also where their bat speed drops off or their swing path creates vulnerabilities. This allows Codify to suggest pitch locations that are even harder for hitters to handle, further optimizing a pitcher's arsenal.

Swing data also offers the potential to identify trends in a hitter's confidence. If a batter begins to consistently swing with success against one of a pitcher's previously dominant pitches, that data can be captured and analyzed to recommend adjustments. Fisher explained, "It's not just about finding weaknesses anymore; it's about recognizing when a hitter is figuring you out and getting ahead of their adjustment curve." Codify could suggest subtle shifts in sequencing, pitch location, or even usage patterns to ensure that a pitcher stays one step ahead of evolving hitter strategies.

As MLB continues to expand the metrics captured by Hawk-Eye and other technologies, the ability to tailor strategies based on hyper-specific hitter tendencies will grow. Fisher observed, "The possibilities are endless. As the game evolves, so do we. We're constantly looking for ways to leverage new data to stay ahead."

15

Baseball once lived in a stat-free wilderness. No hits, no strikeouts, no averages—just stories, wild exaggerations, and barroom debates about who was best. Without numbers, it was all opinion, bias, and myth. The greatest pitcher was usually the one with the loudest, most colorful storyteller in his corner. The lack of structure held baseball back. The sport was growing fast, but without a standard way to track performance, its history was scattered, locked away in newspaper blurbs and fading memories. There was no way to prove how one player stacked up against another, no leaderboard to settle debates, no real way to measure greatness.

Then came Henry Chadwick—the man who saw baseball's future and decided to put it in the box score.

Henry Chadwick didn't need to swing a bat or throw a pitch to change the game forever. Known as the "Father of Baseball," Chadwick was a sportswriter with a vision, turning baseball from a backyard pastime into America's favorite sport. Born in England in 1824 and raised on cricket, Chadwick brought his love for that sport's statistics and structure to baseball. He believed it was perfectly suited for the American spirit, once writing, "Americans do not care to dawdle over a sleep-inspiring game, all through the heat of a June or July day. What they do they want to do in a hurry. In baseball all is lightning; every action is as swift as a seabird's flight."[1]

Chadwick's genius lay in capturing that lightning in a bottle. In 1859, he introduced the first modern box score, documenting stats like runs, hits, putouts, assists, and errors while chronicling the superiority of clubs like the Brooklyn Excelsiors. He even added pitchers' strikeouts to the mix, marking them with the now-iconic *K*. It was the initial spark of baseball's love of data and numbers. According to his biographer, Andrew Schiff, "The box score was the only way of showing the game; there really was no photography. So the writer really was the person at the center between the fans and the player at the game." Chadwick built a bridge between the players on the field and the fans in the stands.

Chadwick's influence went well beyond the box score. He introduced stats like batting average and earned run average (ERA), giving fans and players a new way to evaluate performance. These became tools to measure greatness and fuel debates. Chadwick called the box score baseball's "numerical language," and it became the foundation for how we understand and analyze the game today. By giving the sport a statistical backbone, he made baseball more accessible, turning every game into a story fans could follow and relive.

Chadwick's writing brought those stories to life. Through his columns in nationally read publications like *The New York Clipper* and *Sunday Mercury*, he painted baseball as a game of skill, strategy, and lightning-fast action. His descriptions elevated players to mythical status and gave fans a front-row seat to the drama, even if they weren't at the ballpark. Chadwick's columns made sure baseball's heroes and moments were etched into the cultural memory.

Back in the early days of baseball, before radar guns, spin rates, or even standard rules, the ball itself was, simply put, a chaotic mess. Forget the pristine, meticulously engineered baseballs we know today—nineteenth-century pitchers had to deal with handmade creations that varied wildly in size, weight, and performance. Imagine trying to throw a slider or a cutter when every baseball you pick up feels completely different. Let's dive into some of the unpredictable designs that pitchers had to tame back in the day.[2]

To have any meaningful way of developing consistent pitches with regular movement, you need to have a baseball you can plan for. However, that wasn't really a thing in the mid-nineteenth century. Clubs often used different balls depending on who was hosting the game, and the differences were staggering. Some balls were "live," packed tightly with rubber and wound so taut that they rocketed off the bat like they were spring-loaded. Others were "dead," loosely wound with little to no bounce, turning games into defensive slogs. There weren't factories churning out perfectly symmetrical balls—no Rawlings, no MLB specs, nothing. If you wanted a ball, you improvised. Cobblers often stepped up to the plate (pun intended), crafting baseballs from whatever scraps they could find. The core? Melted-down rubber from old shoes. The cover? Yarn wrapped around the core, sometimes finished with a leather exterior—if you were lucky enough to have one.

And here's where it gets even weirder: in some regions, instead of shoe rubber, sturgeon eyes were used as the core. Yes, actual fish parts. These DIY baseballs varied wildly in size, weight, and bounce, so much so that pitchers often just made their own balls before a game. Imagine trying to throw a slider or curveball with a Franken-ball you stitched up yourself the night before. How do you practice for that? Pitchers had to adjust constantly to these conditions, making it nearly impossible to develop consistent mechanics or reliable pitch design. Imagine trying to work on your slider grip when one ball feels like a stress toy and the next feels like a cannonball. It's no wonder pitchers back then relied more on guts and guile than precision or finesse.

♦ ♦ ♦

THE LEMON-PEEL BALL was the go-to in early baseball, and let's just say it was as unpredictable as a knuckleball in a hurricane. Made from a single piece of leather stitched together in a four-line pattern that resembled a lemon peel, this ball was smaller, softer, and darker than today's regulation baseballs.

For pitchers, the lemon-peel ball was a nightmare. Its small size and softer texture made grip inconsistent at best, and forget trying to generate any meaningful spin. These things bounced like Super Balls and traveled farther off the bat, so in addition to pitch control being a problem, pitchers also had to watch helplessly as balls turned into pinballs in the outfield. And don't even think about throwing a split-finger fastball—your fingers might slide right off the seams.

Maybe the lemon ball is where the saying "he's throwing seeds" and the "squeeze play" came from? Oh, come on, don't be so sour.

Adding to the madness, early baseballs were soft enough to allow for a now-extinct rule called "soaking"—where fielders could throw the ball at runners to get them out. (You probably had this rule in kickball as a kid.) For pitchers, this rule added a whole new layer of pressure. Imagine fielding a bunt, ball in hand, and instead of just tossing it to first, you have the option to *absolutely level* the hitter on their sprint down the line. A poorly aimed throw could knock a runner clean off their feet or ricochet into the crowd, sparking pure mayhem.

♦ ♦ ♦

FOR MODERN PITCHERS, pitch design is all about repeatability—consistent seams, uniform weight, and a precise grip allow them to fine-tune every single pitch. Today's baseballs are engineered to MLB specifications right down to the coefficient of restitution—or, in less nerdy terms, their bounciness.

I've handed big leaguers baseballs, and within seconds, they can tell if something is off. Too heavy, too light, seams too high or too low—they just know. That level of precision makes sense when you realize that even the slightest variation can mess with movement, grip, and command.

Case in point? The 2017 World Series ball controversy.[3] Pitchers—including Justin Verlander and Yu Darvish—claimed the baseballs were slicker than normal, making it harder to spin breaking balls. Verlander, who's known for exceptional command, didn't hold back: "The World Series ball is slicker. It's different. No doubt. I noticed it as soon as I picked it up."

Dodgers pitching coach Rick Honeycutt backed him up, explaining how the difference in grip impacted breaking balls: "The slicker the ball is, the more difficult it is for guys to throw their breaking balls."

Yu Darvish, who struggled in his World Series starts, felt it too. Lance McCullers Jr. added that the baseballs had lower seams and a smoother surface, making them tougher to control: "It's not the same. The balls are slick. You can't get the same grip."

Now, imagine going back in time—before all the science, before MLB standardized baseballs, before pitchers had any real consistency to work with.

Early baseballs? Totally unpredictable. No two balls felt the same. Want to master a 12–6 curveball? Good luck finding a ball with seams you can grip. Trying to develop a changeup? Hope the ball doesn't slip right out of your hand.

Baseball has come a long way, but one thing's for sure: The earliest pitchers had it rough.

It wasn't until the mid-1850s that clubs began agreeing on basic standards, regulating the weight of baseballs to between 5.5 and 6 ounces and their circumference to between eight and eleven inches. Even then, variation persisted. It took decades for manufacturers to perfect the art of creating consistent baseballs, and by then, the game had evolved dramatically.

♦ ♦ ♦

IN 1867, A teenage pitcher named Candy Cummings was quietly revolutionizing how baseball was played. The story is as legendary as it gets. One summer afternoon on a Brooklyn beach, Cummings was skipping clamshells when he noticed something extraordinary—the spin caused the shells to curve midair. That sparked a question that would change baseball forever: "What if I could make a baseball do that?" With that idea, Cummings began a journey that would lead to the invention of the curveball, a pitch that reshaped the art of pitching.

As mentioned earlier, at the time, baseballs were anything but precise. Handmade and often misshapen, they were challenging to control even for the best pitchers. But Cummings was undeterred. He spent hours in secret, testing grips and arm motions to mimic the curving flight of a clamshell. His early experiments were unruly—wild pitches veered unpredictably, and teammates mocked his apparent lack of control. Still, Cummings refused to quit. He fine-tuned his technique until he found the key: snapping his wrist sharply at release to generate the spin needed for the ball to break.

When he finally brought his curveball into a game, it was a revelation. Hitters swung helplessly at a pitch that seemed to defy physics, and fans were awestruck. "I became fully convinced that I had made a new discovery in the art of pitching," Cummings later said. "A surge of joy flooded over me—one I shall never forget. I wanted to shout to the world that I had made a ball curve. It was too good to keep to myself."[4]

This new pitch became a weapon. By adding movement to the equation, Cummings gave pitchers a new advantage, forcing hitters to rethink everything.

The curveball's impact was undeniable, but it didn't come without criticism. Some traditionalists called it deceptive and unsportsmanlike: "Athletics have come to the pass where they are no longer fair and open trials of strength and skill, but on the contrary, as at present conducted, they train the young men to look upon victory as the rewards of treachery and deceit. That this is the case, anyone who has seen the game of baseball as it is played by the so-called best college nines will at once admit. For the pitcher, instead of delivering the ball to the batter in an honest, straightforward way, that the latter may exert his strength to the best advantage in knocking it, now uses every effort to deceive him by curving—I think that is the word—the ball. And this is looked upon as the last triumph of athletic science and skill. I tell you it is time to call halt! when the boasted progress in athletics is in the direction of fraud and deceit."[5] This quote has been attributed to Charles Eliot, president of Harvard University from 1869 to 1909, but according to Richard Herschberger, it more likely came from his cousin, Charles Eliot Norton.[6]

Despite this controversy, the pitch quickly caught on, and by the 1880s, it had become a must-have in any serious pitcher's arsenal.

Henry Chadwick himself praised Cummings' ingenuity and, in 1871, Chadwick named Cummings the most outstanding ball player in the United States.[7]

Cummings bewildered hitters with his new curveball. Over six professional seasons, Cummings compiled a 145–94 record with a 2.42 ERA and seventeen shutouts, proving that his invention was shifting the baseball landscape. His curveball turned pitchers into strategists, elevating their role from facilitators to tacticians. As Cummings later reflected, "But my idlest dreams of what a curved ball would do, as I dreamed of them that afternoon while throwing clamshells, have been filled more than a hundred times. At that time I thought of it only as a good way to fool the boys, its real practical significance never entering my mind. I get a great deal of pleasure now in my old age out of going to games and watching the curves, thinking that it was through my blind efforts that all this was made possible."[8]

While the pitch was groundbreaking, Cummings's grasp of the science behind the curveball was charmingly rudimentary. He explained: "I have often been asked to give my theory of why a ball curves. Here it is: I give the ball a sharp twist with the middle finger, which causes it to revolve with a swift rotary motion. The air also, for a limited space around it begins to revolve, making a great swirl, until there is enough pressure to force the ball out of true line."[9]

Though his explanation was more imaginative than accurate—modern science credits spin and air resistance for the ball's break—Cummings was at least starting to connect his instinctive feel for pitching with a broader understanding of its forces. Obviously, Candy Cummings wasn't an aerospace engineer so his description isn't scientifically perfect.

Cummings's curveball was apparently not only nearly impossible to hit, but it was also extremely tough to call for the umpire. He might have benefited greatly from an automated ball and strike system, declaring: "I would throw the ball straight at the batter; he would jump back, and then the umpire would call a ball. On this I lost, but when I started the spheroid toward the center of the plate he would call it a strike. When it got to the batter it was too far out, and the batter would not even swing. Then there would be a clash between the umpire and batter."

Candy Cummings's curveball was an early form of pitch design. He paved the way for sliders, sinkers, and splitters, proving that movement and deception could be as effective as velocity. With endorsements from Henry Chadwick and a career defined by innovation, Cummings carved his name into baseball history.

♦ ♦ ♦

CANDY CUMMINGS MAY have revolutionized the game with the curveball, but pitchers in the late nineteenth and early twentieth centuries weren't content to rest on their laurels. Competition kept them pushing the boundaries, experimenting with new ways to manipulate the baseball and outwit hitters.

Enter the spitball.

By applying substances like saliva, petroleum jelly, or tobacco juice to one side of the ball, pitchers could create unpredictable, almost supernatural movement. Hall of Famer Ed Walsh was a master of the spitball, and his performance on the mound was the stuff of legend. In 1908, Walsh threw a jaw-dropping 430 innings and posted a 1.82 ERA. His spitball was so filthy that Hall of Famer Sam Crawford once quipped, "Big Ed Walsh. Great, big, strong, good-looking fellow. He threw a spitball. I think that ball disintegrated on the way to the plate, and the catcher put it back together again. I swear, when it went past the plate, it was just the spit went by."[10]

Of course, not everyone was a fan of the spitball. Critics slammed it for being unsanitary and unfair. The idea of pitchers dousing the ball with spit—or worse substances—didn't sit well with baseball's growing reputation as a clean and professional sport. The controversy reached a boiling point, and in 1920, Major League Baseball officially banned spitballs.

However, a grandfather clause allowed pitchers like Burleigh Grimes—one of the pitch's last great practitioners—to keep throwing it until they retired. And let's be honest: Burleigh Grimes sounds like a guy born to throw spitballs. If your name conjures images of someone chewing tobacco on a dusty backroad, you might as well lean into it.

If the curveball was all about precision and the spitball thrived on deception, the knuckleball was pure insanity. Unlike traditional pitches that relied on spin to create movement, the knuckleball was thrown with little to no spin, turning aerodynamics into a pitcher's best (and sometimes only) friend. The result was a pitch that fluttered unpredictably, darting and dipping as if it had a mind of its own. Eddie Cicotte, one of the early pioneers of the pitch, summed it up best: "I began using this ball when I was a kid. It was always impossible to hit, but I found it very hard to obtain control of it. It was not until I joined Boston in 1908 that I began to get control of the 'knuckle ball.' Even then it evaded me for months at a time. When I got it going right I was hard to beat. Even now I often lose control of it."[11]

That unpredictability was both the knuckleball's greatest strength and its Achilles's heel. Hitters were baffled by its erratic movement, often swinging at air or watching helplessly as the ball danced into the catcher's mitt. But for pitchers, mastering the knuckleball required nerves of steel. One slight misfire, and the pitch might hang in the strike zone like a sitting duck, begging to be crushed—or it could move so wildly that it hit the catcher in a very private spot. Good luck getting him to call that pitch again. Were cups even a thing back then?

It was the ultimate high-risk, high-reward weapon—a pitch that could make a journeyman untouchable on his best day and unplayable on his worst.

Early knuckleballers like Cicotte helped the pitch gain a foothold in baseball. These pitchers weren't just experimenting for fun—they were innovators, challenging the traditional notions of what pitching could be. The knuckleball wasn't about overpowering hitters or tricking them with spin; it was about harnessing the unpredictable forces of nature.

It was a pitch that dared hitters to adjust, knowing full well they might never figure it out.

♦ ♦ ♦

IF THE KNUCKLEBALL brought turmoil to the mound, Christy Mathewson's "fadeaway" brought pure artistry. Building on the tradition of innovation that defined early pitching, Mathewson elevated the game with a pitch so precise and deceptive that it left hitters guessing every time they stepped into the box. Known today as a screwball, the fadeaway soon became a weapon that defined an era.

Mathewson's fadeaway was a reverse-breaking pitch that moved away from left-handed hitters, the opposite of what most batters expected from a standard curveball. For right-handed hitters, it broke in at the last second, making it equally devastating. Mathewson's pinpoint control of the fade was legendary, earning him the nickname "Big Six" (likely after New York City's Big Six Fire Company, the fastest to put out the fire) and cementing his reputation as one of the top pitchers of his era.[12]

The fadeaway, with its sharp arm-side break and sink, was also likely an early predecessor to the circle changeup—another pitch that "fades" to the arm side with filthy, late movement similar to a screwball.

The fadeaway remade pitching as a game of strategy. Mathewson used it to outthink hitters, setting them up with a mix of fastballs and traditional curves before unleashing the fade. Hitters were now left lunging at pitches that seemed to vanish or froze as the ball veered off its expected course. The fadeaway was his chess move, and Mathewson played it to perfection.

Unlike a curveball, which relied on wrist action, the fadeaway required a full forearm twist at release, creating the reverse spin that made the ball break. This motion was rumored to have put immense strain on his arm, but Mathewson's meticulous preparation and durability allowed him to wield the pitch with devastating consistency. And wield it he did, to the tune of 373 career wins, three National League pitching Triple Crowns, and a 2.13 ERA over seventeen seasons.

Mathewson's mastery of the fadeaway also came at a turning point in baseball history. His dominance highlighted a shift in pitching's role—from a simple deliverer of balls to a tactician capable of controlling every aspect of the game. The fadeaway was proof that pitching was more than overpowering hitters; it was about outsmarting them. In an era defined by innovation, Mathewson's fadeaway stood out as a pitch that combined physical skill, strategic brilliance, and a deep understanding of the game's evolving dynamics.

Just when hitters thought they'd seen it all—a blazing fastball, a looping curve, even the occasional spitball, knuckleball, and screwball—pitchers unveiled a new weapon that changed the game: the slider. A pitch that blurred the line between fastball speed and curveball movement, the slider came with late, sharp bite that left batters swinging at air and wondering what just happened.

♦ ♦ ♦

THE SLIDER, THAT wicked mix of speed and movement, didn't appear out of nowhere—it was crafted, experimented with, and perfected over decades.

The story begins in the early twentieth century with Charles Albert "Chief" Bender, one of the top pitchers of his era. Pitching for the Philadelphia Athletics from 1903 to 1914, Bender threw what he famously called a "nickel curve," showcasing a perfect example of nominative determinism.

The pitch wasn't quite a curveball and wasn't a fastball; it was somewhere in between. It had the speed to catch hitters off guard and enough lateral bite to make them look silly. Bender's nickel curve helped him rack up 212 wins, including a no-hitter in 1910, and laid the foundation for what would become the slider we know today.

As documented by Rob Neyer,[13] fast forward to the 1920s, when George Uhle of the Cleveland Indians took the concept and put his own spin on it—literally. Uhle's version, which he dubbed a "sailing fastball," used a unique grip that caused the ball to glide off his index finger while his ring and pinky fingers added a subtle twist. This created a pitch with late-breaking movement that left hitters guessing. Uhle's innovation added a whole new layer of deception to his arsenal. Batters couldn't sit on his fastball, without second-guessing themselves, which was exactly the point.

Another pitcher credited with developing the slider was George Blaeholder, who pitched in the 1920s and 1930s. While with the St. Louis Browns, Blaeholder made the slider his signature pitch. Back then, it didn't even have a consistent name. Some called it a "sailor," others a fastball with a mysterious sweep. But the name didn't matter—what mattered was the movement: sharp, late, and devastating. Pitchers began using the slider so effectively that hitters had virtually no chance. Skeptics worried the pitch's torque would destroy pitchers' arms, but that didn't stop it from taking root and changing the balance of power in the game.

Today's modern pitching labs build on these pitch grips and iterate off of them, creating nearly infinite variations of them to fit perfectly within a given pitcher's arsenal.

16

"Driveline was born out of frustration with conventional methods," Kyle Boddy explained to me. "We knew there had to be a better way to evaluate performance and prevent injuries."

Inspired by the book *Moneyball* and frustrated by the lack of scientific rigor in coaching, Boddy combined his technical expertise with a relentless drive to improve both injury prevention and player performance. "It slowly dawned on me that no one really knew how to keep players healthy despite claiming to," he recalled.

That determination to bring real science into player development became the foundation of Driveline Baseball—a facility that would challenge everything baseball thought it knew about mechanics, velocity, and durability.

A self-taught innovator, Boddy combined his background in economics and computer science with a willingness to challenge traditional coaching norms. After moving to Seattle in his early twenties, he began coaching youth and high school teams. However, his traditional coaching career was short-lived; being fired from a high school position for some of his unconventional coaching ideas became a pivotal moment. "I realized that working within conventional team structures wasn't for me," Boddy laughed. This realization drove him to create an independent system where he could challenge entrenched norms and focus on evidence-based training methods.

Before founding Driveline, Boddy honed his analytical skills in an unlikely arena: online poker. At PokerStars, the world's largest online poker platform, he developed tools to optimize player strategies using statistical modeling and data analysis. "PokerStars taught me how to think probabilistically," he explained. "It's about making decisions based on incomplete information, which isn't all that different from baseball." This experience cultivated a mindset of experimentation and iteration—skills he would later apply to baseball training.

   Tom House's book, *The Pitching Edge*, had a significant influence on Kyle Boddy during his early exploration of pitching mechanics and player development. Combining House's experience as both a pitcher and coach with insights from biomechanics, the book provided a detailed framework for understanding the pitching motion and maintaining arm health. "It was the first time I realized that there could be a scientific approach to coaching pitchers," Boddy said. House's emphasis on leveraging biomechanics to enhance performance and reduce injuries resonated deeply with Boddy and played a key role in shaping his approach to player development.

   Boddy acknowledged that while he didn't agree with everything in the book, it taught him to question conventional wisdom and look for answers beyond tradition. "It made me realize there was more to the game than what was commonly accepted," he noted. This mindset became a cornerstone of Driveline Baseball's philosophy.

   Boddy's philosophy was also shaped by influential figures like Paul Nyman and Dick Mills, another online pitching coach, and the grassroots discussions on the Let's Talk Pitching message board. Nyman's pioneering work in biomechanics and rotational force challenged traditional pitching mechanics, resonating deeply with Boddy. "Paul Nyman's ideas about rotational force and movement efficiency completely changed how I thought about pitching mechanics," Boddy later reflected.

   Meanwhile, Mills's emphasis on arm health and efficient mechanics underscored the importance of injury prevention. Boddy synthesized their contrasting ideas, blending them into his own evidence-based philosophy. "What I learned from guys like Nyman and Mills is that no single perspective has all the answers—you have to synthesize and experiment," he explained.

The Let's Talk Pitching internet message board became a pivotal space for collaboration and innovation in the pitching world. It served as a meeting point for forward-thinking minds, connecting Boddy with influential figures like long toss and mental game expert Alan Jaeger, as well as rising strength and conditioning leader Eric Cressey. The forum's open exchange of ideas gave Boddy the freedom to experiment with and refine his concepts while building relationships that would impact his future work.

I can personally attest to the power of that message board, as it's where my own pitching journey took shape. It's where I found myself engaging in debates with Boddy and another aspiring pitcher, Ben Brewster, who would go on to co-found Tread Athletics, discussed earlier. It was clear from the start that Boddy and Brewster were approaching pitching development in an important, new way, using the internet as a tool for connection and innovation. These conversations shaped Boddy's career and also ignited a movement that would fundamentally change the way baseball training is approached.

◆ ◆ ◆

DRIVELINE'S USE OF weighted baseballs, now one of its signature training tools, started by accident. Early in the facility's history, Boddy received a shipment of weighted baseballs by mistake. Rather than returning them, he decided to explore their potential. "They weren't something I ordered or planned to use initially," Boddy explained, "but when they showed up, I started digging into the science behind them and realized they might have untapped potential."

Boddy's curiosity led him to research existing studies on weighted baseballs. Though the research was limited at the time, it suggested that, when used properly, weighted balls could help increase velocity, improve arm strength, and even reduce injury risk by promoting more efficient movement patterns. "The research showed promise, but the application needed careful testing and refinement," Boddy said. This scientific approach helped dispel concerns about the potential for injury. Driveline carefully incorporated weighted balls into their programs, balancing intensity with recovery to improve pitchers' performance while safeguarding their health.

Initially, weighted baseballs were a controversial tool, with many fearing they would lead to arm injuries. However, by blending biomechanics and data analysis, Driveline refined the practice, proving that, when used correctly, through a series of well-designed throwing drills, they could enhance mechanics, increase velocity, and reduce injury risks. This accidental discovery became a cornerstone of Driveline's training philosophy.

Another significant developmental moment for Driveline came from Boddy's consumer-grade Casio high-speed cameras. Unable to afford professional-grade motion capture systems, Boddy turned to these cameras to analyze pitching mechanics of pitchers he was training. Recording at several hundred frames per second, they revealed issues invisible to the naked eye. "At the time, no one was really using slow-motion video to analyze pitching in this way," Boddy said. "It was one of those things where we realized we could see inefficiencies and patterns that even trained coaches couldn't spot in real-time."

The use of these cameras provided athletes with precise visual feedback and also helped establish Driveline's biomechanical approach. By breaking down a pitcher's motion frame by frame, Boddy could pinpoint subtle issues, such as poor hip-shoulder separation or inefficient arm paths, and provide targeted corrections. "It's one thing to tell someone they're leaking energy during their stride," he explained. "It's another to show them exactly how it's happening and what it looks like when they fix it."

Driveline's use of slow-motion video also led to a serendipitous encounter with Trevor Bauer, at the time a highly touted prospect renowned for his limitless curiosity about pitching mechanics. Bauer, then a college star, was experimenting with a Casio high-speed camera to analyze his delivery but encountered technical issues. Frustrated with skipped frames in his recordings, Bauer approached Kyle Boddy for help during a chance meeting.

Boddy quickly diagnosed the problem. "You don't have a Class 10 memory card," he explained to Bauer. "The write speeds aren't fast enough, so it buffers and skips frames. You need to get a Class 10 card." Bauer was impressed by the immediate solution. After implementing Boddy's advice, he texted a couple of weeks later to confirm it had worked. This seemingly minor technical fix sparked a lasting connection between the two innovators. "We just stayed in touch ever since," Boddy recalled.

Their relationship grew as Bauer began training at Driveline. "Trevor's approach to pitching aligned perfectly with what we were doing at Driveline," Boddy noted. Bauer's willingness to experiment and his analytical mindset made him an ideal fit for Driveline. At the facility, Bauer fully embraced tools like slow-motion video, motion capture, and advanced analytics to dissect every detail of his mechanics. His persistent drive to improve mirrored Driveline's philosophy, pushing the boundaries of traditional training methods.

♦ ♦ ♦

TYLER GLASNOW'S VISIT to Driveline Baseball became a defining moment in the facility's early history, as the towering pitcher set a new standard that left the staff in awe. Known for his six-eight frame, overpowering fastball, elite athleticism, and Cillian Murphy–esque looks, Glasnow walked into Driveline and obliterated the facility's plyoball velocity records, instantly cementing himself as a legend in the making. Reflecting on that visit, Glasnow explained, "I just tried to break all the records," demonstrating both his raw power and competitive drive. His visit was encouraged by Trevor Bauer, who had been a mentor to Glasnow. "Trevor was there, and I know Trevor from high school, so I just kind of walked in and had a bullpen," Glasnow recalled.

Boddy was left in disbelief by Glasnow's effortless power. "It was ridiculous," Boddy remarked, highlighting how Glasnow, with no prior exposure to Driveline's systems, walked in and effortlessly surpassed the long-standing records.

The attention from working with some elite MLB arms transformed Driveline Baseball from a small operation into one of the most influential training facilities in baseball. In the beginning, Boddy faced intense skepticism from traditional baseball organizations, many of which resisted the data-driven, scientific methods he was championing. This resistance was rooted in the sport's long-standing reliance on intuition and tradition over hard data. "Teams were reluctant to embrace what we were doing because it challenged their entire structure," Boddy explained. But as players who trained at Driveline began seeing significant, measurable improvements, the skepticism slowly started to melt away.

Before long, more and more professional players were flocking to the facility, attracted by its reputation for producing tangible results. MLB organizations took notice, sending representatives to observe Driveline's ground-breaking methods. Yet, resistance remained; many players shared that their teams actively discouraged visits, fearing Driveline's approach would strip them of control. Boddy recognized this tension, noting, "The adversarial relationship between players and teams worked to our advantage. Players came to us because they wanted to take control of their careers." Despite the pushback, Driveline's success forced teams to reconsider their approach, prompting many to eventually adopt key aspects of Driveline's methods into their player development systems.

Today, Driveline has evolved from a scrappy start-up to a high-tech powerhouse for pitcher development, where biomechanics, data, and raw determination collide. Boddy's drive for innovation sparked a revolution in how pitchers train, challenging old norms and setting a new standard for peak performance. From motion capture systems to state-of-the-art brainwave sensors, Driveline has forever changed how pitchers prepare to dominate, making it clear that the future of pitching is rooted in science, technology, and a resolute pursuit of excellence.

♦ ♦ ♦

AT THE CORE of Driveline's approach is its motion capture lab, a facility equipped with OptiTrack Prime 17W cameras capable of capturing 360 frames per second. This advanced system provides a detailed, three-dimensional breakdown of every aspect of a pitcher's mechanics with unmatched precision.

"The ability to see exactly how an athlete moves in three dimensions is a game-changer," says Boddy. Whether it's refining pitch movement or correcting inefficiencies in delivery, the lab translates raw data into actionable insights, giving pitchers a clear blueprint for improvement.

Driveline's technological arsenal goes far beyond motion capture, boasting tools and data access that could rival NASA's. Bertec force plates measure ground reaction forces during pitching and other movements, offering detailed insights into power generation, balance, and efficiency—looking at how a pitcher is generating force with his lower half during the delivery in an attempt to optimize it. Having this data ensures that each athlete's training program is meticulously tailored to address that player's specific imbalances or inefficiencies.

PULSEthrow sleeve (formerly Motus Global) sensors monitor arm stress and throwing efficiency in real time, enabling pitchers to optimize performance while mitigating the risk of overuse injuries. Additional tools, like Pupil Labs gaze-tracking headsets, analyze an athlete's focus during high-pressure moments, while Emotiv Flex brainwave readers measure stress and mental fatigue, creating a comprehensive profile of both physical and cognitive performance. With this technology, Driveline can precisely diagnose what's happening with a pitcher—and then help him correct flaws, sharpen strengths, or push his performance to the next level.

Driveline also employs Edgertronic high-speed cameras, Rapsodo, and Trackman systems to analyze every pitch's spin rate, velocity, and movement in ultra-slow motion. These technologies empower pitchers to refine their mechanics and even design entirely new pitches. The depth of analysis fosters a data-rich environment.

Driveline's success was built on more than technological advancements—it thrived because of the talent and expertise of its staff. Kyle Boddy recognized that innovation requires both leading-edge tools and skilled professionals to interpret and apply them. That's why he focused on building a team with deep knowledge in biomechanics, sports science, and player development.

Several key individuals who trained at Driveline have gone on to make an impact in Major League Baseball. For example, Eric Jagers, who started as a trainee, now serves as the Vice President of Pitching for the New York Mets. Other former Driveline trainers, like Caleb Cotham, Rob Hill, and Matt Daniels, now hold important positions with the Philadelphia Phillies, Los Angeles Dodgers, and Minnesota Twins, respectively.

Boddy's investment in talent creation has allowed Driveline to maintain its leadership in the field of pitching development. The emphasis on expert trainers who understand both the technology and the athlete has been key to creating personalized, effective training programs that continue to shape baseball's future.

Driveline initially faced significant criticism from the baseball establishment, with skeptics accusing the facility of prioritizing velocity at the expense of command, mechanics, and arm health. Traditionalists feared this velocity-first approach increased injury risks and overlooked the finesse and durability essential for long-term success. Critics dismissed Driveline's methods as shortcuts focused solely on raw power.

In response, Driveline, over the years, refined its mission to encompass every aspect of pitching performance while reducing injury risks. Founder Kyle Boddy acknowledged, "Velocity gets people in the door," but once pitchers joined Driveline's programs, they were introduced to a comprehensive system that included command, biomechanics, and pitch design. By leveraging tools like Edgertronic cameras, Rapsodo, and Trackman, Driveline helps pitchers refine their repertoire with precision and purpose.

Edgertronic cameras, in particular, have transformed pitch design by capturing ultra-slow-motion video of release mechanics, spin, and movement down to how the ball leaves a pitcher's fingers. Paired with real-time data from Rapsodo and Trackman—measuring metrics like spin rate and pitch movement—these technologies create detailed profiles of pitch performance, enabling data-driven adjustments.

One of Driveline's standout contributions lies in integrating the art of pitch design with the science of biomechanics. By tailoring pitches to a player's unique arm slot and spin profile, Driveline helps pitchers create standout pitches that complement their arsenal. As Boddy explained, "We didn't invent any of this, but applying technologies from biomechanics and sports science to create actionable results for pitchers—that's what sets us apart."

This approach has shifted the perception of Driveline from a velocity-first facility to a leader in holistic pitching development.

Evaluating Individual Pitches: Driveline's Stuff+ Model

Driveline's internal Stuff+ model was developed to evaluate the intrinsic quality of a pitcher's individual pitches. Through quantifying factors such as velocity, vertical and horizontal movement, release extension, arm angle, and other biomechanical elements, Stuff+ offers a comprehensive, data-driven assessment of pitch effectiveness.

By isolating these key metrics, Stuff+ provides a standardized, location-independent evaluation of pitch quality, enabling comparisons across pitches and pitchers that were previously impossible. This empowers pitchers to refine their approach with precision, providing valuable insights into how each of their pitches ranks against MLB competition. It essentially shows pitchers how nasty their individual pitches are compared to other pitchers in baseball.

How Stuff+ Transforms Pitch Design at Driveline

Stuff+ assigns a numerical value to each pitch, with 100 representing the league average. A slider that scores 110, for example, is considered 10% better than the average slider. This scoring system provides pitchers and coaches with valuable insights to accomplish the following:

Identify Strengths and Weaknesses: Pinpoint which pitches are effective and which need improvement.

Guide Pitch Design: Refine spin, movement, and release mechanics to tailor pitches to a player's strengths.

Optimize Game Strategy: Use pitch quality data to inform pitch sequencing and matchups.

For instance, if a pitcher's fastball scores high for velocity but low for movement, adjustments can be made to improve its effectiveness. Alternatively, the pitcher can pair it with a higher-scoring secondary pitch, like a curveball or slider, to create a more devastating arsenal. This precision ensures that every pitch in a pitcher's repertoire serves a specific, impactful purpose.

Driveline knew nasty pitches alone don't win games. Arsenal construction is important. Pitching dominance comes when an arsenal plays in harmony. Stuff+ on a pitch is like rating instruments one by one. A killer drummer can't cover for a bad guitarist—the whole band has to be in sync.

This nuanced perspective reflects a paradigm shift in pitching, focusing on arsenal construction rather than isolated improvements as discussed in *Quantifying Arsenal Effects: A New Paradigm in Pitching Models* by Driveline's Jack Lambert and Marek Ramilo. Visualizing arsenals in three-dimensional space—using metrics like vertical break, horizontal break, and velocity differentials—also allows Driveline to map how pitches complement each other. This enables them to identify gaps in a pitcher's arsenal and recommend specific adjustments, such as adding a curveball to expand breadth or refining a sinker to improve tunneling.

♦ ♦ ♦

DRIVELINE EMPHASIZES THE importance of "bridge pitches," which connect a pitcher's repertoire and enhance deception. For example, a cutter with movement and velocity that sits between a fastball and a slider can significantly increase a pitcher's effectiveness by making each pitch harder to predict. Similarly, adding pitches like splitters or changeups can expand an arsenal's range, ensuring the pitcher can keep hitters guessing across all quadrants of the plate.

Michael King's slider serves as a prime example of a "bridge pitch," effectively connecting his sinker and sweeper to enhance the overall deception of his arsenal. King described his smaller slider, or "gyro slider," as a pitch designed for command rather than overwhelming movement, telling me, "It's not one of my sexy pitches, but there are a lot of hitters that take 0-spin pitches at an 85 percent clip." The gyro slider spins, but like a football. It's usually a few miles slower than the fastball, while looking just like the fastball. It has some dip, but none of the horizontal movement of a slider.

The bridge pitch strategy allows King to sequence his pitches more effectively, keeping hitters off balance. He explained how he uses the slider to bait hitters: "I can go backdoor sinker, take strike one, and then slider away off of that. They see the spin, think it's going to stay on the plate, and then I throw the sweeper with ten more inches of horizontal movement, and they swing at it thinking it's going to stay in the zone." By ensuring his slider remains distinct in movement and release from his sweeper, King maximizes deception, illustrating the value of bridge pitches in modern pitching strategy.

Driveline's research extends to understanding how pitch effectiveness evolves over the course of a game. Over-reliance on a single pitch can result in "decay," where hitters become more familiar with its shape and timing, reducing its effectiveness. Even the nastiest pitches can lose their edge if batters see them too often. To combat this, Driveline applies the concept of "buyback," where a well-designed arsenal leverages secondary pitches to "buy back" the effectiveness of primary pitches, keeping hitters off-balance and maintaining unpredictability.

Driveline's optimization framework, known as the Paint Mixer, integrates inputs like Stuff+, Arsenal+, and pitch usage patterns to develop customized game plans for pitchers. This advanced system helps pitchers strategically vary their arsenals, balancing the maximization of utility with the minimization of overuse. By managing pitch sequences and usage strategically, pitchers can ensure their best offerings remain unpredictable throughout the game, preserving their edge against increasingly savvy hitters. Think of it as a poker player shuffling their tells, making sure no pattern gives them away.

♦ ♦ ♦

DRIVELINE'S FOCUS IS quantifying the art of pitching and fine-tuning pitch arsenals to create the most effective combinations for each individual pitcher. Their approach seamlessly blends science and strategy, using data to optimize how pitches interact and complement one another. By leveraging these insights, Driveline is helping pitchers craft arsenals designed to keep hitters off balance—turning good pitches into nearly unhittable weapons. Driveline's philosophy is simple: Once you can measure the art of pitching, you can teach it. And once you can teach it, you can master it so that performance is repeatable and built on skill, not luck.

Command has always been one of pitching's great mysteries. It's easy to see when it's missing, but it's nearly impossible to measure or fix. And, as you'd guess, Driveline's approach to command is to strip away that mystery and turn it into a science. Command, often misunderstood as simply throwing strikes, is defined by Driveline as the ability to hit precise pitch locations with minimal deviation. Their system begins by measuring "miss distance," which tracks the difference between where a pitcher aims and where the pitch actually lands. Tools like Trackman, Rapsodo, and projected strike zones provide real-time feedback, allowing pitchers to fine-tune their mechanics.

Boddy emphasizes understanding natural tendencies: "One degree of variation in release angle can result in a 12-inch difference at the plate." Instead of trying to eliminate these natural variations, Driveline helps pitchers optimize them. They focus on targeting central spots in the zone, letting the pitcher's arm slot and mechanics guide the pitch to the ideal location.

Driveline's training also includes deliberate practice, where pitchers repeatedly throw to specific targets while tracking their miss distances. By analyzing this data over thousands of reps, pitchers learn to align their intent with execution. Command isn't only minimizing misses; it's also about leveraging natural variations to make pitches more deceptive and effective.

Additionally, Driveline uses "execution reports," which visualize where a pitcher's misses occur relative to their target. These reports break down specific miss tendencies and provide actionable adjustments, helping pitchers improve during both bullpens and in-game situations. This method enhances command while teaching pitchers how to perform under the pressure of competition, ultimately transforming raw talent into game-ready precision.

Overall, Driveline's command training strikes a balance between technology and practicality, equipping pitchers with the tools to dominate through sustained, intelligent performance—proving that it's far more than just a "velo factory."

♦ ♦ ♦

DRIVELINE BASEBALL'S IMPACT on the sport is immense, extending far beyond its original flagship facility in Washington. What began as a small, experimental program has grown into a global phenomenon, training thousands of professional athletes each year. With a roster that includes over forty MLB All-Stars, multiple MVP winners, and Cy Young Award recipients, Driveline has become synonymous with superior performance in baseball. Here are some examples of household names who have worked with Driveline:

Clayton Kershaw

Clayton Kershaw, a future first-ballot Hall of Famer, provides compelling evidence for the adaptability and effectiveness of Driveline's approach.

Kershaw's experience with Driveline Baseball highlights the organization's versatility and focus on personalized player development, extending far beyond the commonly associated weighted balls. In a 2020 interview with *The Athletic*, Kershaw shared that his time at Driveline did not involve weighted balls, demonstrating how their methods adapt to the specific needs of each athlete. "They don't force you to do anything. They're very individualized," Kershaw explained. "I didn't even touch a weighted ball while I was there."

For Kershaw, the goal was not to increase velocity but to refine his mechanics and maintain his longevity as one of the best left-handed pitchers ever to play the game. "For me, it was just about getting my body in the right spots," Kershaw added, reflecting the organization's ability to adapt their methodology for different priorities and goals.

Shohei Ohtani

Shohei Ohtani's collaboration with Driveline emphasized his incredible talent and showcased just how much of an outlier he is in every measurable aspect of athletic performance. Even among elite MLB players, Ohtani exists in a league of his own. His sheer physical presence left an indelible impression on Driveline founder Kyle Boddy, who described Ohtani's presence with awe:

"When you're ten feet away from him, it's a f***ing joke. You're just like, 'What the f*** is this man?' In an alternate universe, this dude is the emperor of Japan—it's ridiculous," Boddy said. He noted that seeing Ohtani up close, without the distance of a baseball uniform or TV screen, highlights just how genetically extraordinary he is. Comparing him to other athletic marvels like LeBron James, Boddy added, "It's like seeing LeBron in his prime—you think, 'This guy would've been the king of the world five thousand years ago.'"

Ohtani's dominance extended to the metrics tracked during his time at Driveline, where he topped strength, power, and biomechanical efficiency tests. His explosive power was evident in his force plate data, while his biomechanics revealed near-perfect efficiency in generating velocity and force. Ohtani's greatness goes beyond natural talent—it's his relentless drive to adapt, train, and maximize his potential that sets him apart.

One example of this drive was showcased by his isometric mid-thigh pull test, a measure of raw strength and ability to overcome resistance. Initially, Ohtani's results in this area were surprisingly average. Recognizing the potential for improvement, Driveline prescribed a simple strength training regimen, including deadlifts and other foundational exercises. True to his work ethic, Ohtani returned after training ranked easily in the top three of all athletes tested. The improvement translated directly to his performance, a development that Driveline had predicted and Ohtani realized through meticulous training.

Tarik Skubal

Tarik Skubal's rise to the 2024 American League Cy Young Award winner is a story of growth, determination, and embracing modern technology. A key part of his development was his time at Driveline, where he honed his pitching mechanics using advanced tools like Trackman, Edgertronic cameras, and motion capture systems.

Skubal's success lies in his ability to balance data with the nuances of pitching. "There's a fine line," Skubal shared. "You can look at pitch shapes, release height, and release extension, but sometimes the numbers don't capture the feel." This realization led him to personalize his training and refine his pitch arsenal to match his unique abilities.

His approach involves constant fine-tuning. "It's a lot of Trackman, Edgertronic, and communication with coaches," Skubal explained. These technologies helped him transform his changeup from an inconsistent pitch into one of his most potent weapons. Not only did he refine the changeup itself but he also made sure that pitch tunneled with his fastball to make it even harder for hitters to pick up because they look the same coming out of his hand.

Skubal's commitment to improving his pitches is reflected in the way he integrates data into his training regimen. "I want to know what my pitches are doing, and when they're off, I check the numbers to get back on track."

Alongside technical training, Skubal's pregame work includes Driveline's plyoball drills on the field to improve arm path and strength. These exercises, combined with his focus on pitch mechanics, have made him more efficient and durable on the mound.

Skubal's approach to pitching is a blend of art and science, rooted in data but driven by instinct. Through his work with Driveline, he's evolved into one of baseball's top pitchers, using both his natural talent and cutting-edge analytics to dominate at the highest level.

♦ ♦ ♦

KYLE BODDY'S TRANSITION from running Driveline Baseball to working with MLB organizations highlights his influence and adaptability within professional baseball. His role with the Cincinnati Reds marked a significant step, as he brought his innovative, data-driven approach to one of MLB's oldest franchises. Reflecting on his time there, Boddy remarked on the balance of tradition and innovation: "You forget how important that history is to the people who work there . . . but being able to disrupt and challenge the status quo is crucial."

Boddy's time with the Reds was about more than implementing industry-leading baseball technology—it was also about building unique connections with players. One memorable story involves chess matches with reliever Amir Garrett, a player known for his fiery competitiveness on the mound but who also harbors a surprising talent for chess. Boddy recalled being impressed by Garrett's skills: "Amir kicked the shit out of me in chess," he admitted. When asked where he learned, Garrett responded, "Washington Square Park."

Garrett, who was a basketball standout at St. John's University before transitioning to professional baseball, shared how chess became a way to focus and stay sharp. "Man, you know, I just got to keep that off the field—it just gets me into trouble," he told Boddy, referencing the mental energy chess demanded. For Garrett, chess became a tool to manage the pressures of being a professional athlete.

For Boddy, these matches were a window into the multifaceted personalities of his players and the ways they stayed grounded amid the intensity of baseball. Boddy remarked, "He's brilliant in so many ways, but he knows to stay competitive, he has to keep his mind busy off the field."

Boddy's journey continued as he joined the Boston Red Sox, stepping into the role of Interim Director of Baseball Sciences. With the Red Sox, he has focused on integrating modern technologies, such as K-Motion and force plate systems, into the team's player development framework. His efforts emphasize optimizing performance through data collection and analysis while also managing the complexities of a major MLB organization. "Mostly what I do in Boston now is project management," Boddy explained, highlighting the importance of aligning resources and priorities to maximize the team's potential.

♦ ♦ ♦

DRIVELINE AIMS TO transform baseball at every level, starting with the youngest players. The organization's focus on youth sports began with a critical observation from Boddy: Many of the injuries and inefficiencies in baseball stem from inadequate training and guidance during formative years. Reflecting on his early coaching experiences, Boddy admitted, "When I started coaching Little League and high school, I realized how little I knew about keeping kids healthy and improving their skills. There was no comprehensive answer anywhere—not in books or medical literature."

This insight became the foundation for Driveline's commitment to youth sports, driving the creation of programs designed to teach proper mechanics, prevent injuries, and foster a love for the game. By addressing these issues early, Driveline ensures that young athletes improve their skills and also build a solid foundation for long-term success.

Under the leadership of Deven Morgan, who heads Driveline's youth development initiatives, the organization has made significant strides in introducing high-level methodologies to younger athletes. Morgan has been instrumental in implementing programs that focus on long-term athlete development, emphasizing health, mechanics, and incremental progress over the all-too-common push for early specialization. "If we can start anywhere, it's by keeping these kids healthy," Boddy emphasized.

Morgan's work includes creating accessible versions of Driveline's high-tech tools, such as lightweight plyometric balls and foundational strength exercises, tailored to younger players. These tools help teach proper movement patterns while ensuring training remains engaging and age appropriate. By focusing on foundational skills, Driveline ensures that youth athletes develop the mechanics and strength needed for long-term success, not just short-term gains.

Both Boddy and Morgan share a vision of improving youth baseball through structured, science-backed programs. "When you're coaching kids, you quickly realize how much they can benefit from structured, well-informed programs," Boddy noted. Driveline's efforts, driven by Morgan's leadership, aim to bring the same level of innovation seen at the professional level to the grassroots of the sport. Together, they are ensuring the next generation of players grows up healthier, stronger, and better prepared for the challenges of baseball, while fostering a love for the game that prioritizes fun and development.

Driveline Baseball's impact on modern baseball cannot be overstated. Yankees pitching coach Matt Blake described it as "a laboratory for innovation" that disrupted traditional norms and championed data-driven decision-making. "Driveline brought credibility to the private sector," Blake explained, "because it showed that you could measure outcomes, test new methods, and actually track improvement in a way that hadn't been done before." He emphasized its role in empowering athletes: "It gave players a way to take control of their own development, to ask questions, and be active participants in the process."

Driveline's influence reached far beyond individual athletes, compelling Major League Baseball organizations to rethink their approach to player development. As Blake noted, "They forced MLB teams to look at what was working in the private sector and ask why they weren't doing the same." By blending science with tradition, Driveline ushered in an era where technology and evidence-based practices became indispensable tools in player development.

Driveline soon became synonymous with innovation, especially in the hugely important area of velocity development for pitchers, through more efficient mechanics. Motion capture systems dissected pitching mechanics with millisecond precision, pinpointing inefficiencies that could hinder performance or lead to injury. Weighted baseballs were paired with advanced analytics to enhance velocity and command, while force plates measured ground reaction forces during pitching and hitting. These technologies allowed Driveline to develop personalized training programs tailored to each athlete's unique needs and goals, enabling pitchers to throw harder, recover faster, and perform better.

Driveline's methods upended the entire baseball landscape. High school programs, collegiate teams, and MLB franchises began adopting its methodologies and training techniques, recognizing its reputation as a hub for revitalizing professional careers. By prioritizing measurable outcomes and embracing continuous experimentation, Driveline merged science with a sport long rooted in tradition and intuition.

18

Despite the clear advantages of high-speed cameras, ball-tracking systems, and biomechanics-driven pitch design, for years most MLB teams remained committed to traditional, feel-based coaching. Pitchers looking to refine their movement profiles or develop new pitches had little choice but to seek out private facilities like Driveline or experiment blindly on their own. While Bauer demonstrated that pitch design could be enhanced with the right tools, there was still no system for integrating this into MLB clubhouses.

That's when Eric Jagers emerged as the Johnny Appleseed of pitch design, spreading its influence throughout Major League Baseball.

Jagers honed his skills working alongside Bauer, whose meticulous approach pushed him to refine new training methods. "Trevor was using Edgertronic and Rapsodo together . . . really the only person in the entire world doing that at the time," Jagers recalled. "Every time I was there, I was watching Bauer throw 150 to 200 pitches off the mound daily."

What started as a niche experiment at Driveline—where Jagers and Bauer pushed the boundaries of pitch design—has since become a pillar of modern pitcher development. Jagers was among the first to recognize pitch design could be scaled across an entire MLB organization to create a deeper, more effective pitching staff. He understood that elite pitchers weren't simply born with unhittable stuff; they could craft it through technology. And if teams could integrate pitch design into their development systems, they would gain a competitive edge on the field.

Through his work with Bauer, Jagers began systematizing pitch design into a scalable training model. Moving beyond individual experimentation, he developed methods that could be applied across different players and levels of the game. "It was important to me to provide that to more than just Trevor or the top-tier MLB guy," Jagers said. "I saw the impact it could have on players at all levels." By combining high-speed cameras, Rapsodo, and advanced data sources like Baseball Savant, he reverse engineered effective movement profiles. "If you know what pitch profiles work, you can tweak grips or manipulate spin direction and axis to replicate them," Jagers explained.

Jagers's career exemplifies the broader evolution of pitch design—from a niche concept to a cornerstone of modern pitching strategy. Once jokingly calling himself a "designated pickoff expert" during his playing days, Jagers had little formal knowledge of pitch design but became an authority through hands-on experimentation and collaboration at Driveline. After a labrum injury ended his playing career, he immersed himself in pitching mechanics and training methodologies, eventually transitioning from player to coach and helping reshape how modern pitchers develop.

"Nobody really knew what they were doing, but everybody in that space wanted to get better and figure it out," Jagers recalled to me. "We knew there was opportunity in front of us, and we were just trying to find the best version of ourselves. For a long time, if your breaking ball wasn't great, you just didn't throw a great breaking ball. Now, we don't accept that. We can build something better."

MLB teams took notice of Jagers's leadership in pitch design, leading to key roles in professional baseball, first as the Cincinnati Reds' assistant pitching coach and later as the New York Mets' vice president of pitching. Along the way, he helped elevate pitch design from an overlooked concept to a fundamental aspect of pitcher development, showing teams how tools like Rapsodo, Edgertronic cameras, and advanced analytics could systematically craft unhittable pitches.

"At first, a lot of teams were hesitant," Jagers admitted. "It was a tough sell to get organizations to buy in because so much of pitching was feel-based. But once you could show tangible improvements—guys adding movement, reshaping their pitches, or getting more swings and misses—it became undeniable."

Sonny Gray's resurgence with the Cincinnati Reds serves as a prime example of how expertise in pitch design can transform a pitcher's arsenal. After struggling with the New York Yankees, where he was encouraged to rely more on four-seam fastballs and sliders, Gray found new life in Cincinnati, thanks in large part to the advanced pitch design techniques used by the Reds' development staff. By integrating high-speed Edgertronic cameras, Rapsodo data, and biomechanical analysis, they optimized his two-seam fastball and curveball—both of which better suited his natural movement profile. Instead of forcing a high-spin, four-seam fastball-heavy approach, they helped Gray unlock the movement potential in his sinker and breaking pitches. As a result, Gray's strikeout rate spiked, his ground-ball percentage improved, and he regained the elite form that had once made him an All-Star.

At times, pitch design tweaks delivered immediate results—even moments before a game. "I remember making an adjustment with a guy on his slider in pregame as he was warming up, and then he goes out in the game and gets a punchout on it," Jagers said. "That was like, oh man, now I see the value—you can improve something and get results."

Jagers helped shape the modern approach to pitcher development, one that goes beyond velocity training to refine movement profiles, sequencing, and deception. His career reflects baseball's shift toward a more analytical future, where independent research and professional coaching seamlessly merge to push the boundaries of what a pitcher can achieve.

Perhaps Jagers's most lasting impact came from helping uncover an insight that changed how we understand baseballs in flight—pushing the boundaries of what pitch design could achieve.

♦ ♦ ♦

FOR OVER A century, pitchers, coaches, and researchers believed they had fully unraveled the mystery of pitch movement. The answer seemed simple: the Magnus effect. Rooted in fluid dynamics, this principle explained how spin created pressure differences on opposite sides of the ball, causing it to curve, sink, or rise. The idea was so universally accepted that entire pitch-tracking systems—Rapsodo, Trackman, and others—were built around the assumption that all pitch movement stemmed from Magnus force.

Because of this, early pitch design revolved almost entirely around spin efficiency—ensuring that as much of a pitch's spin as possible translated into movement. Coaches pushed pitchers to maximize that efficient spin: a fastball with perfect backspin rides up in the zone like a plane catching lift, while a 12-6 curveball with tight topspin falls straight down like a falling elevator. By pairing those two opposites, pitchers created an illusion that kept hitters guessing and that turned spin into a weapon of deception. This strategy became a cornerstone of modern pitch design, leveraging Magnus-dominant movement profiles to deceive hitters.

But something didn't add up.

Some pitches moved in ways that Magnus models couldn't fully explain. Facilities like Driveline observed that while certain two-seam fastballs behaved as expected, others darted unpredictably to the side. Yet, pitch-tracking technology that relied on Magnus Force calculations registered them as having identical movement. Similar inconsistencies appeared in changeups and breaking balls, where some pitches defied traditional expectations of spin and movement.

Pitchers who weren't maximizing spin efficiency still generated significant movement—but no one knew why. The movement was obvious, yet the technology designed to measure it, meant to counter the deception of the human eye, couldn't explain its cause.

It took another enterprising outsider to crack the code—Dr. Barton Smith, a mechanical and aerospace engineering professor at Utah State. A baseball fan and amateur beer brewing enthusiast with no formal ties to the sport, Smith uncovered a flaw in how baseball had understood pitch movement for over a century. As Dr. Barton Smith put it, "Our eyes have limitations. Tech has limitations too—just different ones. The key is knowing when your eyes are lying and when the tech is lying."

◆ ◆ ◆

TREVOR BAUER WAS one of the first modern pitchers to recognize these unexpected movement patterns—some two-seam fastballs had significant movement, while others, despite identical characteristics like spin rate and velocity, moved far less. Though he didn't fully understand the science behind it at the time, he noticed the distinct arm-side run on some of his two-seamers and hypothesized that it was caused by laminar flow—a phenomenon where fluid moves smoothly in parallel layers without turbulence. Convinced that this airflow was responsible for the unusual movement, he dubbed the pitch the Laminar Express.

"We had pitches thrown with very similar mechanics, spin rates, and spin axes, but they were moving differently," Eric Jagers recalled. The term "laminar flow" initially seemed like a logical explanation.

In November 2018, I played matchmaker for science and baseball by sharing a presentation from Professor Smith's early findings on Twitter, my small but proud role in the discovery of Seam-Shifted Wake.

That post sparked debate across the baseball world and led to Smith's connection with Driveline Baseball, bridging academic aerodynamics with practical pitch design. Eric Jagers and others at Driveline saw my post and reached out to Dr. Smith at Utah State, determined to uncover the mystery force once and for all. Jagers captured the mix of skepticism and excitement: "I was over my skis telling a PhD that I didn't agree with what he was saying."

Intrigued, Jagers and a team from Driveline traveled to meet with Smith and conducted tests, painstakingly throwing baseballs into a particle image velocimetry (PIV) system—a laser-driven, high-speed camera setup designed to visualize airflow. The goal: to find this unexpected force that was acting on baseballs.

The process, however, was far from smooth. "This was a truly ridiculous operation," Jagers recalled. "Bart had this machine that would measure the flow of the air on the ball, but you had to absolutely hit a gnat's ass for it to read." The team spent hours hurling baseballs into the setup, tweaking grips and angles in an effort to generate meaningful data. "We were throwing for hours, maybe over a thousand pitches, and we only got like four that actually registered," Jagers said. Each failed attempt raised doubts about whether they could ever get a clean read.

Then, finally, the breakthrough. "We got one," Jagers said. "The wake on the ball was up, and it was the best thing ever. Bart printed out a huge copy of it, and the ball had our signatures on it. It was a huge moment." After hours of trial and error, the PIV had validated a new force that had a profound impact on pitch movement. And a new force in pitch design was born.

What was the missing piece? Aerodynamically, it wasn't just spin that dictated movement—seam orientation played a crucial role. The position of the seams as the ball was thrown had an extraordinary impact on airflow, creating movement that traditional Magnus-based models failed to explain.

For years, traditional pitch design ignored the role of seam orientation in influencing airflow around the ball. It wasn't until Dr. Smith and his team discovered Seam-Shifted Wake that baseball finally began to understand how seam orientation could manipulate movement in ways Magnus effect alone never could.

Unlike the Magnus effect, which depends solely on spin to generate lift or lateral motion, Seam-Shifted Wake disrupts airflow asymmetrically, creating movement that was once considered unexplainable. This discovery reshaped how pitchers and coaches approach pitch design, providing a powerful new tool to craft pitches with unexpected and highly deceptive movement.

♦ ♦ ♦

TO UNDERSTAND SEAM-SHIFTED Wake, imagine a large, flat boat moving through water. The boat leaves a wake behind it, and the shape of that wake depends on the boat's design and movement.

Now, picture that same boat with bumps or ridges on one side. If the ridges stick out more on one side than the other, they divert the water flow unevenly, causing the wake to shift. As a result, even if the engine is pushing the boat straight, its path may curve slightly.

In baseball, a pitcher's grip and release create a similar effect. The ball is like the boat, and the seams act like the ridges, influencing how air moves around it. As the ball spins, the seams interact with the air asymmetrically, altering its trajectory in ways batters don't expect. Just like the boat's wake shifts due to uneven water pressure, the air around the baseball creates movement based on seam orientation—that's Seam-Shifted Wake.

Using a baseball, here's how Seam-Shifted Wake works:

- As a baseball spins through the air, its seams interact with the airflow.
- Depending on their orientation, the seams can disrupt smooth airflow on one side more than the other.
- This imbalance creates pressure differences, similar to how a scuff on a ball alters its flight.

The outcome was pitch movement that defied traditional Magnus-based models.

By strategically gripping and releasing the ball, pitchers can position the seams in ways that manipulate airflow, producing unexpected movement. As Dr. Barton Smith explained: "The seams act like scuffs or irregularities, creating unique forces on the ball as it spins. When they disrupt airflow asymmetrically, they generate unexpected and highly effective movement."

It's difficult to overstate the impact of this discovery on pitch design. Seam-Shifted Wake gave pitchers a new way to manipulate movement, independent of traditional spin-based/Magnus force. With Seam-Shifted Wake, they could now craft deceptive horizontal and vertical breaks, unlocking movement patterns that had previously been misunderstood or entirely overlooked. Suddenly, they weren't just throwing pitches.

They were painting masterpieces on the canvas of the strike zone with colors hitters didn't even know existed. Even before Seam-Shifted Wake was fully understood, pitchers intuitively recognized that surface imperfections could dramatically alter movement. As Barton Smith explained, a scuffed baseball breaks in the direction opposite the scuff by disrupting airflow—much like Seam-Shifted Wake influences pitch movement.

Greg Maddux once described to me how he exploited a scuffed baseball to devastating effect, turning what seemed like an insignificant detail into a competitive advantage. He recalled a pitch where a scuff from the previous play created extraordinary movement, veering in the opposite direction of the blemish. "If you want it to sink, you want the scuff facing the left-handed batter's box, and you just launch it," Maddux explained. The result was a pitch so filthy that it left batter Moises Alou and fans alike questioning how it was even possible. Even Maddux was amazed, calling it "absolutely filthy," maybe the filthiest pitch he ever threw. He was dismayed when the scuffed ball was later taken out of play.

The key difference between a scuffed baseball and Seam-Shifted Wake is control and accessibility. Every baseball has seams, while a scuffed ball is either a rare find—one that happened to be marked and left in play—or an outright violation if intentionally altered. With Seam-Shifted Wake, pitchers can deliberately create similar movement on every pitch, eliminating the need for luck or bending the rules.

Maddux's ability to manipulate even the smallest variables was part of his mastery. If he had understood the science behind Seam-Shifted Wake, there's no telling how much further he could have pushed his already Hall of Fame stuff.

The idea that a baseball's seams could unexpectedly influence a pitch's movement wasn't entirely new. Some pitchers had long noticed that certain throws produced unpredictable movement, but without a clear explanation, they often chalked it up to luck or one of baseball's enduring mysteries—more black magic than science.

With the discovery of Seam-Shifted Wake, the mystery is finally solved. Understanding why movement occurs gives pitchers a systematic way to harness it for intentional pitch design, transforming what was once seen as random chance into a repeatable skill.

Long before the term Seam-Shifted Wake entered the baseball lexicon, pitchers like David Cone noticed its effects, even without understanding the physics behind them. Reflecting on his career, Cone recalled, "I used to call it catching a seam. Well, I must have caught a seam with that one because it really took off right to left." He described how his pitches sometimes behaved in ways that defied traditional mechanics or spin rates, often catching him by surprise. "It's like the ball just did something extra," he said, capturing the natural yet misunderstood impact of seam orientation on airflow. At the time, however, it was viewed as a stroke of luck rather than a deliberate aspect of pitching.

Today, this newfound understanding empowers pitchers to intentionally create movement that was once thought to be a fluke. As Cone noted, "Everything that I thought I was doing, I now know how this happened and why it happened." This revelation has turned what was once seen as chance into a cornerstone of modern pitch design, giving pitchers a powerful new tool in their arsenals.

Of course, this precision wasn't always possible in baseball. You might remember that the lemon-peel ball and early baseballs were far from aerodynamic marvels. With irregular shapes and haphazard stitching, they looked more like someone's first attempt at quilting than tools for high-performance pitching. Seam-Shifted Wake? Forget about it. The only thing those seams consistently offered was sore fingers for pitchers and excuses for fielders blaming bad hops. Predicting movement with those baseballs was as futile as predicting the path of a drunk butterfly—it just wasn't happening.

♦ ♦ ♦

THE FINDINGS FROM Smith's and Driveline's collaboration set the stage for a new era in pitch design. Seam-Shifted Wake expanded the possibilities for pitchers, enabling them to create pitches with movement profiles that defied traditional Magnus-based models.

Seam-Shifted Wake blew the doors off what we thought was possible, creating movement that defies the old rules of pitch design. For instance, experiments at Driveline revealed that sliders known as "sweepers" can gain up to *nine* inches of additional horizontal movement solely by optimizing seam orientation to disrupt airflow. This enhanced movement makes pitches more deceptive and increases their effectiveness against hitters.

The "sweeper" has become the hallmark of Seam-Shifted Wake's impact on modern pitching. A slider variant with exceptional horizontal break, it gained widespread attention for its success in Major League Baseball. Shohei Ohtani's sweeper, in particular, exemplified its potential. By leveraging Seam-Shifted Wake, Ohtani achieved unparalleled lateral movement, turning his sweeper into one of MLB's most dominant and valuable pitches during the 2022 season, as highlighted by Baseball Savant.

Lucas Luetge's sweeper, which boasted the second-most horizontal break in 2022 at 19.3 inches, is an example of how subtle adjustments can lead to extraordinary results, even if the pitcher himself doesn't understand how Seam-Shifted Wake works. As Luetge explained to me, "It's just a two-seam grip, but I throw it like a curveball." Surprisingly, he admitted he didn't fully understand why it worked so well. "This one's a little above my head," he said, adding, "It makes no sense to me how I can throw two balls the exact same way . . . and one moves side to side while the other's almost straight down."

That year Luetge's curveball had only ten inches of horizontal break despite being thrown with the same release, with the sole difference being how the seams of the ball were positioned in his hand. Reflecting on the difference between his curveball and his sweeper, Luetge noted, "It's about the seam orientation. The curveball is going end over end, but this one stays on the side."

Key to developing the pitch was a unique coaching approach during the offseason. The Yankees sent Luetge baseballs with large black dots drawn on them to indicate where the seams needed to be visible during the throw. "When you throw it, you need to see a black dot here and here," Luetge recalled, emphasizing how the seam orientation created the sweeper's exceptional movement. Through trial and error, including solo sessions in the batting cage, Luetge finally mastered the grip and spin needed to make the pitch one of the most unhittable in baseball.

Beyond the sweeper, Seam-Shifted Wake has transformed pitches like sinkers and changeups. By strategically aligning seams to disrupt airflow, pitchers have enhanced the vertical drop on sinkers and introduced lateral or unexpected vertical movement to changeups, making them even harder to hit. Detroit Tigers pitching coach Chris Fetter emphasized how this discovery reshaped pitch design: "Seam orientation gives us a way to create shapes that spin rates alone couldn't achieve. It's also later movement, right when [the ball] finally does catch that seam." Imagine a bowling ball sliding on oil and then suddenly swerving into the pocket—this type of "late" movement is now a reality in baseball.

In 2024, both Tarik Skubal and Chris Sale dominated the league with their changeups, using Seam-Shifted Wake to make their pitches virtually unhittable.

Despite their success, neither Skubal nor Sale fully grasped the intricate physics behind Seam-Shifted Wake. Skubal openly admitted, "I don't quite understand all the cool seam-shifted stuff, but I do it." His focus was on simplifying his motion and allowing the natural orientation of the seams to work for him, often cutting the ball slightly to enhance its movement.

Similarly, Sale recalled his initial skepticism when a coach suggested cutting his changeup instead of pronating it. That means instead of turning his palm away to impart spin, he would turn his palm inward, toward his glove side, to impart spin.

"I looked at him like he had nine eyeballs in his head," Sale told me. "But I threw it, and it was good. I did it again, and it did it again. I just kept doing it." Like Skubal, Sale admitted to having little understanding of the underlying science. "I know none of this stuff," he confessed. "I just throw it."

By cutting their changeups at release, the seam orientation of the baseball allowed Seam-Shifted Wake to influence the pitch's movement in unexpected ways. Instead of cutting (moving glove side), these changeups ended up running arm side, creating movement that defied traditional expectations. For both pitchers, the results were nothing short of mind-blowing.

For both Skubal and Sale, their willingness to experiment with Seam-Shifted Wake concepts led to almost immediate results: Skubal achieved career-best marks en route to his AL Cy Young Award, and Sale revitalized his career, earning the NL Cy Young Award. The success of their changeups highlights the transformative power of Seam-Shifted Wake, marking a pivotal shift in how MLB pitchers develop their arsenals.

Logan Webb's use of Seam-Shifted Wake is a demonstration of how pitchers can tailor their approach to create unique movement profiles, and it transformed him from a promising prospect into one of Major League Baseball's most consistent starters.

Drafted by the San Francisco Giants in 2014, Webb worked his way through the minor leagues, debuting in 2019. Early in his career, he showed flashes of potential but struggled with consistency. However, Webb's ability to master Seam-Shifted Wake—especially in crafting a sinker that generates elite ground-ball rates—helped him transition from a solid starter to the ace of the Giants' rotation. His standout 2021 season, during which he posted a 3.03 ERA with 158 strikeouts over 148.1 innings, set the stage for even greater success in subsequent years. In 2023, Webb cemented his status as an Ace, leading the majors with 216 innings pitched and finishing with a stellar 3.25 ERA and 194 strikeouts.

Working with Brian Bannister in San Francisco, Webb explored the potential of Seam-Shifted Wake through a practical and innovative training method. Like the Yankees did with Luetge, Bannister explained, "We put black dots on either side of the ball and focused on ensuring they would pass through the correct orientation. That's how the seams would take over." This visual feedback helped Webb align the ball's seams to influence airflow deliberately, transitioning him from throwing high-spin, rising fastballs to becoming one of the best sinkerball pitchers in baseball.

By embracing Bannister's scientific approach, Webb harnessed seam orientation to create unpredictable and exceptional movement. Bannister emphasized, "The right seam orientation can generate movement that completely confounds hitters," and Webb's devastating sinker is a testament to that. This willingness to adapt and leverage advanced principles has solidified Webb's status as one of the most effective ground-ball pitchers in the game today.

◆ ◆ ◆

SEAM-SHIFTED WAKE HAS opened new opportunities for pitchers who struggle with spin efficiency, particularly those with gyro spin on their fastballs. Gyro spin, which resembles a football's spiral, doesn't contribute to Magnus Force movement and was traditionally seen as a disadvantage. But with Seam-Shifted Wake, pitchers can create effective movement by optimizing seam orientation rather than relying on spin efficiency.

Barton Smith explained, "Seam-Shifted Wake decouples the dependence on spin efficiency, allowing pitchers to achieve effective movement through a completely different mechanism." This breakthrough has redefined what's possible, allowing pitchers without elite spin rates—once at a disadvantage—to generate movement profiles previously out of reach.

Magnus Effect movement is directly tied to a pitcher's arm angle, meaning the spin axis—and therefore the break—is largely dictated by release point. A lower arm slot typically produces more horizontal movement, while an overhand delivery results in vertical break.

Seam-Shifted Wake, however, operates differently. "Unlike the Magnus Effect, Seam-Shifted Wake isn't as tied to arm angle," Smith noted. "Instead, it relies on seam orientation to disrupt airflow and create asymmetric pressure forces." This decoupling from arm angle allows pitchers to generate unique and deceptive movement, making it harder for hitters to predict pitch behavior. By leveraging Seam-Shifted Wake, pitchers can craft unexpected break patterns and develop nearly unhittable pitches—regardless of their release point.

Technology has revolutionized the way baseball teams design pitches, analyze player performance, and develop strategies. However, it also carries inherent risks when misunderstood or misapplied.

One of the most significant cautionary tales comes from Detroit Tigers pitching coach Chris Fetter, who admitted how early reliance on tools like Rapsodo, which couldn't measure Seam-Shifted Wake, limited his ability to optimize pitchers' arsenals. "I was telling guys that their two fastballs were the same because Rapsodo couldn't differentiate them, even though my eyes were telling me something different," Fetter reflected. This disconnect between what technology could measure and what coaches observed with their own eyes led to missed opportunities for pitchers to fully leverage their unique strengths. Only with later, more advanced versions of Rapsodo and Trackman—and now Hawk-Eye—could Seam-Shifted Wake be accurately tracked. Once quantified, these previously overlooked differences became actionable, unlocking "unbelievable" new possibilities for designing pitches that were both more effective and more deceptive.

A similar example of technology's limitations was discussed earlier with respect to Sonny Gray's struggles with the New York Yankees. Armed with some of the highest spin rates in the league, Gray was directed to throw high fastballs, a strategy designed to exploit the "carry" typically associated with elite spin. Yet this plan failed to account for Gray's natural mechanics. His fastball lacked the vertical lift expected from high-spin pitchers due to his spin axis and arm slot. "Yes, my four-seam spins like nobody's business," Gray admitted, "but it's not carrying above their barrel—it's actually flattening out and finding barrels instead."

The Yankees' rigid reliance on spin rate as a primary indicator of success, as was the common practice at the time, forced Gray to adopt a pitching strategy that clashed with his strengths, undermining his confidence and effectiveness. "I was never a guy that was like, 'Hey, throw your fastball up in the zone.' It was always down and away to righties, down and in to lefties," Gray explained.

The one-size-fits-all approach "took away from who I was," leaving him frustrated and underperforming. Gray rediscovered his dominant form only after moving to the Cincinnati Reds, where both his arsenal and the technology used to measure it were better understood.

19

For most of baseball history, training meant showing up in person. You found a local coach—maybe a former pro, maybe just the loudest guy with a clipboard—and hoped for the best. Improvement depended on geography, word of mouth, and a little bit of luck. Then the internet blew the doors off that.

Suddenly, you didn't need pedigree or proximity—you needed curiosity, a Wi-Fi connection, and the drive to get better. A new generation of self-made pitchers emerged, bypassing the old-school gatekeepers and building arsenals through eBooks, YouTube tutorials, pitch design forums, and slow-motion overlays. They weren't waiting to be taught. They were learning grips at midnight, designing sliders in their garage, and turning themselves into monsters—one filthy click at a time.

Paul Nyman didn't have a Major League résumé, a blazing fastball, or a Hall of Fame pedigree—but that didn't stop him from changing how baseball approached pitching by making pitching mechanics eBooks and products available for the masses over the Web, so pitchers could teach themselves rather than have to have a coach by their side.

Nyman took a purely engineering-based approach. He wasn't interested in gut instincts or "feel"—he wanted efficiency that could be measured and repeated.

Nyman's foundation for this nontraditional approach wasn't forged in a bullpen but in classrooms and laboratories. With a degree in electrical engineering and a minor in physics from the University of Massachusetts, Nyman also competed as a high jumper in track and field. This combination of analytical precision and athletic experience shaped his philosophy on movement. Instead of asking, "How does it feel to throw hard?" he asked, "What makes the human body generate maximum velocity?" Inspired by Cold War–era Russian training techniques emphasizing overload and underload principles, Nyman began breaking down how the best athletes optimized movement, even as the baseball world clung to tradition.

Nyman's background as a pitcher was unremarkable. A relatively low-level high school player, he struggled with velocity and was baffled by how smaller, less physically imposing teammates could throw harder. This frustration sparked a lifelong quest to uncover the mechanics behind velocity. For Nyman, the focus was on uncovering what set the best apart, rather than pursuing greatness on the mound himself.

♦ ♦ ♦

BEFORE REVOLUTIONIZING PITCHING mechanics, Paul Nyman applied his engineering expertise to golf, working with a company called Sports Technology Inc. to develop the Golf Swing Analyzer. Although not a golfer himself, Nyman approached the project with the same analytical precision that later defined his contributions to baseball. His challenge was to decode the mechanics of a golf swing, focusing on the exact moment the club struck the ball and translating that data into actionable insights on a computer—a complex task that required dissecting intricate sequencing, timing, and biomechanical efficiency.

Much like pitching, the golf swing relies on precise mechanics to generate power and accuracy. Nyman's engineering mindset thrived on unraveling these complexities, breaking down the relationship between the golfer's body, the club, and the ball. This early work sharpened his ability to analyze movement and sequence efficiency, laying the groundwork for his future innovations in pitching biomechanics software to arm pitchers with the ability to teach themselves how to be world class throwers.

In 1995, Nyman founded SetPro, which produced both eBooks and related products dedicated to developing pitching mechanics through an engineering-based framework. His work was deeply influenced by Russian physiologist Nikolai Bernstein, whose theories on motor control and movement science reshaped Nyman's understanding of how the body learns and refines complex physical tasks. Central to his philosophy was the Bernstein Principle: "The body will organize itself based upon the ultimate goal of the activity."

This principle flipped traditional coaching on its head. Instead of forcing pitchers into rigid mechanics or fixed positions or checkpoints, Nyman believed in creating training environments that encouraged the body to naturally find its most efficient and effective way to move. Tools like weighted baseballs were instrumental in this approach, forcing the body to adapt and self-organize. For Nyman, this was about refining sequencing, efficiency, and command.

Paul Nyman introduced the concept of "intent to throw hard," a revolutionary shift in pitching philosophy that emphasized the body's natural ability to organize itself into optimal mechanics when striving for maximum velocity. This marked a sharp departure from traditional coaching, which often prioritized "just throwing strikes" and hitting spots over physical intensity. Nyman's approach acknowledged the raw, aggressive effort required to generate high-end velocity, a philosophy that echoes the immortal words of Hall of Famer Bob Gibson: "Have you ever thrown a ball a hundred miles an hour? Everything hurts. Even your ass hurts. I see pictures of my face and say, 'Holy shit,' but that's the strain you feel when you throw. I had one of those faces you look at and say, 'Man, he's an asshole.' Could be, depends on if you pissed me off or not."

Nyman's focus on intent changed how pitchers approached velocity and also highlighted the mental and physical strain inherent in high-level pitching.

Nyman's early use of weighted baseballs was particularly groundbreaking. Drawing on historical examples, such as Bob Feller's unconventional training methods, Nyman pointed out to me, "Feller used to throw a steel ball, almost like a small shot put, against a barn wall for hours." He used this as evidence to support his belief that weighted implements could enhance strength and mechanics by engaging the kinetic chain more efficiently. By applying principles of modern sports science, Nyman demonstrated how weighted ball training could help pitchers unlock velocity and improve durability when used correctly. His approach challenged the long-standing fear that weighted balls inherently led to injury, instead positioning them as a powerful tool for performance optimization.

Paul Nyman was among the first to use video analysis and software to study pitching mechanics through a purely engineering lens. While his approach had surface similarities to Tom House's early work, Nyman's focus was rooted entirely in physics and biomechanics. By slowing down footage frame by frame, he uncovered flaws in conventional teachings that had spread unimpeded for decades.

His analytical approach shed light on key movement patterns such as scapular loading, pelvic rotation, and kinetic chain sequencing, giving pitchers a clearer blueprint for optimizing mechanics and maximizing efficiency. These concepts, now staples in modern pitching development, helped pitchers refine their mechanics and unlock their full potential.

Nyman's dedication to understanding pitching went far beyond mere video analysis. He pushed the boundaries further by creating 3D models of legendary pitchers like Nolan Ryan and Bob Feller. Using available footage and painstaking research, Nyman constructed virtual representations of their mechanics to study how their movements generated velocity and efficiency. These models gave him a deeper understanding of how elite pitchers utilized their bodies to produce exceptional power while minimizing stress on their arms. Through this process, he was able to distill the mechanical principles that made Ryan's explosive delivery and Feller's iconic fastball timeless examples of pitching excellence.

Although Paul Nyman didn't directly coach a large number of pitchers, his influence on MLB pitching was profound. Through his SetPro eBooks, Nyman's teachings reached a wide audience, shaping a generation of coaches and players. His work coincided with the rise of online learning and discussions about sports mechanics, making him one of the pioneers in leveraging the internet to revolutionize how athletes and coaches approached pitching development.

Prominent leaders in the new school of data-driven pitching development—such as Kyle Boddy of Driveline Baseball, Ron Wolforth of the Texas Baseball Ranch, and Ben Brewster of Tread Athletics—as well as legendary MLB pitching coach Brent Strom all credit Paul Nyman's eBooks and engineering-driven approach as a cornerstone of their philosophies and development.

One of Paul Nyman's most notable projects was his work with Robert Stock, a two-way phenom from Southern California. Stock's raw athleticism and cannon-like arm made him a standout prospect, but inconsistencies in his mechanics kept him from reaching his full potential. Seeking a data-driven approach, Stock's father—an engineer with no baseball background—turned to Nyman, believing his analytical, biomechanics-based methods could refine Robert's talent.

Their collaboration proved pivotal. Nyman helped Stock understand that pitching is a rotational athletic movement, a breakthrough that unlocked his velocity and improved his efficiency.

Stock's journey to the big leagues highlights just how crucial velocity is in catching the attention of MLB teams. On December 19, 2017, he famously posted a YouTube video of himself throwing on an empty field, a radar gun positioned behind home plate. With no scouts or fanfare—just him and the gun—Stock hit a remarkable 101.3 mph, prompting shouts of "1-O-fn-1 mph, dude!" from off-screen. The video showcased his elite velocity and caught the attention of MLB teams, earning him a professional contract. This unconventional moment underscores Stock's belief in the value of velocity while also showcasing the power of social media and video, reflecting the evolving ways modern players get noticed in baseball's digital era.

Stock made his MLB debut with the San Diego Padres in 2018, where he impressed with his triple-digit fastball. Over his career, he has pitched for multiple teams, consistently showcasing the elite velocity that has defined his game. The value of Nyman's work—emphasizing movement efficiency, weighted ball training, and biomechanical precision—is evident in Stock's progression.

Wes Johnson, former pitching coach of the Minnesota Twins and LSU Tigers, emphasized Paul Nyman's lasting influence on modern pitching. Johnson credited Nyman with introducing and popularizing key concepts such as weighted ball training and biomechanics in the early 2000s, laying the groundwork for today's pitching development.

"If people aren't talking about a guy named Paul Nyman—whether you like him, whether you agree with him, or whether you don't—they just don't understand the history of where this thing has come from," Johnson stated.

According to Johnson, Nyman's engineering-based approach changed how pitching mechanics were viewed and distributed to the masses. His ideas shaped the careers of countless coaches and players. Johnson pointed to Nyman's direct impact on training methods, recalling, "We started throwing weighted balls in '03 because of Paul."

The ripple effects of Nyman's work continue to drive technological and biomechanical advancements in baseball today.

◆ ◆ ◆

TAKING THE BATON from Paul Nyman and bringing pitching mechanics from eBooks to the smartphone, in 2019, Tom House and Rocky Collis co-founded the Mustard app with a mission rooted in democratizing access to high-level coaching, particularly for young athletes. The app's concept was inspired by House's groundbreaking contributions to pitching mechanics and his lifelong commitment to making baseball knowledge accessible. According to the co-founders, their vision was to "put Tom House in a phone," providing young players access to his decades of expertise and allowing them to receive personalized coaching through state-of-the-art technology for a fraction of the cost of private lessons.

House's career laid the groundwork for the app's design. Collis, inspired by his brother's experience training with House, emphasized that their aim with Mustard was to ensure every kid could experience top-tier coaching, helping them improve their game and stay in sports longer.

The Mustard app leverages motion capture technology, artificial intelligence, and House's comprehensive database of 3D models collected over decades to provide personalized analysis and feedback to athletes. By focusing on young players and local teams, the app addresses common barriers to entry in sports, such as access to quality coaching and financial constraints. With hundreds of thousands of users and millions of swings and pitches analyzed, Mustard is rapidly becoming a transformative tool in youth sports.

The Mustard app isn't designed to give generic tips; instead, it uses advanced AI to offer personalized, specific mechanics coaching tailored to each athlete. Tom House explained that the app analyzes biomechanics using motion capture and identifies inefficiencies in a player's movements, providing targeted drills to correct them.

Co-founder Collis summarized their approach as "fun, fast, and free," a mantra designed to keep young athletes engaged while removing barriers to entry. The app both gives athletes insights into their mechanics and also tracks their progress over time, creating a positive feedback loop that fosters improvement and confidence.

As you might remember, House once faced personal and financial challenges due to the immense cost of building his own biomechanics lab—a bold investment in understanding pitching mechanics. At the time, such a facility was groundbreaking and prohibitively expensive, accessible only to a privileged few. Today, the Mustard app has revolutionized this landscape, offering the same level of analysis from a simple smartphone. "With just a smartphone, you can receive analysis that used to require a multimillion-dollar lab," House remarked.

House and Collis have been clear about their ambitious vision for the Mustard app, emphasizing both its rapid growth and its ability to transform youth sports. House explained, "Our goal is to make sports science accessible to everyone, not just the elite athletes who have the resources to work with top-tier trainers." He sees the app as a way to connect professional-level coaching with young athletes who might otherwise lack access to quality instruction. "By putting these tools into the hands of kids, their coaches, and even their parents, we can democratize sports and keep kids playing longer," House remarked.

Collis echoed House's sentiments, noting how the app has grown exponentially since its inception. "We've already analyzed millions of pitches and swings, and what's exciting is how it's helping athletes of all ages and skill levels," Collis said. He emphasized the importance of using technology to create a supportive ecosystem that empowers athletes. "Mustard is not just about fixing mechanics; it's about giving athletes confidence and keeping them engaged in the sports they love," he added. Collis also highlighted the community aspect of Mustard, explaining how users can learn not only from the app but also from each other, fostering a sense of collaboration and shared growth among athletes and coaches alike.

Even MLB stars have turned to Mustard for guidance, highlighting its value for athletes at every level. Toronto Blue Jays pitcher José Berríos used the app to refine his mechanics after identifying inefficiencies in his delivery. "Mustard helped me see the details I needed to adjust," Berríos explained, crediting the app's visual tools and actionable insights for helping him regain consistency on the mound.

Similarly, another veteran pitcher, Walker Buehler, turned to Mustard as part of his recovery process following his second Tommy John surgery. "It's a great tool," Buehler said in a testimonial, noting how the app's analysis helped him focus on key mechanical adjustments during his rehab.

Looking ahead, both founders are focused on expanding Mustard's reach and capabilities across multiple sports, from golf to soccer and beyond. As Collis summarized, "The potential for Mustard is limitless. If we can help a generation of athletes get better and stay in the game longer, then we've done something truly impactful." For House, the mission is equally personal: "At the end of the day, it's about creating better experiences for athletes and their families. If we can achieve that, then we've accomplished our mission." By breaking down barriers and fostering inclusivity, Mustard has democratized coaching and reshaped what's possible for athletes worldwide.

20

Social media isn't a traditional "pitching lab," but its impact on modern pitching development has been just as game-changing. It democratized access to once-guarded secrets—grips, drills, mechanics, tunneling—and fed a new generation of information-hungry, self-taught pitchers.

Before social media, if you wanted to see a filthy slider or perfectly tunneled heater, your options were limited: live games, a few SportsCenter highlights, or a grainy word-of-mouth scouting report.

Inside knowledge—how to grip a changeup, create spin, or tunnel pitches like a pro—was locked inside clubhouses and private labs. If you were a kid with big-league dreams in the middle of nowhere, tough luck. That curtain wasn't getting pulled back.

Even MLB's own marketing machine tended to sideline pitchers, focusing on bat flips and bombs. The arms that were quietly dominating with insane movement profiles or cutting-edge techniques flew under the radar—unless you were already deep in the weeds.

That started to change when baseball social media began to take off. And I was part of that shift—as PitchingNinja.

What started as a personal passion project turned into a revolution in how pitching is viewed, analyzed, and celebrated. By breaking down tunneling, sharing grips, and highlighting the nastiest pitches, my

PitchingNinja account has given fans, players, and analysts a new way to appreciate the art and science of pitching.

But, for me, it was always about more than pure education—it was about making pitching fun.

♦ ♦ ♦

FROM VISUALIZING PITCH tunneling to sharing grips that unlock the secrets behind the nastiest pitches, my goal has always been to highlight the beauty and complexity of pitching, as well as the lighter side of baseball.

Social media has shifted the way pitching is taught and shared, transforming it into a digital bullpen where players, coaches, and fans collaborate to exchange knowledge, insights, and inspiration. My journey is just one example of how social platforms can amplify the conversation around pitching, breaking down barriers and making advanced techniques accessible to anyone with a passion to learn.

There are countless brilliant baseball social media accounts that deserve recognition, but for now, I'll focus on my own experiences to illustrate this broader trend—because I've lived it firsthand.

In 2014, I began using social media as an outlet to share the lessons I had gathered from my coaching journey. Learning alongside some of the game's most innovative new-school coaches gave me a perspective I felt was worth passing on, and social platforms offered a way to give back to the sport that had given me so much.

For a few years, I posted MLB breakdowns without much pushback. I was flying under the radar. Then, in 2018, MLB decided it wanted to stringently crackdown on fans or coaches sharing game clips, and my account was briefly shut down. The move sparked an uproar. Front office executive Brian Bannister and several high profile MLB pitchers publicly blasted the decision and argued that my account wasn't hurting baseball and that it was expanding the game with a thriving new online fan base. What began as MLB's attempt to shut me down ended up cementing my place in the pitching community, and proved just how much value fans and players saw in what I was doing. Soon after, MLB reversed course—realizing the content was good for the sport—and officially embraced it. That's when things really took off.

As the audience grew, my content became more creative and expansive. Beyond breaking down pitchers' mechanics, something I had done for years, I began interviewing pitchers and giving them a platform to share insights. They opened up about everything from pitch grips and mechanical tweaks to mental cues and training philosophies. The account evolved into a hub of pitching knowledge, a place where everyone, from youth players to seasoned MLB pitchers, could learn and exchange ideas.

At first, I was hesitant to reach out to MLB pitchers, worried I might be bothering them. That hesitation didn't last long. Soon, pitchers were eager to collaborate and share their secrets with the baseball world through my platform.

What followed was a series of remarkable conversations with a who's who of baseball greats, past and present. I had the privilege of interviewing legends like Nolan Ryan (my interview with Ryan was even included in the Blu-ray edition of the documentary *Facing Nolan*), Greg Maddux, Roger Clemens, and Billy Wagner. I also connected with current stars such as Clayton Kershaw, Chris Sale, Jacob deGrom, Gerrit Cole, Max Scherzer, Yu Darvish, Shane Bieber, Tyler Glasnow, Carlos Rodón, Tarik Skubal, Logan Gilbert, Bryan Woo, George Kirby, Sonny Gray, Blake Treinen, Kodai Senga, Marcus Stroman, Edwin Díaz, Corbin Burnes, and Paul Skenes, among many others. My account had become the ultimate pitching resource, a place where the game's best could share their wisdom, and a new generation of players could learn from the masters.

♦ ♦ ♦

AS I MENTIONED earlier, my quest has been to make quality pitching knowledge accessible to everyone, so I compiled a collection of MLB pitching mechanics and pitch grips, gathered from my pitcher interviews and other sources, into a free Dropbox—an online treasure trove for aspiring pitchers seeking to refine their craft. This resource became a tool for players at all levels to uncover the secrets of greatness, and it played a surprising role in the rise of 2024 Cy Young Award winner Tarik Skubal.

As a college pitcher, Skubal was drawn to the raw power and mechanics of Aroldis Chapman, one of the most unhittable pitchers in the game. "In college, I would go through the Dropbox link on your Twitter and just look at Aroldis Chapman—how he moves, how he throws so hard," Skubal recalled. For hours, he analyzed slow-motion clips, marveling at how Chapman coiled into his back leg and unleashed explosive power through perfect hip rotation. "I tried to get those same feels, even if it didn't look exactly the same," Skubal said, inspired by Chapman's ability to create seamless energy transfer and devastating velocity.

Skubal's meticulous study of Chapman's mechanics paid dividends, as he incorporated key elements into his own delivery. This dedication to self-improvement helped transform him from a college pitcher with potential into one of the premier arms in Major League Baseball, including throwing a fastball over 101 mph in 2024 during his Cy Young Season and 102.6 mph in 2025. His rise underscores the value of accessible resources for players willing to put in the work to unlock their potential.

The pitching Dropbox exemplifies the philosophy behind *Unhittable*: democratizing the tools and knowledge that can turn good pitchers into elite ones. Skubal's journey proves that with the right resources and indefatigable dedication, the next generation of unhittable pitchers can emerge, no matter where they start.

♦ ♦ ♦

THE RIPPLE EFFECT of content from my account and my pitching Dropbox has directly influenced some of baseball's brightest stars, reshaping their arsenals in surprising and impactful ways. George Kirby of the Seattle Mariners revealed during a national broadcast with Joe Davis that he learned his splitter grip from watching my interview with Kevin

Gausman. "I had to try it," Kirby said, crediting the insight as a key addition to his repertoire. This small, actionable piece of knowledge, gleaned from social media, transformed a grip into an effective weapon on the mound.

Similarly, Jake Diekman discovered his slider grip through my content. In an article on MLB.com,[1] Diekman explained how he stumbled upon a clip of Chaz Roe's slider on my account and decided to adopt the grip. "It was eye-opening," Diekman said, underscoring the power of visual learning and experimentation sparked by shared insights.

In Tokyo, during the Dodger-Cubs series in 2025, I interviewed Clayton Kershaw about his slider grip—a pitch that Cy Young winner Tarik Skubal had previously told me he wished he had in his arsenal. Skubal admired how Kershaw's slider mirrored his fastball before darting away at the last moment.

When I mentioned this to Kershaw, he laughed and said he wished he had Skubal's changeup grip—a pitch he'd love to be able to throw. I posted both grips on social media, and soon after, Skubal replied privately to me that he was going to try Kershaw's grip in his next bullpen session—and also replied publicly with a "note-taking" emoji.

Even seasoned professionals like Collin McHugh credited my Pitching-Ninja account as a resource for improvement. In August 2021, McHugh tweeted, "In all seriousness. I got better by watching dudes pitch on @PitchingNinja. Nobody gets better by accident. We saw/heard something and tried it for ourselves." It's a statement of how accessible pitching content can inspire growth at every level of the game, from young players to seasoned veterans.

One of my favorite pitch-grip stories involves the man who has more pitch grips than any other pitcher, Yu Darvish. In August 2020, I was out to dinner with my wife, Patricia, enjoying a quiet evening at a local restaurant. Midway through the meal, my phone buzzed with a direct message (DM) from Twitter. Normally, I wouldn't dare text or DM during dinner—it's one of those unwritten rules of good manners. Okay, who am I kidding? I regularly text during dinner. But this time, when I glanced at my phone, it wasn't just to check the score or send a quick meme. This message made me pause mid-bite—fork in one hand, phone in the other, and suddenly, dinner felt a lot less important. It was from Yu Darvish, one of the most talented and innovative pitchers in the MLB. His message read: "Do you have Bieber's curveball release and my curveball release?"

Patricia noticed me typing away and asked, "Why are you texting during dinner?"

Sheepishly, I replied, "Umm . . . Yu Darvish needs help with curveball grips." To her credit, knowing my obsession with baseball and my work with pitchers, she gave me a knowing smile and let it slide.

Darvish, a pitching perfectionist always looking for an edge, wanted to study the grip and release of Shane Bieber's knuckle curve, one of the best pitches in baseball at the time. I quickly pulled up videos of Bieber's grip and release from my archives and sent them over to Darvish. It felt surreal—helping one of the game's greatest pitchers refine his arsenal in real time, all while sitting at a cozy table at a local restaurant.

A few days later, Darvish put the grip into action. While he adapted Bieber's knuckle curve into more of a slider, the results were immediate and jaw-dropping. In his first game using the pitch, Darvish threw twenty-five sliders and racked up thirteen whiffs, completely baffling hitters. His catcher, Victor Caratini, remarked through a translator, "The slider, the way he was throwing it today, he was throwing it like never before." After the game, Darvish sent me a message with the Statcast data, letting me know the success was because of the grip I had shared.

The story didn't end there. In a later press conference, Darvish shared the backstory with the media, telling the world he had gotten the grip from me via Twitter. For me, it was a moment that perfectly captured the blending of modern technology, social media, and baseball innovation—a reminder of how something as simple as a DM during dinner could help make one of the game's most unhittable pitchers even harder to hit.

It's incredible to think that what started as a way to share knowledge and passion has had such a tangible impact on the careers of pitchers at every level, helping them take their games to the next level and, ultimately, making them unhittable.

Creating a vibrant pitching community has always been one of my main goals. I wanted to establish a space where fans could rally around the art of pitching, players could draw inspiration and learn, and pitchers—both aspiring and professional—could sharpen their skills by learning from each other. By making pitching the centerpiece of discussions, highlights, and education, this community has elevated the role of pitchers in the game, inspiring more players to take the mound and refine their craft.

♦ ♦ ♦

MY SOCIAL MEDIA influence also helped create a new MLB statistic to measure both pitcher dominance and hitter embarrassment: the Sword. Swords are those hilariously bad swings where hitters chop at the ball and stop mid-swing, looking utterly defeated. I've always loved coming up with nicknames. Over the years, I've coined plenty, from the "Airbender" for Devin Williams's high-spin-rate changeup to the "Volunteer Fireman" for flamethrower Ben Joyce. But "Sword" might be the most widely used of them all, and its origin traces back to a cult comedy classic. The idea struck me while watching *The Benchwarmers*, a 2006 movie about a group of misfit adults taking on Little League teams. In one scene, a character critiques a batter by shouting, "Don't chop at it! It's not a sword!" David Spade's deadpan response—"You're not a sword"—was so absurd that it stuck with me. I thought, why not call those hilariously bad, chopped-off swings "Swords" as a nod to the movie? So, in June 2017, I coined the term on Twitter after a particularly ugly swing on an unhittable Lance McCullers curveball.

The term caught fire. Fans, pitchers, and broadcasters adopted Sword as the go-to descriptor for embarrassing swings. "That's a Sword! I learned it from PitchingNinja!" Yankees announcer David Cone exclaimed during a broadcast. It became a way for players to bond over the art of pitching and for fans to laugh while appreciating truly unhittable pitches. A few years later, in 2021, Trevor Bauer rolled out his "Sword K Strut," a strikeout celebration complete with an imaginary blade and on a national broadcast described it as an homage to the term I had brought to life. What started as a niche reference has evolved into a cultural phenomenon, adding levity to the game while celebrating the pitchers who create those Sword-worthy moments.

By 2024, the term "Sword" had become so ingrained in baseball culture that MLB officially adopted it as a tracked statistic and gave me credit for it:

A "sword," as popularized by Rob "the Pitching Ninja" Friedman, is "when a pitcher fools a hitter so badly that he forces a noncompetitive swing, one where a batter either regrets his choice or can't stop himself from taking a hack that looks so ugly it ends up going viral on social media."[2]

The inclusion of Sword as an official MLB stat on Baseball Savant reflects its organic rise from a social media quirk to a universally recognized part of the sport. It's another illustration of the creativity and camaraderie that define the pitching community—and proof that even the quirkiest ideas can leave a lasting mark on the game.

♦ ♦ ♦

SOCIAL MEDIA DIDN'T just change how pitchers train and share things like pitch grips—it changed how they get seen.

For decades, getting scouted meant waiting to be "discovered" by a coach, a recruiter, or some clipboard-wielding guy with a radar gun. Now? Pitchers can take control of their own narrative. Post your stuff online, build a following, and let the filth speak for itself.

Travel ball and showcases still dominate the scouting scene—but they come with a price tag that would make a closer flinch. How much can your family shell out to chase the dream?

For many families, the dream of a pro contract feels like a lottery ticket worth chasing. So they pour thousands into showcases, private coaching, and travel teams, hoping their kid beats the odds. But for countless others, the cost slams the door shut before it even opens.

The system favors the wealthy and punishes everyone else. Showcases can cost thousands, with no guarantee of meaningful exposure. Overlooked arms, late bloomers, and small-school standouts often vanish in a world that rewards connections over raw ability.

And it's not just about money—geography plays a huge role.

If you grow up in a baseball hotbed like Florida, Texas, Georgia, or California, scouts are everywhere. You get noticed just by showing up. But if you live in a small town or under-scouted region, you're invisible. Doesn't matter how nasty your stuff is—if no one sees it, does it even happen?

♦ ♦ ♦

FLATGROUND WAS CREATED to tear down these barriers and give every pitcher a fair shot.

It provides a free, social-media-driven platform where pitchers can showcase their talent, connect with coaches, and get noticed—without the financial burden of traditional scouting events. By eliminating the pay-to-play model, FlatGround has given overlooked players a direct path to opportunity, where talent—not money or geography—determines who gets a chance.

In late 2018, I launched FlatGround with a simple yet powerful mission: to help pitchers showcase their skills and connect with scouts, coaches, and recruiters, regardless of their resources or location. Too often, talented players missed out on opportunities because they couldn't afford expensive showcases or didn't live in heavily scouted areas. FlatGround aimed to level the playing field, ensuring that no player's dreams were derailed by circumstances beyond their control.

FlatGround extended the mission of PitchingNinja by democratizing access to baseball opportunities. "There's so much talent out there that goes unnoticed because players can't afford to attend showcases or live in areas that don't attract scouts," I told *Forbes* in 2019. Using social media, players could post videos of themselves pitching, put in measurables such as radar gun readings or information from Trackman, and tag @FlatGroundApp or use the #FlatGround hashtag to directly reach scouts, coaches, and MLB executives who followed the platform. The concept was straightforward—let talent speak for itself—and it became a boon for players seeking exposure.

The inspiration for starting FlatGround came from observing the financial struggles many families face in supporting their kids' baseball dreams. Playing in showcases, purchasing equipment, affording high-level coaching, and taking time off work to travel for tournaments often come at a significant cost. At the heart of this issue is the expense of training and networking, which can make clinics, development opportunities, and even the chance to get noticed unaffordable for many families.

With FlatGround, my goal was to use the connections I've built to provide players with development tools and opportunities—completely free of charge. Baseball shouldn't be a sport reserved for those who can afford it. Limiting access to quality coaching and equipment based on financial resources not only hurts the future of the game but, to me, is also fundamentally unfair.

Since I knew my PitchingNinja account was already followed by most college coaches and MLB organizations, I realized I could leverage that existing audience to build FlatGround as a platform for showcasing talent. By directing those same followers to FlatGround, I created a space where scouts and recruiters could easily discover promising players who might otherwise go unnoticed. This shift both democratized access to opportunities and flipped the traditional power dynamic—scouts and recruiters were no longer in control of dictating the terms. Instead, they found themselves competing in a feeding frenzy for the latest hot prospect posted on FlatGround, giving players more leverage and visibility than ever before.

Due to this democratization and feeding frenzy, thousands of young high school pitchers have credited FlatGround with helping them land college offers, but its impact has reached beyond the amateur level. Professional pitchers like Justin Topa, Taylor Grover, Chris Nunn, Nathan Patterson, and Logan Sawyer have publicly credited FlatGround for connecting them with Major League organizations. The platform has become a transformative tool for both scouting and player development, reaching areas that traditional recruiting methods often miss.

◆ ◆ ◆

NATHAN PATTERSON'S JOURNEY from a stadium radar gun booth to signing with the Oakland Athletics is perhaps FlatGround's most famous success story. In 2019, Patterson—a 23-year-old former high school player working a regular job—attended a Colorado Rockies game and decided to test his arm in the stadium's radar booth. To everyone's amazement, he threw multiple pitches clocking in at 96 mph. His brother captured the moment on video, and it went viral.

Recognizing Patterson's potential, I amplified his story by sharing the video through FlatGround and PitchingNinja. The simplicity of the footage—a raw display of untapped talent—resonated with scouts and executives. The story received the widespread attention of the news media, including appearing in *The Wall Street Journal* and *USA Today*.[3]

Within months, the Oakland Athletics signed Patterson to a professional contract. Reflecting on his unexpected journey, Patterson said, "The exposure I got from PitchingNinja and FlatGround was incredible. It gave me the chance to live out my dream."

Patterson's signing captured national attention, becoming a symbol of FlatGround's ability to change lives. It demonstrated how raw talent, when paired with the right platform, can lead to opportunities once reserved for players already in the system. For me, Patterson's story validated FlatGround's mission: that great talent can come from anywhere and deserves to be seen. Today, FlatGround is run day-to-day by Josh Rudd, whose philosophy closely mirrors my own. But I remain involved, and the platform stands as one of my proudest achievements. In the end, the internet and social media did for baseball what it did for the rest of the world: tore down gates, amplified voices, and let talent prove itself in public. The players who put in the work can no longer be ignored.

21

Today's pitchers are throwing harder, nastier, and smarter than ever. But if you had every tool in baseball's arsenal—every camera, sensor, lab, and pitch grip known to man—could you build the perfect pitcher? And if you could... what kind of filth would that unleash?

The ultimate pitcher would be a rare fusion of physical dominance, mental sharpness, and unshakable confidence—a force on the mound that would make them virtually unhittable. They would throw with overwhelming velocity, routinely hitting triple digits, forcing hitters into split-second decisions. But velocity alone wouldn't be enough. Their pitches would feature devastating movement—a fastball that explodes through the zone, a breaking ball that drops like it's falling off a table, and a changeup that vanishes from a hitter's swing path.

Every pitch would be perfectly tunneled, looking identical out of the hand before darting unpredictably, leaving hitters guessing—and often swinging at air.

Yet dominance on the mound isn't just about pure stuff—it's about adaptability. The ultimate pitcher would be a student of the game. They would use advanced data and cutting-edge technology to unlock even greater potential, fine-tuning every aspect of their game. But with all that openness to improvement, they would still have the confidence to trust their abilities, executing pitches under pressure with precision and fearlessness.

Of course, they would also be surgical with command. The ultimate pitcher wouldn't just overpower hitters; they would dictate at-bats, locating pitches with pinpoint accuracy, exploiting weaknesses, and keeping hitters off balance at all times. Intelligence would be just as crucial as talent—this pitcher wouldn't just throw; they would think two steps ahead, setting up hitters like a chess master, anticipating adjustments, and countering them with deadly precision.

Above all, the ultimate pitcher would be relentless—never satisfied, always obsessed with improvement. They would refine mechanics, perfect new pitches, and master the mental side of the game. This pitcher wouldn't just be built to compete—they would be engineered to dominate.

In short, the ultimate pitcher looks a lot like Paul Skenes.

Paul Skenes exemplifies the blueprint for the modern pitcher—a seamless blend of physical size and athleticism, technical mastery, and mental fortitude. At LSU, Skenes solidified his reputation as a generational talent, leading the Tigers to a College World Series title and earning the prestigious Dick Howser Trophy as the national college baseball player of the year. His overwhelming performance on the collegiate stage propelled him to become the first overall pick in the 2023 MLB Draft by the Pittsburgh Pirates, a decision the organization's leadership would quickly see validated.

Skenes's rookie season in 2024 was nothing short of historic. He posted an 11–3 record with a 1.96 ERA across twenty-three starts, striking out 170 batters in just 133 innings. His ability to keep hitters off balance was evident in his .198 batting average against and a sparkling 0.95 WHIP. These incredible numbers earned him unanimous National League Rookie of the Year honors and a spot as a finalist for the NL Cy Young Award—a rare accomplishment for a first-year player. He also became the first Pirates rookie to make the All-Star team since 1997 and the first rookie pitcher to start the All-Star Game since 1995, solidifying his rapid ascent to MLB stardom. In 2025, he again posted an ERA under 2.00, cementing himself as perhaps the best pitcher on the planet. He also became only the fourth pitcher in the live ball era (since 1920) to have an ERA that low in his age-twenty-three season or younger.

Physically, Skenes is the epitome of an unhittable pitcher. Standing at a towering six foot six with a huge frame, his sheer size is impossible to ignore. When I stood next to him at the 2024 All-Star Game, I felt that I looked a bit more like his kid than someone who could be his dad.

More importantly, Skenes's "stuff" on the mound is otherworldly. He combines a triple-digit fastball with devastating movement, including a slider that breaks late and sharp and a changeup that disappears from hitters' swing paths. As Skenes described his arsenal, "My fastball is unique because of the combination of ride and run," making it nearly impossible for hitters to square up. His ability to tunnel his arsenal of seven distinct pitches effectively adds another layer of deception, ensuring every pitch looks identical coming out of his hand. Another benefit of a diverse arsenal is that Skenes isn't limited to overpowering hitters with pure heat; he can outthink them, too, which could help extend his career and protect his arm.

When I first sat down to interview Paul Skenes while he was still in college at LSU, it was immediately clear how exceptional his talent was. As we discussed his meticulous approach to the game, his advanced understanding of pitch sequencing, and his relentless commitment to improvement, it struck me how much better he could still get. At the time, Skenes had been a full-time pitcher for less than a year, and his "low mileage" arm—a rarity for a pitcher of his caliber—meant that his ceiling was even higher than most powerful college pitchers.

Paul Skenes's humility is one of his defining traits, even as he skyrocketed to stardom. Despite being the first overall pick in the MLB Draft and winning the Dick Houser Trophy as the nation's best college player, he never put personal accolades above team success.

When I interviewed him at LSU, he consistently downplayed his own achievements, often redirecting praise to his teammates. When I asked if he thought he should be picked ahead of his teammate and fellow LSU star Dylan Crews, who was drafted immediately after him, Skenes didn't hesitate: "Not really, just because I've seen him play for three years now. Played with him with Team USA the last couple of summers and obviously being his teammate now—I don't know that anyone deserves it more than him. He's just such a great human being and such a special player. It's been really cool to play with him."

Adding to his natural gifts is also his unique background. As a former two-way player at the US Air Force Academy (catcher and pitcher), Skenes developed a deep understanding of the game from multiple perspectives. This experience gave him an edge in reading hitters, recognizing their tendencies, and making in-game adjustments with ease. Despite his relatively short time focusing solely on pitching, his command came naturally—a rare trait for a power pitcher.

"I've always been able to put the ball where I wanted to, even at a young age," Skenes said. That ability sets him apart from most young flamethrowers, as command is typically one of the last things to develop for hard throwers. But Skenes isn't like most pitchers. His pinpoint control, combined with his continuous drive to improve, made it clear to me that he's still only scratching the surface of his potential.

What perhaps struck me most, talking with him both at LSU and in MLB, is his insatiable hunger to get better. Skenes spoke with excitement about refining his mechanics, mastering pitch sequencing, and experimenting with new grips like his devastating "splinker" (a hybrid between a splitter and a sinker). His confidence wasn't arrogance; it was a calm assurance rooted in disciplined preparation and tangible results.

Watching him overpower hitters at LSU and as a rookie in MLB while knowing how much room he still had to grow made me wonder: With increasing exposure to the advanced technology and data available in today's game, could Paul Skenes become an all-time great? Even though he's still extremely young, it's hard not to see the potential for Skenes to transcend the usual expectations for outstanding young pitchers and etch his name among the greatest to ever play the game.

♦ ♦ ♦

COREY MUSCARA'S PERSPECTIVE on Paul Skenes during the NCAA Tournament highlights a fascinating juxtaposition of competition and admiration. From the opposing dugout in the College World Series, in one of the biggest and most viewed college baseball matchups of recent times, Muscara admitted to initially drinking "a little bit of haterade," as his competitive instincts kicked in when preparing to face Skenes. However, as the game progressed, his feelings shifted to awe and respect. Muscara described watching Skenes and Wake Forest's Rhett Lowder go head-to-head as a "one-of-one game," marveling at the execution and composure of both pitchers under the intense pressure of the College World Series.

Muscara reflected, "I might be in this game for thirty more years and never see anything like that again." He likened the duel to "Larry Bird and Michael Jordan playing a game of H-O-R-S-E." What stood out most to Muscara was Skenes's superior command, efficiency, and ability to maintain velocity deep into the game, which he attributed to Skenes's biomechanical efficiency and strategic use of his pitches. By the later innings, Muscara was no longer solely focused on strategizing against Skenes and LSU; he was also an observer and fan, captivated by the historic display on the mound.

Muscara praised Skenes's mechanics as a key factor behind his success, emphasizing their biomechanical efficiency and repeatability. From the opposing dugout, Muscara observed how Skenes's delivery allows him to maintain velocity and command deep into games. "His mechanics are incredibly clean," Muscara noted, highlighting how Skenes's ability to stay within his movement patterns not only minimizes wear and tear but also ensures consistent execution. This efficiency enables Skenes to harness his immense physical tools—such as a fastball that holds triple digits late into outings—while also maintaining pinpoint accuracy. Muscara remarked that Skenes's mechanics are a foundational element of his success, allowing him to both overpower hitters and outlast them with precision and consistency.

Muscara was particularly impressed by Skenes's exceptional command and his ability to use all four quadrants of the strike zone with his fastball. Muscara noted how Skenes's blazing velocity is amplified by his precise control, making his fastball nearly unhittable. "He can dot the edges of the zone and elevate at will," Muscara said.

By working up, down, in, and out, Skenes keeps hitters guessing and neutralizes their ability to sit on any one location. This command both elevates the effectiveness of his fastball and, additionally, sets up his secondary pitches, as hitters struggle to adjust to his ability to exploit every part of the strike zone. Muscara highlighted this skill as a hallmark of Skenes's dominance, saying it's rare to see a pitcher with such a potent combination of velocity, movement, and surgical accuracy.

Similarly, New York Yankees Pitching Coach Matt Blake observed Skenes's exceptional execution and diverse arsenal when his team faced the Pirates. Reflecting on the matchup, Blake noted, "The level of execution he's getting to is just incredible. It's not just the stuff—his fastball, his breaking balls—it's the way he commands them. He understands how to move the ball in different ways to counter hitters' approaches."

One pitch that stood out to Blake was Skenes's mastery of the front-door fastball, a rare and challenging weapon. (This is a running fastball thrown at the hitter that breaks just enough back into the strike zone for, ideally, a called strike.) Blake remarked, "Skenes has the ability to throw the front-door fastball to lefties with precision, which is something you don't see often. That's a weapon that can completely neutralize a hitter's approach."

Blake further emphasized how Skenes's ability to adapt during games enhances his unpredictability. "He's got an understanding of what guys are trying to do to him, and then he moves his plan around off of that," Blake remarked. "The confidence he has in throwing that pitch in big situations speaks volumes about his approach. It's not just about the stuff; it's about knowing how to use it in the right moments," Blake added.

♦ ♦ ♦

WHEN SKENES TRANSFERRED from the US Air Force Academy to LSU, he found himself immersed in one of the most advanced pitching development environments in college baseball. At the heart of this transition was LSU's pitching lab and the expertise of pitching coach Wes Johnson, widely regarded as one of the top pitching minds in the sport. Skenes, who had limited exposure to advanced tools like Trackman before arriving at LSU, described the experience as transformative. "I'd never had anything like that in my life," Skenes said. "I didn't understand what made my stuff good or why I got hitters out." LSU's lab provided him with unparalleled resources, including analysis of his spin rate, velocity, and release point, alongside a team of number crunchers to interpret the information.

Johnson played a pivotal role in helping Skenes unlock his full potential. "What Coach Wes is so good about is he gives the how—how to do something—so that everyone can understand the why," Skenes explained. This approach allowed Skenes to refine his mechanics, improve his velocity, and optimize the movement on his pitches.

A key element of Skenes's development was LSU's state-of-the-art motion capture lab and force mound, which provided detailed insights into his mechanics and performance. The lab allowed Johnson and Skenes to analyze every aspect of his delivery in three dimensions, pinpointing inefficiencies and opportunities for improvement. Using data from motion capture, with the help of Jimmy Buffi's company Reboot Motion, Johnson identified subtle but impactful adjustments to Skenes's front-side landing mechanics, helping him generate more force with each pitch. "It's all about finding the small details that make a big difference," Johnson noted. These refinements were keys to boosting Skenes's velocity and enhancing his ability to command pitches across the strike zone with precision.

The force mound, another critical tool, measured how Skenes utilized ground reaction forces during his delivery. Johnson leveraged this information to optimize Skenes's energy transfer from the ground up, ensuring every ounce of force translated into velocity and pitch movement. This holistic approach to biomechanics and performance gave Skenes a clear plan for maximizing his physical capabilities. Reflecting on his progress, Skenes described how these technological tools and

Johnson's coaching came together to elevate his game: "It was really cool to see how everything came together."

Skenes first reached 100 mph during a practice session, a milestone that marked a turning point in his development. Johnson recalled the moment vividly, emphasizing its significance. "When he hit a hundred for the first time, you could see everything we worked on clicking," Johnson said. This milestone was the embodiment of the synergy between technology, focused coaching, and Skenes's continuous drive to improve.

The combination of LSU's advanced facilities and Johnson's coaching expertise gave Skenes the tools to succeed and the confidence to excel. This comprehensive approach enabled him to perform at a near legendary level in college, and additionally prepared him for a seamless transition to professional baseball, setting the stage for his historic rise in MLB. Johnson summed up his philosophy succinctly: "We weren't just preparing Paul for the next game. We were preparing him for the next level."

♦ ♦ ♦

SKENES'S TRANSFORMATION INTO one of the top pitchers in baseball has been fueled by his willingness to learn and adapt, often using resources like my PitchingNinja social media account to refine his craft. Skenes shared with me how he began understanding the concept of pitch tunneling by watching my videos that broke down elite pitchers' sequences. "I remember seeing your breakdown of a fastball up and a curveball down—how they tracked perfectly—and thinking, 'That's why hitters take that pitch,'" Skenes said, referring to an at-bat featuring Freddie Freeman and Zac Gallen during the MLB Playoffs. These videos helped Skenes grasp the importance of making every pitch look identical on their way to the plate to deceive hitters.

The idea of pitch tunneling became central to Skenes's approach, and he began consciously integrating it into his game. "Sometimes I'm thinking about tunneling in-game, using my misses to set up pitches," he explained to me. Skenes recognized that even a so-called waste pitch could have value if it was used to bait hitters into poor decisions, stating "there is no waste pitch, if you use it." This strategic layer of his game has made him even more difficult to face, as hitters struggle to differentiate between his fastball and breaking pitches until it's too late.

Skenes's splinker has become one of the most intriguing weapons in his pitching arsenal—a hybrid pitch that he perfected after his time at LSU and during his transition to professional baseball. Initially thrown more like a traditional sinker, Skenes refined the grip and delivery to create a pitch with exceptional late movement and a unique spin profile. "It's just how my body moves naturally," Skenes explained. Skenes's splinker's unpredictability makes it a nightmare for hitters to barrel up.

Pirates catcher Henry Davis was impressed by the pitch's devastating movement in spring training and became one of its biggest advocates. "You'll see it on PitchingNinja," Davis confidently predicted after catching Skenes during a spring training session. His belief in the splinker proved well-founded, as the pitch has since become a highlight-reel feature, earning admiration from analysts and striking fear into opposing hitters.

The splinker's development was an evolution of Skenes's commitment to pushing the boundaries of pitch design. After experimenting with grips to achieve rightward movement, Skenes inadvertently released the ball off his middle finger. This reduced the spin rate while maintaining velocity, resulting in the pitch's distinctive late drop and sharp break. Averaging 94 mph, the splinker combines sinker-like velocity with splitter-like movement, creating a dynamic weapon that confounds hitters.

Corey Muscara also marveled at the pitch. "It's not just the velocity; the late movement makes it almost impossible for hitters to barrel up," Muscara noted. He highlighted how Skenes seamlessly tunnels the splinker with his high-octane fastball, amplifying its deception and leaving hitters guessing until it's too late. Muscara praised Skenes's adaptability and dedication, pointing out how quickly he mastered the pitch after turning professional—an indication of his persistent work ethic.

Skenes's development of his splinker is emblematic of his ability to blend innovation with execution. Perfected after his collegiate career, the pitch now serves as a cornerstone of his arsenal, complementing his high-velocity fastball and sharp breaking ball. Its development highlights Skenes's commitment to refining every aspect of his game, while its in-game effectiveness cements his reputation as one of baseball's most exciting young pitchers.

Skenes takes a unique and highly adaptable approach to his game strategy. Often basing his plan on what feels effective during his bullpen sessions, Skenes adjusts his focus based on the strengths that emerge that day. "When you have five pitches, you throw each of them a few times in a fifteen-pitch bullpen, and that helps you figure out what might be a weapon today," Skenes explained to me before the All Star game in 2024. This adaptability keeps hitters guessing. Armed with seven pitches in 2025, he's unpredictable and dominant, shifting gears mid-game and always finding the pitch that plays best when it matters most.

A prime example of this flexibility was his unexpected changeup-heavy approach against the Cubs. Cubs analyst Lance Brozdowski observed the mid-game adjustment, noting, "He took what was essentially his fourth pitch and threw it 40 percent of the time in that game—completely out of nowhere." By deviating from his usual patterns and capitalizing on the strengths that emerged, Skenes exemplified the art of pitching, blending instinct, data, and preparation to maintain an unpredictable edge over opponents. Whether it's a sharp slider in one game or a Bugs Bunny changeup in another, Skenes's ability to adapt makes him a dynamic and formidable presence on the mound.

Johnson praised Skenes's exceptional hand control, a skill he believes sets Skenes apart as a pitcher capable of adapting his strategy in real time. "Paul has such an elite hand feel," Johnson explained. "You're going to see him come out, and today he's going to throw curveballs and throw 40 percent of them because that day he's got elite command of it." This ability allows Skenes to determine his most effective pitch during pregame bullpens and adjust his game plan accordingly. Johnson highlighted how this rare talent, combined with Skenes's mental acuity, enables him to dissect lineups with a tailored approach: "The good ones understand that knowing their stuff that day and being able to command a pitch that's moving the way theirs does—you can't put a price on that."

♦ ♦ ♦

SKENES EMBODIES THE modern blueprint of an overpowering, unhittable pitcher, and his meteoric rise has drawn comparisons to some of the most transformative athletes in sports history. Ben Brewster, founder of Tread Athletics, likened Skenes to one of the greatest athletes of all time: "Paul is the LeBron James of baseball in the sense that he's maximized every factor of success—genetics, work ethic, understanding of his craft, and access to elite resources."

Brewster emphasized that Skenes has all of the tools and talent to be an all-time great, but the open question is whether he has the physical ability to stay healthy and sustain dominance. "He has the potential to be one of the greatest pitchers of all time. That's not hyperbole—it's just a longevity question," Brewster stated. Noting that Skenes is already pitching at a level comparable to the best in the game, Brewster added, "He's pitching on par with some of the greatest pitchers there are. The challenge is, can he do that consistently?" He pointed to the difficulty of maintaining peak performance in a demanding role, saying, "Chris Sale is a great pitcher, but how many years has he been this dominant in his entire career? It's very difficult to sustain that level."

What also sets Skenes apart, according to Brewster, is his ability to learn and adapt. "Every step of his career has been a clear progression. He identifies what he needs to improve, and then he attacks it with precision." This disciplined approach, paired with his incredible physical tools and advanced understanding of pitching, positions Skenes as a generational talent capable of redefining the standard for modern pitchers. However, as Brewster noted, the ultimate question for Skenes will be his ability to remain healthy and productive over time. "If he stays healthy, he has everything it takes to go down as one of the all-time greats," Brewster concluded.

Chris Fetter, the highly regarded pitching coach for the Detroit Tigers, offered a glowing assessment of Paul Skenes after facing him in 2024 when the Tigers squared off against the Pirates. Fetter was in the opposing dugout, getting a firsthand look at Skenes's impressive stuff. "He has all the tools," Fetter said. "The ability to throw a hundred miles an hour, he's learned the splinker in the matter of a couple months—he seems adaptable, he seems in control of himself on the mound."

Fetter also pointed out how Skenes's consistency in his approach and work ethic sets him apart. "The best guys in our game are consistent—in their approach, in their daily work—and that's what it appears like from the outside with Skenes." Fetter was particularly impressed with how Skenes has maximized his fastball. "When you throw a hundred, a hundred one, it's gonna play—especially with his ability to utilize a splinker now, which only makes it that much better." Coming from a pitching mind as respected as Fetter, this praise underscores the complete package that Paul Skenes brings to the mound: adaptability, preparation, and a devastating arsenal of pitches.

Brozdowski points out that Skenes's ability to command his pitches at such a high velocity is rare and crucial to his success. "You could argue most pitchers with that kind of velocity aren't also showing elite command," Brozdowski observes. This combination sets Skenes apart from many high-velocity pitchers who may struggle with accuracy.

Brozdowski also emphasizes how Skenes's physicality—standing at six six—plays a significant role in his deceptive delivery. His release point, aided by his height and arm angle, generates a unique look that contributes to his effectiveness on the mound. "It's not just about raw stuff with him; it's how his body moves and how he hides the ball," Brozdowski explains.

Wes Johnson expands on this, noting the parallels between Skenes and tall pitchers like Randy Johnson. Despite his towering frame, Skenes delivers from a lower arm slot, which enhances his deception and disrupts hitters' timing. "A lot of tall pitchers are taught to throw downhill, but with Paul, we worked on letting his arm naturally swivel out of his delivery. This approach not only maximizes his velocity but also creates a unique visual for hitters that they're not accustomed to," Johnson explains. He likens this attribute to Randy Johnson, who famously utilized his height and a lower arm slot to vanquish hitters. "When you pair that with Paul's ability to command his pitches, it's a combination that's exceptionally hard to prepare for as a hitter," Johnson adds.

♦ ♦ ♦

BRENT STROM PRAISED Skenes for his immense talent and potential, describing him as a "meteor on the rise" and expressing admiration for his blend of size, intelligence, and work ethic. Strom shared an anecdote from the 2024 All-Star Game, where he provided Skenes with scouting notes on the first six hitters of the opposing lineup. Skenes responded with confidence, saying, "I won't need it. I'll get the three of the first four guys out, I won't need all the way to six."

Now working as the assistant pitching coach for the Pittsburgh Pirates, Strom expressed excitement about coaching Skenes regularly, saying, "He's trying to change the entire culture of that team as a twenty-two-year-old. He's not just about the pitching staff—it's about elevating the entire team with his approach." This speaks to Skenes's leadership and the high expectations surrounding him as he continues to establish himself as one of the most exciting pitchers of his generation.

After several months working side-by-side with Skenes in Pittsburgh, Strom told me how impressed he was: "He is very dedicated to his routines and always has a plan, which might be a residual from his time at the US Air Force Academy. He's also highly aware of his movements during drills and mound work, and he takes a deep interest in scouting reports." Strom told me he'd rank Skenes right up there with the best he's ever coached—including Cy Young winners and likely Hall of Famers Justin Verlander, Gerrit Cole, and Zack Greinke—when it comes to raw talent and relentless drive to improve.

Johnson expressed high regard for Paul Skenes being coached by Brent Strom, emphasizing Strom's deep knowledge and unique ability to blend old-school and modern approaches to pitching. Johnson stated, "Strom's a mentor for me. We've known each other a long, long time. He helped me a ton when I first broke in with the Twins." He pointed to Strom's experience coaching some of the best pitchers in the game, including Justin Verlander, and expressed confidence in Strom's ability to further develop Skenes. "I think the Pirates have a chance to have some of the best young pitching staff in baseball next year, and Brent is a huge part of that," Johnson added.

Paul Skenes has garnered significant attention both for his eye-popping on-field performance and also for his distinctive pregame warm-up routine. This meticulously structured 35-minute regimen is designed to enhance body awareness, refine mechanics, and ensure optimal readiness for each start.

Skenes begins his routine with a series of drills focused on activating his core and honing his mechanics. Using equipment such as resistance bands and water bags, he meticulously rehearses his pitching motion, alternating between right-handed and left-handed movements to promote balance and coordination. This comprehensive approach, influenced by his collegiate career at LSU, also incorporates techniques inspired by pitchers like Yu Darvish, who famously practiced opposite-handed throws to enhance balance and adaptability.

Skenes's preparation has drawn praise from across the baseball world. Chris Fetter noted the precision of his regimen, commenting, "You look at his routine before he gets on the mound, it's pretty special. It seems like every aspect of his life is pretty dialed in."

Trevor Bauer, a trailblazer in the use of unorthodox pitching methods, sees clear parallels between his own groundbreaking routines and Skenes's methodical approach. Reflecting on the changing landscape of pitching preparation, Bauer remarked, "People are suddenly okay with this kind of warm-up routine now that Paul Skenes is doing it, but when I started, I was told it was unnecessary or weird." His point underscores how individualized warmup protocols—once mocked—are now standard. Bauer believes he was the lightning rod who absorbed the backlash years earlier, clearing the path for pitchers like Skenes.

Wes Johnson, Skenes's former pitching coach, agrees that Bauer helped pave the way. He called Bauer a "first through the wall" figure who took heavy criticism for pushing practices like elaborate warm-ups and weighted ball training, innovations that are now the bedrock of modern pitching development.

Yet it isn't just Bauer's defiance that normalized these methods. Skenes's humility and collaborative style have also been key. Where Bauer's unapologetic edge often divided opinion, Skenes's approachable, team-first demeanor has allowed him to fold advanced routines seamlessly into the clubhouse and to earn both trust and buy-in from those around him.

As Yankees pitching coach Matt Blake observed, "Paul's approach is different—he's methodical but humble. Trevor often defied norms outright, which wasn't always received well. Paul works within the team structure, blending modern preparation with an approachable personality."

Bauer also emphasized the intentionality behind Skenes's routine, saying, "Skenes's routine is focused and detailed—it's built to get him into the exact state he needs to dominate." For Skenes, the process is not merely about warming up; it's about ensuring that every movement and every throw serves a purpose in the larger framework of performance optimization.

Bauer further highlighted the sustainability embedded in Skenes's methods. "It's not just about the warm-up," Bauer explained. "It's about building a foundation that allows you to sustain dominance, outing after outing. Paul's doing that at such a young age, and it's impressive."

Paul Skenes's blend of both traditional and modern methods sets the standard for the next generation of baseball players.

♦ ♦ ♦

SKENES'S UNIQUE APPROACH to pitching includes an element that has intrigued fans and analysts alike: his incorporation of football into his training regimen.

Wes Johnson introduced Paul Skenes to football throwing as a unique training tool halfway through the season, drawing inspiration from the methods of Tom House. "I'm big on football throws," Johnson said, crediting House's work as an influence. The football throws were tailored to help Skenes achieve a natural arm swivel, emphasizing efficiency and comfort in his throwing mechanics. Johnson explained, "I want your arm to swivel naturally out of your sequence delivery, wherever that is."

The football drills allowed Skenes to feel the natural swiveling motion of his arm while throwing, which was critical to refining his mechanics. Johnson noted that Skenes preferred throwing the football with his fingers off the laces to prevent blisters, highlighting how personalized this approach became. This method contributed to Skenes's efficient arm action and helped him understand and improve his overall pitching mechanics sequence.

According to House, this aspect of Skenes's preparation is far from unconventional—it's rooted in science and tradition.

House, widely regarded as one of the pioneers of modern pitching mechanics, has long advocated for throwing a football to build rotational strength, refine throwing mechanics, and reinforce proper arm angles. "Throwing a football activates the same muscles you use in pitching," House has explained in the past. "It's about functional strength and improving efficiency in the kinetic chain."

House emphasized that Skenes's football throws and background as a multiposition player have given him a unique edge and make him, in House's words, a "prototype athlete." He told me, "Paul's football work helps create better arm action and balance, and I've been advocating that for decades. He's a former catcher, and catching is the purest form of what a pitcher needs—it teaches quick, efficient footwork, balance, and the ability to throw from different arm slots under pressure. That's why playing multiple positions can make you a better pitcher."

Interestingly, House points out how athletes like Tom Brady have also incorporated similar nontraditional principles into their training regimens. "Paul's understanding of his body and his willingness to embrace unconventional methods shows why he's special," House remarked. "He's not just a great athlete; he's a student of the game, and that's why he's excelling at such a young age."

Skenes's use of football in his training is a statement about his commitment to finding every possible edge. House believes this forward-thinking mindset will keep Skenes ahead of the curve, adding, "Paul's willingness to try new things while staying true to what works for him is why he has the potential to become one of the all-time greats."

Wes Johnson acknowledges Skenes as having the potential to be a once-in-a-generation pitcher but also urges caution in making such declarations too early. Johnson points to Skenes's unique blend of physical talent, mental discipline, and work ethic, which set him apart from most players. He remarked, "When you look at what he's able to do and his ability to push himself, not just physically but mentally, it's different. That's what makes him who he is."

Johnson noted that Skenes has consistently demonstrated the ability to push his mind to uncomfortable levels daily, a trait that separates him from others. "It's never been easier to be great at baseball, but it's never been harder to manage distractions," Johnson shared, adding that Skenes has the rare capacity to focus intensely while balancing the demands of high-level competition. While Johnson refrained from labeling Skenes definitively as a generational talent, he did affirm that "everything trends to say yes" if Skenes stays healthy and continues on his current trajectory.

Skenes certainly appears to represent the archetype of the ultimate modern pitcher, seamlessly blending modern technology and data with timeless qualities like work ethic, adaptability, and a constant desire to improve. His journey—from an unpolished talent at the US Air Force Academy to the first overall pick in the MLB Draft and a spectacular professional rookie—is a case study in the evolution of pitching. Through his use of advanced tools, his willingness to embrace unconventional methods, and his deep understanding of the game's mental and physical demands, Skenes has built a skill set that sets him apart in today's baseball landscape.

What truly distinguishes Skenes is his ability to combine old-school grit and new-school analytics. While he utilizes state-of-the-art technologies, such as motion capture systems, high-speed cameras, and pitch-tracking tools, he doesn't allow data to overshadow the fundamentals. His development of the "splinker" highlights this balance. By experimenting with grips and applying biomechanical insights, Skenes transformed the pitch into a devastating weapon. However, it's his old-school traits—meticulous preparation, an unparalleled work ethic, and a hunger to learn—that enabled him to refine and master it in such a short period.

Guided by top-notch coaching and armed with both patience and tech, Skenes treats every bullpen, workout, and training session as a workshop—always tinkering, always finding ways to get nastier. From throwing footballs to enhance his mechanics to fine-tuning his pitch tunneling based on video breakdowns, Skenes reflects the essence of a modern athlete who leaves no stone unturned in the pursuit of excellence.

Moreover, his mental acuity and leadership set him apart as more than just a pitcher; he's a culture changer. Whether it's his calm demeanor under pressure—shaped by his military background—or his collaborative relationship with coaches and teammates, Skenes embodies the ideal blend of humility and confidence. His success highlights the growing trend in baseball of leveraging technology not to replace traditional values but to amplify them, making players both more effective on the field and also better prepared for long-term success.

The evolution of pitching, as seen through players like Paul Skenes and the technological advances explored throughout this book, has undeniably transformed the balance of power in baseball. From state-of-the-art biomechanics to real-time game data and meticulously developed pitch designs, the tools available to pitchers today are staggering in their precision and impact. Combined with the mental resilience, adaptability, and leadership exemplified by athletes like Skenes, it's no wonder that pitching is experiencing an unprecedented golden age of dominance.

But with this revolution comes an inevitable question: Can hitters ever catch up?

22

"I'd hit .200 in this day and age."

That's what Hall of Famer Chipper Jones told me—and he wasn't joking. But let's be real: Chipper was probably selling himself short. One of the most complete hitters of his generation, he could hit in any era. Still, as a Braves hitting consultant, he sees just how nasty the modern game has become. "That's some filthy stuff coming out," he said, watching a wave of high-velocity, high-movement arms dominate the league.

Chipper was a switch-hitting third baseman who spent his entire nineteen-year career with the Atlanta Braves. He finished with a .303 career average, over 2,700 hits, 468 home runs, and the 1999 National League MVP award. He was also an eight-time All-Star and a World Series champion. And yet—even with all that—he thinks today's pitchers might have him overmatched.

Chipper played in an era with elite pitching—he faced Randy Johnson, Pedro Martinez, and prime Roy Halladay—but he's adamant that today's pitchers are a different animal altogether. "It's a hundred-mile-an-hour heat and strikeouts. Nobody pitches to contact anymore," he said. "Now there's four or five guys on each staff throwing a hundred."

He told me that hitters used to be able to look for something in the zone, work the count, and make contact. Now the game has shifted to raw velocity and wicked movement, and pitchers aren't pitching to contact to get outs—they're trying to miss bats entirely—trying to embarrass you. "Their secondary stuff is a lot better nowadays than it was twenty years ago," Chipper told me. "You could time a fastball, but now you've got to worry about a slider that starts at your hip and ends up in the other batter's box."

The unpredictability of modern stuff has turned hitting into what he called a "guessing game." "You've got to sit on one or the other," he said. And if you guess wrong, you're done. There's no recovering from 100 mph at the top rail followed by a sweeper that dives out of the zone.

Chipper also admitted, not without a little pain, that it's not exactly fun for him to watch. "It's not necessarily a good thing to watch for a dinosaur like me," he said. "There's not a whole lot of baseball being played out there—just a lot of punchouts and homers."

And yet, he respects it. He understands how the game has evolved—and how pitchers, with tools like high-speed cameras, pitch design software, and biomechanical feedback—have unlocked a new level of dominance. "That's what makes them so hard to hit," he said. "They've got weapons we didn't even know existed."

In Chipper's eyes, today's hitters aren't worse. The pitchers are just better. Faster. Nastier. Smarter. Unhittable, even for a legend like him.

◆ ◆ ◆

BASEBALL HAS ALWAYS been about balance—pitchers versus hitters, power versus finesse, a battle of chess moves played out on dirt and grass. But right now, pitchers are holding all the cards. It's not just a fastball anymore; it's a high-spin, rising fastball that seems to climb uphill. It's sliders that vanish into thin air and splitters that fall like they've hit an eject button. Thanks to Edgertronic cameras, Rapsodo machines, and Trackman data, pitchers are essentially engineers, fine-tuning pitches into weapons so devastating they make hitters look like they're swinging pool noodles.

On top of that, advanced scouting reports and heat maps are turning pitching into a sniper operation. Pitchers know where hitters struggle, and they attack those weaknesses with surgical precision.

As A. J. Pierzynski, a nineteen-year Major League hitter and former catcher, put it to me: "As a pitcher, you're in control of the ball, so you can manipulate how you want to manipulate it. With hitting, you're kind of at the mercy of the pitcher. Pitching analytics are way ahead of hitting analytics . . . You can move your finger a quarter inch on a fastball and get more ride. You can't do that with hitting." That's the brutal truth of the modern game—hitting has become pure counterpunching. Baseball is the only major sport where the defense controls the ball, and in today's version of the game, that control has evolved into domination. With pitchers dictating both velocity and movement, location and sequencing, hitters are left guessing—and often guessing wrong.

While hitters haven't had access to the same depth of tools and resources as pitchers, new technologies are starting to help close the gap. One is Trajekt, a pitching machine that uses advanced algorithms and motion capture data to replicate the delivery, velocity, spin, and movement of specific pitchers. With Trajekt, hitters can face a digital version of an opposing ace during batting practice, giving them unprecedented opportunities to prepare for even the best pitching. Tools like these allow hitters to train for the exact challenges they'll face in a game, potentially helping to reduce the overwhelming advantage pitchers currently hold. It's like a flight simulator for hitters—it lets them practice against turbulence before they ever leave the ground.

But as A. J. Pierzynski told me, even cutting-edge tools have limits. "You can't simulate game-on-the-line, ninth inning . . . You're facing the best closer, he throws a hundred with cutters—one away, one in, one off the plate—with the crowd going crazy. I love the Trajekt machine, it simulates [a pitcher's] motion, but it's never the same . . . you don't know what's coming in a game." There's still no substitute for the chaos of live pitching.

Beyond Trajekt, other technologies such as bat sensors, biomechanical motion analysis, and high-speed cameras for swing diagnostics are beginning to reshape hitting development. While not yet as prevalent as pitching labs, these tools aim to give hitters the ability to fine-tune their mechanics, improve their timing, and better understand their swing paths. The question remains, however, whether these advances can close the gap created by the rise of data and technology in pitching—or if the game is destined to remain in the grip of engineered pitching perfection.

As the game continues to evolve, hitters must both adopt new tools and also find innovative ways to apply them, much like pitchers have done. Whether the balance of power can shift back toward offense remains one of the most compelling questions in modern baseball.

♦ ♦ ♦

HISTORY REMINDS US that this isn't the first time pitchers have flexed their dominance. In the early 20th century, baseball was all about small ball and hustle plays—bunting, stealing bases, scratching out runs. Then Babe Ruth came along and said, "What if I just hit the ball five hundred feet?" Suddenly, the home run era was born.

Pitchers pushed back in the 1960s, turning the game into a strikeout fest when MLB expanded the strike zone. Scoring plummeted so much that MLB had to step in and level the playing field by lowering the mound. Fast forward to the late 1990s and early 2000s—the Steroid Era blew offense through the roof. Home runs were popping off like fireworks, and it felt like pitchers might never catch up.

But here we are. In 2024, offense scraped the bottom of the barrel. Batting averages fell from .264 in 2008 to .243. League-wide OBP dipped from .333 to .310. Slugging percentage, which peaked in the home-run-happy 2019 season, tumbled back under .400. And the stat that says it all? Whiff rates jumped from 20.8 percent to nearly 26 percent in just over a decade.

This is a game where the pitcher throws 94.3 mph on average—not a "rarity," but average. Combine that with wicked sliders, disappearing splitters, and tunneling—where every pitch looks identical out of the hand before veering in unpredictable directions—and you start to understand why hitting feels impossible.

♦ ♦ ♦

IF YOU WANT to understand how tough modern pitching has become, just ask Brent Rooker. A two-time All-Star and one of the best hitters in baseball in 2024—batting .293 with thirty-nine home runs and 112 RBIs—even he admits: It's a nightmare out there.

Rooker described the inherent imbalance in the pitcher-hitter matchup, noting how hitters are often at the mercy of pitchers who control the action. "Even though hitting is called offense and pitching is called defense, in the one-on-one matchup, hitting is almost more defensive than pitching because they're the ones with the ball. They're controlling what's happening, and we just have to react and try to beat them at what they're doing," Rooker explained.

He talked of the growing difficulty for hitters as pitchers continue to train to throw harder and use advanced pitch design to make pitches move unpredictably. "They have the technology to kind of make pitches do whatever they want now and play off each other better," he added. While Rooker acknowledged the potential for hitters to counteract by swinging harder, he wasn't certain about whether that approach would provide a meaningful advantage. Still, Rooker believes in the cyclical nature of the game, suggesting that at some point, "there will be a swing back in the offensive."

When asked about the hardest part of hitting, Rooker didn't hesitate. "It's the tunneling," he said. "The pitches all look the same out of the hand, and then . . . they're not. Fastballs, sliders, splitters—everything looks identical until the last moment. You can't plan for that."

Rooker added, "You used to face guys who had one pitch that was elite. Now, every guy has three or four pitches that are elite. Even their worst pitch is still nasty because they've optimized everything."

Adding to the difficulty is the sheer variety of pitches pitchers now command. Rooker faces four-seamers that ride up, sinkers that fade late, cutters that jam him, and even Seam-Shifted Wake pitches that defy traditional movement patterns. Unlike traditional breaking pitches, where the spin and movement align in predictable patterns, Seam-Shifted Wake pitches deceive hitters by creating movement that doesn't match the visual cues. Rooker explained, "With a standard slider or curveball, you see the spin, and it processes in your head like the spin is what's causing that movement, and those two things are kind of matching up."

In contrast, Seam-Shifted Wake disrupts that intuitive connection. "With Seam-Shifted Wake . . . the pitches look weird because it doesn't look like the spin that it has should be causing the movement that it is," Rooker observed. This disconnect forces hitters to "re-register it in [their] brain," adding another layer of complexity to an already impossible task.

Rooker points to two specific examples. The sweeper, with its exaggerated horizontal movement, and the cutter, which mimics a four-seam fastball's spin but deviates unexpectedly, are particularly deceptive. "The seam-shift cutter that guys throw just kind of looks like four seamers because of the way they're spinning, but then obviously the way that it's catching the seams is causing all the movement," he explained. This movement isn't generated by spin axis alone but by the airflow disrupted by seam orientation, creating a new level of unpredictability.

For hitters, these pitches redefine how they process the visual cues of spin and movement. As Rooker put it, "It's not necessarily the shape of the spin or the axis of the spin causing the movement," which upends the traditional logic hitters rely on to anticipate a pitch's trajectory. As a result, hitters are left grappling with a pitch profile that forces them to rethink their approach in real time. Suddenly, the road signs they've trusted their whole life are pointing the wrong way.

To compete, Rooker turns to technology. He studies heat maps, expected wOBA (weighted on-base average), and exit velocity zones to maximize his strengths. "I use my own heat maps a ton . . . I can manipulate my approach, stance, or where I'm looking in the box to better fit what I already do well," he said. Tools like K-Vest further refine his mechanics, allowing him to analyze inefficiencies in real time and make precise adjustments. "To see where the inefficiencies are and what I need to correct," Rooker added, describing how understanding energy transfer helps him optimize power and consistency.

Reflecting on the modern hitter's evolution, Rooker explained how biomechanics and advanced tools have reshaped hitting instruction. "You can now kind of design swings that best fit you biomechanically, or best fit your movement profile, or body profile—whatever it is," he said. "You can now kind of look at how you move, look at how you're built, look at the way that your body can maneuver, and things like that, then design a swing that should theoretically play the best based on those different variables."

However, even as hitters catch up, new challenges loom, like the proposed automated strike zone. Rooker sees it initially favoring hitters, as fewer borderline pitches will be miscalled. But he believes pitchers will adjust. "You'll see big curveballs that clip the very top of the zone," he predicted. "It's unhittable because, by the time it drops into the zone, it's so high in the swing path that you can't do anything with it."

For a hitter like Rooker, who already battles 100 mph fastballs and unpredictable movement, this future of precision pitching feels like yet another battle in an endless war. Yet, he finds solace in shared struggles. Watching PitchingNinja clips, Rooker admitted, often puts things in perspective. "It makes me feel better a lot of times. If I have a bad strikeout and I see an overlay clip, I'm like, well, obviously I missed those pitches—they were perfect. And when I see someone like Mookie [Betts] looking bad on a pitch, it reminds me that even the best hitters in the world struggle sometimes."

♦ ♦ ♦

ERIC HOSMER—WORLD SERIES champion, 1,700+ hits, a career .276 hitter—spent over a decade in the majors. For him, the difference in today's game is crystal clear.

"Every pitcher has a weapon for your weakness now," Hosmer told me. "They know exactly where to go, and they're throwing with so much conviction because the data backs it up."

Pitchers have eliminated bad pitches from their arsenal. They've fine-tuned sliders, ditched flat fastballs, and learned to dominate with confidence. "The last couple of years, I saw so many pitchers learn a new pitch, and suddenly it was elite. It's crazy how fast they improve now."

A. J. Pierzynski has seen the evolution of pitching development up close, and one of the biggest differences today is just how prepared young pitchers are the moment they reach the majors. "These kids are so advanced now," he told me. "They come up with a plan . . . they know what their ball does, they know how they're trying to attack you, they know what works for them."

That level of self-awareness used to take years to develop—often through trial, error, and time in the minors. Now, thanks to high-speed cameras, spin data, and individualized training, twenty-two-year-olds arrive with polished arsenals and advanced pitch sequencing strategies. "When I came up, guys didn't know why their slider moved the way it did. Now they've seen 3D models of it in a lab before they've even debuted," Pierzynski said. Now, there's a league full of young pitchers throwing elite stuff with the confidence and command of veterans.

♦ ♦ ♦

AS TECHNOLOGY EVOLVES, hitters now have tools to at least attempt to combat the nastiest pitchers. Take Trajekt, for instance—a machine capable of replicating any pitch from any pitcher in the game. Corey Muscara, Wake Forest's pitching coach, notes that as hitters face these simulated pitches more often in practice, they're getting better at solving once-unhittable problems.

"If a hitter sees enough of any pitch, they can adjust," Muscara explained. "Trajekt and tools like it let hitters face elite fastballs, sliders, and splitters over and over until they start to 'see it.' The pitch loses its outlier advantage."

The outcome? Pitches that once were outliers and, due to that, hard to hit—such as high-ride fastballs, sweepers, or devastating splitters—would become familiar enough for hitters to anticipate and attack. The edge pitchers held when hitters were reacting to something new or unpredictable has eroded. "You've got hitters training against everything," Muscara said. "If all you have is one pitch or one quadrant you can attack, they'll sit on it and punish you."

For pitchers, this signals a shift: Arsenal diversity and command matter more than ever. It's no longer enough to throw one pitch exceptionally well. Now, pitchers need multiple pitches—two fastballs, breaking balls, off-speed offerings—that can tunnel together and attack all areas of the strike zone. The game of cat and mouse continues.

"The new wave is fastball variation," Muscara said. "Guys are throwing four-seamers and two-seamers to different quadrants. It's about creating problems hitters can't solve by changing lanes, speeds, and shapes."

He used former Wake Forest standout Rhett Lowder as an example. Lowder's individual pitches might not rank as exceptional on their own—his two-seam and four-seam fastballs grade average in isolation—but their interplay creates chaos for hitters. "When you pair those fastballs with elite command and mix in his secondaries, it's a nightmare," Muscara explained. "He can throw to any quadrant, in any count, with different movement profiles."

This adaptability is the future of pitching. A pitcher who can command the strike zone while seamlessly blending pitch shapes and speeds becomes unpredictable again, even against hitters who train on advanced machines like Trajekt.

"It's not just about pure stuff anymore," Muscara said. "The sum of the parts is greater than the whole. The guys who win today are the ones who can pitch—truly pitch—and keep hitters guessing every at-bat." In other words, rather than simply chasing pure "stuff," advancements in hitting technology may force pitchers to rediscover the art of pitching.

Yankees Pitching Coach Matt Blake agreed. Blake discussed the evolving battle between hitters and pitchers, noting that while pitching technology and techniques have given pitchers the edge for now, hitters are steadily catching up. He pointed out that hitters have historically adjusted to every so-called revolutionary pitching trend—like the rise of high fastballs—by refining their training with tools such as high-velocity pitching machines and Trajekt simulations designed to replicate real in-game pitching. "The league evolves; hitters adjust to trends, and they're getting smarter and better equipped to counter what pitchers throw at them," Blake remarked.

Blake illustrated this point by highlighting one of the game's most exceptional hitters, Juan Soto, whom he had the opportunity to watch closely in 2024 on the Yankees. Reflecting on Soto's approach, Blake marveled at the discipline and precision that set him apart. "When you watch Soto," Blake noted, "you see how he controls the at-bat. He doesn't expand the zone—he forces pitchers to come to him."

Soto's ability to recognize and react to pitches is unmatched, according to Blake. "He's not just reacting; he's dictating. It's like he's two steps ahead of the pitcher." This tactical mastery frustrates pitchers, putting immense pressure on them to execute perfectly, knowing that even the smallest mistake could be punished.

Blake also praised Soto's fearlessness at the plate, describing him as someone who thrives in high-pressure situations. "He knows his strengths, he knows your weaknesses, and he's going to make you pitch to him. That confidence is what separates good hitters from great ones."

Blake's insights reflect the cyclical nature of baseball strategy, where pitchers innovate to dominate, only for hitters to adapt and catch up. While discoveries like Seam-Shifted Wake and innovations such as advanced pitch design keep pitchers on the cutting edge, hitters are continually improving their ability to read and respond, ensuring the game remains both competitive and evolving.

♦ ♦ ♦

WHILE PITCHERS HAVE been using technology to design custom pitches, hitters have turned to tech to craft custom bats aimed at combating those nasty weapons. One of the most intriguing innovations is the "torpedo bat," a design that has recently gained attention in Major League Baseball. Developed by Aaron Leanhardt, a former MIT physics professor and onetime Yankees analyst, the torpedo bat features a distinctive bowling-pin shape. The design redistributes weight lower in the barrel, concentrating mass where hitters are most likely to make contact—effectively increasing the chances of squaring up high-velocity pitches.[1]

The Yankees prominently showcased the bat during their 2025 Opening Day Series against the Milwaukee Brewers. With Jazz Chisholm Jr. and Anthony Volpe swinging the new model, New York launched a franchise-record nine home runs in a single game. The sudden surge in offense sparked both intrigue and outrage across baseball. Some see the torpedo bat as the natural counterpunch in the sport's ongoing arms race. Others—particularly pitchers—are less enthusiastic.

One of them is Brewers reliever Trevor Megill, who fumed after watching his team give up a barrage of home runs: "I think it's terrible. We'll see what the data says. I've never seen anything like it before. I feel like it's something used in slo-pitch softball. It's genius: Put the mass all in one spot. It might be bush [league]. It might not be. But it's the Yankees, so they'll let it slide."[2]

The bats, though controversial, are currently within MLB's rules. According to Rule 3.02, a bat must be "a smooth, round stick not more than 2.61 inches in diameter at the thickest part and not more than 42 inches in length. The bat shall be one piece of solid wood." And by those standards, the torpedo bat qualifies.

Former All-Star Eric Hosmer sees the torpedo bat as a turning point for hitters, a philosophical shift. "It feels like a point back in the offensive direction," he told me. Hosmer has long compared hitter meetings to golf strategy sessions: In today's game, hitters need multiple swings to counter a pitcher's mix of high-spin fastballs, sweepers, sinkers, and cutters—much like golfers need different clubs for different lies and distances. "Hitting coaches used to say you need multiple swings to combat various pitches in a pitcher's arsenal," he said. "Now, with these new bats, it's like getting fitted in golf. You can keep the same swing—we just change the club to fit it."

For Hosmer, who traditionally struggled with pitches moving in on him—right-handed cutters or left-handed sinkers—the torpedo bat could help him stay through the ball more effectively. "The hitting coach can now function more like a caddy," he said. "If I'm facing Paul Skenes and his fastball with ride, I'm bringing a driver. If I'm facing a guy with horizontal movement, maybe we break out the nine iron." With this new bat design approach, instead of needing a sinker swing, a cutter swing, or a sweeper swing, a hitter might finally get to focus on one consistent "A" swing—and just pick the right tool for the job.

Using technology to customize bats is less a gimmick than an inevitable response. Baseball is now a full-blown technology arms race—and what's good for the goose is good for the gander.

Kyle Boddy, who in recent years expanded Driveline's mission to train hitters, told me that pitchers are ahead because they embraced technology first. Boddy explained, "Hitters need to adopt the same level of detail pitchers are using now—every inefficiency in pitching has been addressed, and hitters have to catch up."

As Tom House, one of pitching's greatest minds put it: "Pitching has the edge now because we've been working with science for years. But hitters will catch up—they always do. It's baseball."

23

Unfortunately for MLB hitters, pitchers' tech advantage keeps creeping further upstream—and hitters are still chasing. Advanced technology is now filtering down to lower levels of baseball, creating a steady pipeline of pitchers engineered for dominance, entering pro ball with refined mechanics, optimized velocity, and the tools to make hitters miserable from day one.

Wake Forest's Pitching Lab is a glimpse into the future of college baseball. Built for $8 million, it's a high-tech facility designed to sharpen every edge of a pitcher's game. Outfitted with high-speed cameras, motion capture sensors, force plates, and advanced radar systems, it captures everything—delivery, movement, mechanics—frame by frame. Like the LSU lab that helped propel Paul Skenes to stardom, Wake's lab turns raw arms into refined weapons. It helps pitchers maximize their strengths and clean up their flaws.

◆ ◆ ◆

THEN PITCHING COACH Matt Hobbs, recognized as one of the premier pitching minds in college baseball, was instrumental in shaping the foundation of Wake Forest's state-of-the-art pitching lab. Corey Muscara highlighted Hobbs's pivotal role in the lab's early development, noting his significant input in designing its layout and selecting the state-of-the-art systems and technology that have become integral to its success. From advanced cameras to sophisticated tracking tools, many of the core components that define the lab today were chosen under Hobbs's guidance during its formative stages.

Muscara has embraced data-driven evaluation and development as a cornerstone of the program's success. One of the tools Muscara has developed is the "Shove Score," a comprehensive metric designed to assess a pitcher's overall effectiveness that is used for everything, including deciding playing time. The Shove Score incorporates a variety of data points, including velocity, pitch movement, spin efficiency, strike percentage, and other advanced metrics captured by the lab's modern tools like Trackman and Edgertronic cameras. Think of it as a pitcher's report card: Velocity, spin, and command are the subjects, and the Shove Score is the final grade that indicates if you're honor-roll material.

The Shove Score also serves a competitive purpose within the team. Muscara ranks pitchers weekly based on their Shove Scores, fostering a competitive environment where players are incentivized to improve. "When players see their names on that ranking board, it creates a culture where everyone wants to get better," Muscara said. This system ensures that pitchers constantly strive to refine their mechanics, command, and pitch design, all with the goal of climbing the internal leaderboard. The competitive dynamic creates better individual players, but it also elevates the entire pitching staff, making Wake Forest one of the most formidable programs in college baseball.

Muscara uses analytics both to gauge the current performance of his pitchers and to serve as a valuable tool during the recruitment process. Muscara explained the innovative system: "When we have a prospect camp, we could see guys in high school coming in. We could see all these projections, and we have all these same percentile ranks and things that we do just from prospects. So if we see a kid that's fourteen years old and we put them into all this, we have all of our models, and now we're projecting out where they're going to be." This ability to project long-term development provides a significant recruiting advantage for Wake Forest, enabling the program to identify and nurture young talent with high potential.

Wake Forest's approach isn't confined to the walls of the lab; it extends seamlessly into game situations. By integrating KinaTrax motion capture technology with Edgertronic cameras during live games, the program captures biomechanical data in real time, offering a detailed view of how a pitcher's mechanics evolve under stress. This real-time analysis provides insights into critical factors such as arm speed, release consistency, and overall efficiency, enabling Muscara and his staff to complement lab-based assessments with in-game observations. "The combination of real-time game data and lab data helps us paint a complete picture of a pitcher," Muscara explained.

◆ ◆ ◆

TO ENSURE THIS advanced data could be effectively applied, Muscara collaborated with Jimmy Buffi and his company, Reboot Motion. Buffi's expertise was instrumental in transforming the raw data from KinaTrax into actionable insights for development. His ability to distill complex biomechanical metrics into clear, digestible feedback allowed both players and coaches to make meaningful adjustments. "Jimmy helped us connect the dots," Muscara noted. "We could take what we saw with KinaTrax and translate it into adjustments that improved mechanics, reduced injury risk, and enhanced performance."

This seamless integration of advanced tools into player development would not be possible without a strong foundation of support, including Wake Forest's robust team of twenty-two student data analysts. These analysts play a vital role in interpreting and applying the information, ensuring the data gathered through technologies like KinaTrax and Edgertronic is transformed into actionable strategies for improvement.

The program's student analysts not only assist with player development but also gain hands-on experience to help further their own careers. "Our analysts have gone on to work for MLB organizations because of the experience they get here," Muscara noted. Their work helps convert raw data into actionable coaching plans, ensuring that players and coaches alike can maximize the benefits of Wake Forest's advanced technological infrastructure.

Muscara integrates advanced analytics and technological insights into his coaching philosophy, but he makes it clear that these tools are not the sole drivers of success. Muscara tailors his approach to each pitcher, recognizing that every player processes information differently. "Some guys respond better to data, and others need a feel-based approach," he said. By blending technological insights with individualized coaching strategies, Muscara ensures that the data is actionable and relevant for each athlete. For example, while motion capture and biomechanical analysis might reveal inefficiencies in a pitcher's delivery, Muscara uses that information to create drills and adjustments that align with the player's unique strengths and learning style." Technology is a tool to help us understand what a pitcher does well and where they can improve," Muscara explained. "But at the end of the day, it's about coaching the individual, not just the numbers."

◆ ◆ ◆

MUSCARA'S APPROACH TO coaching goes beyond the mechanics and metrics of pitching; he takes a holistic view, incorporating mental resilience, emotional intelligence, and even gratitude exercises into his program at Wake Forest. While data and technology play a significant role in refining physical performance, Muscara recognizes that success on the mound also requires a strong mental foundation. "Pitching is as much mental as it is physical," Muscara explained. "If you don't have the mindset to compete and adapt, all the tools and data in the world won't help you."

To foster mental resilience, Muscara works with his pitchers to embrace challenges and learn from adversity. He frequently incorporates mindfulness and gratitude exercises into his training regimen to help players maintain perspective. "We ask our guys to reflect on what they're thankful for," he said. "It's not just about being a better pitcher; it's about being a better person. Gratitude keeps them grounded and focused, especially in high-pressure situations."

"We want our pitchers to not just react but respond to adversity," Muscara noted. By helping players build mental toughness and emotional balance, he equips them to perform consistently, even when the game doesn't go as planned. By taking this holistic approach, combining modern technology with exercises that emphasize mindfulness, resilience, and gratitude, Muscara develops well-rounded athletes who are equipped to handle the demands of the game both on and off the field.

At Wake Forest, continuous innovation is a philosophy that drives their pitching program to remain at the forefront of player development. Muscara and his team consistently refine their systems, models, and training techniques to ensure they are maximizing every pitcher's potential. This iterative process allows them to stay ahead in a rapidly evolving game where new technologies, like biomechanics trackers and AI-powered analytics, are constantly redefining how performance is understood and improved. "We're never satisfied with where we are," Muscara said. "Once you create a model, you refine it, and then you create another one. It's about building something that grows exponentially."

As Muscara put it, "If you're not innovating, you're falling behind. In this game, you have to be willing to adapt every single day." This mindset attracts top pitching recruits to Wake and ensures their pitchers are prepared to succeed at the next level when they leave the program.

◆ ◆ ◆

WAKE FOREST'S PLAYER Development Seminar is a unique initiative that also shows how the lines between MLB and College technology have blurred. Muscara described the seminar as an opportunity to provide players with insights from MLB executives, scouts, and analytics professionals. "It's not just about what they're doing now; it's about what's going to happen in professional baseball," Muscara explained. By bringing in experts from twenty-four of the thirty MLB teams, the seminar ensures players are exposed to the latest trends and expectations in the professional baseball world.

For example, the 2024 Wake Forest Player Development Seminar brought together an impressive roster of speakers from all corners of the baseball world, emphasizing its commitment to preparing players for success at every level. The lineup included MLB pitching coaches like Matt Blake of the New York Yankees, Caleb Cotham of the Philadelphia Phillies, and Derek Johnson of the Cincinnati Reds—each renowned for their innovative approaches to pitching development. Ben Brewster, the co-founder of Tread Athletics and a leading voice in pitcher performance optimization, also shared his expertise. Additionally, the seminar featured industry-leading biomechanists and presentations on the latest technologies reshaping the game.

Muscara highlighted the unique value of the seminar, saying, "It's not just about teaching our players what the next level looks like—it's about creating an environment where they can engage directly with the best minds in the industry." The event included fireside chats, giving players and staff the opportunity to ask questions and gain deeper insights into the trends and tools driving modern baseball.

"These fireside chats are where the magic happens," Muscara noted. "Players can ask MLB coaches, biomechanists, and analysts about their own development, about what they see in the big leagues, or even about how to use the latest technologies. It's an open forum, and that level of access is invaluable." By fostering such direct engagement, the seminar educates players and also equips them with the knowledge and confidence to excel in the rapidly evolving landscape of professional baseball.

♦ ♦ ♦

WAKE FOREST'S COMPREHENSIVE approach to training is perhaps best illustrated through the success stories of its players, churning out First Round draft picks like Rhett Lowder and Chase Burns. Both pitchers leveraged the lab's state-of-the-art resources and data-driven coaching to refine their mechanics, develop new pitches, and elevate their performance to unprecedented heights. Their transformations stand as an illustration of the innovative and personalized training that has become the hallmark of Wake Forest's program.

Wake pitcher Rhett Lowder, the seventh overall pick in the 2023 MLB Draft by the Cincinnati Reds, credits the Wake pitching lab for his transformation into one of college baseball's best pitchers.

Arriving as a tall, skinny high school pitcher who topped out at 84 mph, Lowder relied on his ability to pitch intelligently rather than overpower hitters. However, through strength training, biomechanics analysis, and pitch refinement, he significantly increased his velocity and sharpened his arsenal. "I put on about twenty pounds my freshman fall, started throwing harder, and the lab played a huge role in that progression," Lowder explained.

The lab also played a pivotal role in helping Lowder develop his slider, a pitch he did not have in high school. "You can go in the lab with the Edgertronic cameras, mark it all up, and search for one ideal pitch shape. Then you work backward from that," Lowder shared. Using advanced motion capture and pitch-tracking systems, he tailored the shape and velocity of his slider to complement his changeup and fastball, creating a dynamic arsenal that consistently baffled hitters. Reflecting on his slider's evolution, Lowder said, "We looked at all my results for my sliders, the shapes that got the best outcomes, and I tried to just match that one consistently."

"I feel really comfortable talking about and interpreting the data now, and that's something I credit Wake for," Lowder said. His collaborative relationship with the coaching staff and the lab's analytics team allowed him to approach his development with a level of sophistication rarely seen at the college level. "If you're a high school kid who wants to reach your maximum potential, Wake Forest is the place to be," he confidently stated.

Chase Burns, a standout right-handed pitcher from Wake Forest, was selected second overall by the Cincinnati Reds in the 2024 MLB

Draft. He inked a record-breaking $9.25 million signing bonus, surpassing the previous high of $9.2 million set by Paul Skenes in 2023.

During his junior year at Wake Forest, Burns earned the ACC Pitcher of the Year title, posting a 10–1 record with a 2.70 ERA and striking out 191 batters over one hundred innings. His arsenal includes a high-velocity fastball, reaching up to 102 mph, and a sharp slider, both of which contributed to his high strikeout rates.

Burns's decision to transfer from the University of Tennessee to Wake Forest his junior year was influenced by the university's advanced Pitching Lab, renowned for developing standout pitchers like Lowder. He noted, "You look at what Wake Forest has done with guys like Rhett Lowder, Teddy McGraw, and Seth Keener—the list goes on. I knew they could help me develop into a more complete pitcher."

Upon arriving at Wake Forest, Burns dove headfirst into the lab's technology and coaching resources. "When I got here, they told me I wasn't using my glove side as well as I should," he explained. "Once I raised my slot, learned to rotate my back foot, and cleared my hips, everything became more directional. My fastball got more ride, my slider became sharper, and my curveball developed—all just from moving better."

Through the lab's advanced tools, including motion capture, Edgertronic cameras, and force plates, Burns visualized and refined his movements. He joked about the immersive process: "You get in your underwear, they put all these little dots on you, and you see yourself as a skeleton on the screen." Despite the awkwardness, Burns emphasized the value of the feedback. "Every bullpen, every game of catch, it's videotaped, analyzed, and compared to what you feel in the moment. That feedback was huge for me." Burns made his MLB debut in June 2025 and immediately made a statement, striking out ten hitters in four of his first eight games. He later told me that Wake Forest had prepared him so well the jump to the majors felt "almost seamless."

Programs like Wake Forest demonstrate how advanced technology, when combined with personalized coaching and holistic development strategies, can unlock a pitcher's full potential, even before they get to the Majors. The ability to analyze mechanics, refine pitch design, and develop mental resilience allows players to achieve consistent success while mitigating injury risks. Moreover, the integration of data-driven approaches into recruiting and training underscores how technology is reshaping player evaluation and development at every stage.

This movement reflects a broader shift in how baseball views player development. Colleges with advanced facilities have become pipelines for MLB-ready talent, producing athletes already fluent in the tools and analytics that drive today's game. As the sport continues to evolve, the influence of data and technology at the collegiate level will only grow, setting a new standard for what it takes to succeed at every level.

And now, pitching labs have gone global. Japan—long defined by tradition and discipline—is embracing the revolution with a sprawling new facility in Tochigi City. Inspired by American pioneers like Driveline and collegiate labs, the Agekke complex is equipped with cutting-edge tools like Trackman, Rapsodo, motion capture, force plates, and AI-powered analysis—all aimed at optimizing mechanics, refining pitch design, and reducing injury risk. Spearheaded by visionary Masahiro Sato, the lab marks a cultural shift in Japanese player development—from intuition to innovation. The goal: to build on Japan's pipeline of elite arms—including Yu Darvish, Shohei Ohtani, Shōta Imanaga, and Yoshinobu Yamamoto—and prepare the next generation to dominate in both NPB and MLB.

The arms keep coming—from every level and corner of the globe—and they're only getting nastier.

24

Baseball is a game of adjustments. Right now, pitchers are winning. They're smarter, nastier, and more prepared than ever before. But hitters? They're not done yet. The tools are coming—VR simulators, high-speed training, biomechanical breakthroughs—and when hitters figure it out, the balance will shift again.

It always does.

As Tom House reminds us, "Baseball always corrects itself." It's a tug-of-war as old as the game itself. Today's pitchers are throwing pitches that look unhittable, but somewhere, there's a hitter waiting to break the code.

Because no matter how nasty a pitch is, no matter how overwhelming the pitcher on the mound seems, baseball is still baseball. And hitters? They always fight back. They have to—for the sport to stay alive.

As A. J. Pierzynski told me: "I think baseball wants offense. I think front offices want offense. I think TV wants offense. You need scoring to keep people engaged. Nobody wants to see nine innings of two hits and seventeen strikeouts. It's cool for the pitching nerds, but that's not what people show up for."

Baseball is an endlessly evolving battle. It's always been a game of balance—between pitchers and hitters, power and finesse, chaos and control. But today, we're in an age where pitchers have taken the upper hand. With spin rates cranked to the max, sliders that disappear like they hit a glitch in the matrix, and 100 mph fastballs that explode out of nowhere, hitters are living in a nightmare. Pitching has become, in many ways, unhittable. The numbers don't lie—strikeouts are through the roof, and offense sometimes feels like it's been left behind.

Let's be real—this isn't the first time pitchers felt untouchable. Every time pitchers took the lead, hitters found a way to punch back. Maybe that's the beauty of baseball—no edge ever lasts forever. For every new pitch design, tech breakthrough, or biomechanical tweak, there's a hitter somewhere dreaming up their counterpunch.

There's also a price tag: Those sliders and 100 mph heaters don't come free. Arms are pushed to the limit, ligaments shredded, and careers shortened. Tommy John scars have become pitchers' battle tattoos, and for every success story, there's a flameout who never made it back. How much can we ask of pitchers before the human body says enough?

Longevity might be the toughest skill of all. It's the pitchers who can dominate not just today but a decade from now, still throwing fire, who become the legends. Velocity will always matter. It is baseball's most intoxicating weapon. But the next wave of aces won't be defined by the radar gun alone. They'll be the pitchers who outthink as well as overpower and build arsenals deep enough to keep hitters guessing. Some will trade a few ticks of heat for years on the mound. That might be the next revolution.

Tech has given us everything—velocity, spin rates, release points, mechanics mapped down to the millimeter. We have gone from using data to know what happened to shaping what could happen next. But at the end of the day, baseball is still played by humans. No algorithm can capture the intimidation of Randy Johnson glaring in from the mound, or the quiet genius of Greg Maddux carving up a lineup with surgical precision. The numbers can shape a pitch—but they can't measure fear, presence, or the sheer will it takes to own a moment when everything's on the line.

The game still lives in those moments—a full count in the ninth, a pitch that looks like it's coming for your head and ends up painting the black. Most fans don't tune in for the numbers, the gadgets, or the trends. They show up to see human beings compete, to witness something they've never seen before. That's the magic. Every game, every pitch, there's a chance for something unforgettable.

And here's the truth: This isn't the end. It's just another chapter. Baseball never stops evolving. Hitters will adjust. Maybe they'll fight back with their own tech—bat sensors, biomechanical swing designs, or AI-driven approaches. Or maybe we'll see radical changes in the rules—a smaller strike zone or even moving the mound back. Who knows? Baseball always finds a way to balance itself out. And it has to, because it's that equilibrium that keeps the game compelling.

Whatever happens, the battle between pitching and hitting rolls on. As long as there's baseball, someone will be pushing the limits. Someone will find a new edge. And someone will rise to meet the challenge.

For all the science and spin rates and 3D pitch modeling, baseball is still the same beautiful battle it's always been. A pitcher. A hitter. A fastball that hums. A curveball that buckles knees. And somewhere out there, a hitter who refuses to back down.

The moments are what matter—the ones that leave us speechless and get passed down through generations. Candy Cummings dreaming up the curveball. Walter Johnson throwing unhittable heat before radar guns existed. The rise of a generational talent like Paul Skenes. And whoever's out there right now, working on a pitch the world hasn't seen yet.

Because no matter how perfect pitching becomes, no matter how unhittable it feels, there's always a hitter—just one swing away—reminding us that nothing is ever truly untouchable.

Baseball is a never-ending story. It is a balance. Art and science. History and innovation. Pitchers today are the ultimate engineers, mastering physics and mechanics to make hitters look foolish. But the game isn't done. The story isn't over. The revolution keeps going, the game keeps evolving, and that's what makes it great.

Because at its core, baseball is still unpredictable. Still wild. Still beautiful. And on any given day—whether it's a 105 mph fastball, a wicked slider, or a hitter who squares it up against all odds—anything can happen. And that's why we love it.

ACKNOWLEDGMENTS

First and foremost, thank you to my wife, Patricia, who somehow put up with this obsession (and me) through the many late nights, baseball trips, and hours spent trying to explain why a certain pitch sequence was so nasty. Your patience and support made this possible, even when I was talking about pitch grips instead of having a normal dinner conversation.

To my son, Jack, your pitching journey helped light the fuse. Watching you train, fail, grow, and throw flames made me realize how deep this game can go. And to my daughter, Madeline, thank you for reminding me that baseball is supposed to be fun, especially when you're mic'd up and trash-talking your dad in videos. You both inspire me more than you know, and humble me (much to my chagrin).

To my parents, Ira and Ellen, thank you for always being my biggest fans. To my sister, Mindy, thank you for being in my corner always, and for your sense of humor and style. And to my brother, Perry, I miss you, and I wish you could see this.

To all the coaches, trainers, analysts, and pitchers I've had the honor of learning from, and to the pitchers I've coached, thank you. You didn't just help me understand the game better; you helped change the game itself. This book is built on your innovation, your curiosity, and your willingness to explain things to me five different ways until I got it.

Big thanks to Eric Nelson, my editor at HarperCollins, for taking this project seriously (and putting up with some of my bad puns in chapter titles). Your feedback made this book smarter, sharper, and better, and probably saved me from at least a dozen tangents.

To Rob Kirkpatrick, my agent, thank you for helping bring this book to life.

And finally, to the fans, followers, and baseball nuts who've supported PitchingNinja over the years, you're the reason I do this. Whether you're a pro pitcher, a high school coach, or just someone who likes watching wicked sliders that bend like video game glitches, I'm grateful you're along for the ride.

This book isn't about me. It's about all of you who love pitching, and who believe, like I do, that "unhittable" is both a goal and a mindset.

NOTES

1

1. Rob Friedman (@PitchingNinja), "Randy Johnson gushing about Paul Skenes . . . and also his advice to Skenes," X (formerly Twitter), July 28, 2024, https://x.com/PitchingNinja/status/1817525900855886180.

2

1. Nolan Ryan, "On Beef and Baseball," interview by Jesse Mullins Jr., *American Cowboy*, June 7, 2010, https://americancowboy.com/lifestyle/interview-nolan-ryan/.
2. Talmage Boston, "Nolan Ryan," SABR Baseball Biography Project, Society for American Baseball Research, https://sabr.org/bioproj/person/nolan-ryan/.
3. Rob Rains, *Nolan Ryan: From Alvin to Cooperstown* (Sports Publishing LLC, 2001).
4. Jonathan Hock, writer and director, *Fastball*, Gravitas Documentaries, 2016, 1 hr., 26 min., 26 sec., https://www.youtube.com/watch?v=5ogJvlzwxQs.
5. Rob Friedman (@PitchingNinja), "99 mph Fastballs from 33 Year old Nolan Ryan . . . ," X (formerly Twitter), January 6, 2025, https://x.com/PitchingNinja/status/1876249613650235517.

3

1. Charles Carey, "Walter Johnson," Society for American Baseball Research Biography Project, Society for American Baseball, accessed August 2025, https://sabr.org/bioproj/person/walter-johnson/.

2. Ty Cobb quoted in Kevin Larkin, "August 2, 2007: The Train Departs the Station: Walter Johnson Makes Major-League Debut," SABR Baseball Games Project, Society for American Baseball Research, November 13, 2020, https://sabr.org/gamesproj/game/august-2-1907-the-train-departs-the-station-walter-johnson-makes-major-league-debut/.
3. David Schoenfield, "#TBT: How fast was Bob Feller's fastball?," *SweetSpot* (blog), ESPN.com, April 16, 2015, https://www.espn.com/blog/sweetspot/post/_/id/57040/tbt-how-fast-was-bob-fellers-fastball.
4. "Feller's Speed Measured at 98.6 Miles Per Hour," *New York Times*, August 21, 1946, https://www.nytimes.com/1946/08/21/archives/fellers-speed-measured-at-986-miles-per-hour.html.
5. Pat Jordan, "The Wildest Fastball Ever," SI Vault, *Sports Illustrated*, October 12, 1970, https://vault.si.com/vault/1970/10/12/the-wildest-fastball-ever.
6. Michael Avallone, "Dalkowski Was the Original 'Wild Thing,'" MiLB.com, May 6, 2020, https://www.milb.com/news/orioles-steve-dalkowski-was-the-original-wild-thing-313365878.

5

1. "Official Baseball Rules: Rule 10.00—The Official Scorer," Baseball Almanac, accessed June 30, 2025, https://www.baseball-almanac.com/rule10.shtml.
2. Nathan Michael Corzine, *Team Chemistry: The History of Drugs and Alcohol in Major League Baseball* (Univ. of Illinois Press, 2016), 64.
3. Alan H. Levy, *Rube Waddell: The Zany, Brilliant Life of a Strikeout Artist* (McFarland, 2000).
4. William Blewett, *The Science of the Fastball* (McFarland, 2004), 110.
5. Andy McCue, "Branch Rickey," Society for American Baseball Research (SABR), accessed June 30, 2025, https://sabr.org/bioproj/person/branch-rickey/.
6. McCue, "Branch Rickey."
7. Pat Jordan, "Tom Terrific and His Mystic Talent," *Sports Illustrated*, July 24, 1972, https://vault.si.com/vault/1972/07/24/tom-terrific-and-his-mystic-talent.
8. Nolan Ryan with Jerry B. Jenkins, *Miracle Man: Nolan Ryan: The Autobiography* (Thomas Nelson, 1993), 86.
9. Nolan Ryan, Tom House, and Jim Rosenthal, *Nolan Ryan's Pitcher's Bible: The Ultimate Guide to Power, Precision, and Long-Term Performance* (Simon & Schuster, 1991).

7

1. Jeff Passan, *The Arm: Inside the Billion-Dollar Mystery of the Most Valuable Commodity in Sports* (HarperCollins, 2016).
2. "MLB Releases Report on Injuries to Pitchers," MLB.com, December 17, 2024, https://www.mlb.com/news/mlb-releases-report-on-pitcher-injuries-2024.

9

1. Brendan Hall, "Tiny Tim No More," *Worcester Telegram & Gazette*, December 24, 2009, https://www.telegram.com/story/news/local/east-valley/2009/12/25/tiny-tim-no-more/51758756007/.
2. Evan Grant, "How Texas Rangers' Max Scherzer Has Learned to Balance a Competitive Fire with Patience," *Dallas Morning News*, March 15, 2024, https://www.dallasnews.com/sports/rangers/2024/03/15/how-texas-rangers-max-scherzer-has-learned-to-balance-a-competitive-fire-with-patience/.

12

1. "Fielding Independent Pitching (FIP)," MLB Glossary, MLB.com, accessed June 30, 2025, https://www.mlb.com/glossary/advanced-stats/fielding-independent-pitching.
2. Rob Neyer, "Greinke Learns from the Nerds?" *SweetSpot* (blog), ESPN.com, November 18, 2009, https://www.espn.com/blog/sweetspot/post/_/id/1447/.

15

1. Andrew J. Schiff, "Henry Chadwick: The 'Father of Baseball' Was a Sportswriter," *National Pastime* 28 (2008), https://sabr.org/journal/article/henry-chadwick-the-father-of-baseball-was-a-sportswriter/.
2. Jimmy Stamp, "A Brief History of the Baseball," *Smithsonian*, June 28, 2013, https://www.smithsonianmag.com/arts-culture/a-brief-history-of-the-baseball-3685086/.
3. Jerry Crasnick, "Dodgers, Astros Say World Series Baseballs Are Slicker than Regular-Season Balls," ESPN.com, October 28, 2017, https://www.espn.com/mlb/story/_/id/21189661/houston-astros-yet-lose-home-october-ever-world-series-vs-los-angeles-dodgers.
4. "Candy Cummings," National Baseball Hall of Fame, accessed July 1, 2025, https://baseballhall.org/hall-of-famers/cummings-candy.

5. "Give the Batsman a Chance," *New York Clipper*, 31, no. 44 (January 19, 1884): 744, col. 3, https://idnc.library.illinois.edu/?a=d&d=NYC18840119.2.10&srpos=1&e=-------en-20--1--txt-txIN-%22Give+the+Batsman+a+Chance%22---------.

6. Richard Hershberger, "With a 'Deliberate Attempt to Deceive': Correcting a Quotation Misattributed to Charles Eliot, President of Harvard," *Baseball Research Journal* (Spring 2017), https://sabr.org/journal/article/with-a-deliberate-attempt-to-deceive-correcting-a-quotation-misattributed-to-charles-eliot-president-of-harvard/.

7. "Candy Cummings," National Baseball Hall of Fame.

8. "Candy Cummings," National Baseball Hall of Fame.

9. Mark Pestana, "October 7, 1867: Candy Cummings Debuts the Curve," Society for American Baseball Research, SABR Baseball Games Project, accessed July 1, 2025, https://sabr.org/gamesproj/game/october-7-1867-candy-cummings-debuts-the-curve/.

10. "Ed Walsh," National Baseball Hall of Fame, accessed June 30, 2025, https://baseballhall.org/hall-of-famers/walsh-ed.

11. Eddie Cicotte, quoted in Ben McGrath, "Project Knuckleball," *New Yorker*, May 17, 2004, https://www.newyorker.com/magazine/2004/05/17/project-knuckleball.

12. The nickname for Mathewson ("the Big Six") is noted in Frank Graham, *The New York Giants: An Informal History of a Great Baseball Club* (G. P. Putnam and Sons, 1952), 30.

13. Rob Neyer, "The Slider: A Concise History," ESPN.com, April 20, 2004, https://www.espn.com/mlb/columns/story?id=1786104.

20

1. David Adler, "Pitcher Got a Nasty New Slider . . . from Twitter," MLB.com, August 4, 2020, https://www.mlb.com/news/jake-diekman-chaz-roe-slider-pitching-ninja.

2. "Sword," MLB.com Statcast Glossary, MLB.com, accessed June 30, 2025, https://www.mlb.com/glossary/statcast/sword.

3. Jared Diamond, "A Regular Guy Hit 96 MPH in a Speed-Pitch Booth: A Viral Video Turned Him into a Prospect," *Wall Street Journal*, August 6, 2019, https://www.wsj.com/articles/a-regular-guy-hit-96-mph-in-a-speed-pitch-booth-a-viral-video-turned-him-into-a-prospect-11565262000; Chris Bumbaca, "Fan Who Threw 96 mph to Sign Major League Deal with A's Describes Journey to Contract." *USA Today*, August 7, 2019, https://

www.usatoday.com/story/sports/mlb/athletics/2019/08/07/mlb-nathan-patterson-describes-journey-contract-oakland-as/1943803001/.

22

1. Jeff Passan, "What Is a Torpedo Bat? Inside MLB's Next Big Thing," ESPN.com, March 31, 2025, https://www.espn.com/mlb/story/_/id/44477141.
2. Dan Martin, "Brewers Closer Fumes over Yankees' New 'Bowling Pin' Bats: 'Never Seen Anything Like It,'" *New York Post*, March 30, 2025, https://nypost.com/2025/03/30/sports/brewers-closer-fumes-over-yankees-new-bowling-pin-bats/.

INDEX

Aaron, Hank, 6
ABCA conference, 85
Aberdeen Proving Ground, 23
accessibility of talent discovery, 197–200
Adler, David, 66
Agekke, 240
Alou, Felipe, 124
Alou, Moises, 173
Andrews, James, 14
Arizona Diamondbacks, 85, 96–97, 122
The Arm (Passan), 54
arm conditioning, injury prevention and, 56
Atlanta Braves, 6, 220

Baltimore Orioles, 23
Bannister, Brian, 58, 61, 191
  on Codify, 131
  family background, 108–9
  Grienke partnership, 111–13
  pitch advisory roles, 114–15
  at USC, 109
  use of FIP, 113–14
  use of PITCHf/x, 110–11, 116
  Webb's work with, 177–78
Bannister, Floyd, 108
baseball
  analytics, 40–41

aversion to science, 39–41
balance between pitchers and hitters, 221, 224, 241–42
  historically, 35–39
  unpredictability of, 244
baseballs
  cobbler-made, 136
  handmade, 135–36, 138
  lemon-peel, 136–37, 174
  precision-made, 137
  Seam-Shifted Wake effects on, 170–79
  standards for, 138
  sturgeon-eye cores, 136
  weighted, xiv, 48, 56, 87, 91–92, 148–49, 184, 186
  World Series controversy, 137–38
Baseball Savant, 63–71, 125, 127, 132, 197
bat technology, 229–31
batting average, 135
bat waggle, 123
Bauer, Trevor, xviii
  baseball career, 93–95, 96–97
  Boddy and, 149–50
  controversies, 87
  Cy Young Awards, 87, 92–93, 107
  Driveline Baseball, 150
  extreme long toss, 87, 91, 107

254 ♦ INDEX

Bauer, Trevor (*cont.*)
  family background, 88
  health tracking, 102–3
  influence of, 106–7
  injuries, 90
  injury prevention approach, 57
  Laminar Express, 170
  MLB exile, 94–95
  Momentum, 105–6
  pitching methodologies, 95–97
  science background, 88–90
  on Skenes, 214–15
  social media use, 103–4
  Sword K Strut, 196–97
  training principles, 101–2
  use of technology, 98–101, 104, 149–50, 166
Bauer, Warren, 88
Bay, Max, 72
The Benchwarmers (film), 196
Bender, Charles Albert "Chief," 144–45
Bernstein, Nikolai, 183
Bernstein Principle, 183
Betts, Mookie, 107, 226
Bichette, Dante, 70
Bieber, Shane, 99, 192, 195
biomechanics, xviii, xix
  analysis services, 51–52
  Driveline's use of, 149–50, 151–53, 155
  for hitters, 222–23, 225–26
  House's lab, 5, 7, 8–9
  injury risk reduction and, 45–49, 55–58, 68
  Nyman's use of, 184, 186
  personalization and, 49–50
  Trend Athletics' use of, 30–31
Blaeholder, George, 145
Blake, Matt, 84–85, 99–101, 164, 206, 215, 228–29, 237
Blanco, Henry, 97
Boddy, Kyle, xii, xviii, 28
  Bauer and, 149–50

on Bauer's influence, 107
coaching background, 146
Driveline Baseball, 46, 146–47, 148–49, 151–53, 154–55, 158, 163–64, 185, 231
House's influence on, 147
injury prevention approach, 55
Let's Talk Pitching (forum), 27, 147–48
pitching philosophy, 147–48
poker background, 147
work with MLB teams, 162–63
Bonds, Barry, 123
Boston Red Sox, 6, 114–15, 163
box scores, 134–35
Brady, Tom, 18, 217
Brees, Drew, 18
Brewster, Ben, xii, 107
  injury prevention approach, 57
  pitching journey, 26–28
  on Skenes, 211–12
  Tread Athletics, 26, 28–31, 33, 148, 185, 237
bridge pitch strategy, 156–58
Brooklyn Dodgers, 40, 41
Brozdowski, Lance, 71–72, 210, 212
Buffi, Jimmy, 46–49, 51–52, 207, 235
Building the 95 MPH Body (Tread Athletics), 28–29
Burnes, Corbin, 64, 192
Burns, Chase, 237–39
buyback concept, 157

Caratini, Victor, 195
Chadwick, Henry, 134–35, 140, 141
Chapman, Aroldis, 12, 193
Chicago Cubs, 210
Chicago White Sox, 115
Chisholm, Jazz, Jr., 230
Cicotte, Eddie, 142
Cincinnati Reds, 162, 167, 168, 180, 237, 238

INDEX ◆ 255

Cishek, Steve, 80
Clemens, Roger, 192
Cleveland Indians, 21, 97, 99–100, 117, 144
Clevinger, Mike, 99, 100
Cobb, Ty, 20
Codify, 124–33
Cole, Gerrit, 121, 192, 213
Collins, Tim, 79–80
Collis, Rocky, 186–88
command training, 41, 158–59
conditioning, injury prevention and, 14
Cone, David, 50–51, 75–76, 174, 196
consistency, 101
Copping, Corey, 48
Cotham, Caleb, 153, 237
Crawford, Sam, 141
Cressey, Eric, xii, 28, 148
   Cressey Sports Performance (CSP), 54, 76, 79–85
   injury prevention approach, 54–55
   with New York Yankees, 83–84
   powerlifting background, 77
   rehabilitation approach, 81–82
   strength training emphasis, 74–75, 77–79
   tennis background, 75
Cressey Power Test, 78
Cressey Sports Performance (CSP), 54, 76, 79–85
Crews, Dylan, 203–4
cross-pollination, 72
Cummings, Candy, 39, 138–41, 243
curveballs, 138–41, 175, 243
cutters, 110, 225
Cy Young Award, 3, 50, 57, 69, 80, 81, 87, 92, 100, 107, 121, 161, 177, 193

Dalkowski, Steve, 23–25
Daniels, Matt, 153
Darvish, Yu, 137–38, 192, 194–95, 214, 240

Davis, Henry, 209
Davis, Joe, 193
Dedaux, Rod, 5, 109, 117
deGrom, Jacob, 65, 71, 192
Detroit Tigers, 11, 48, 49–50, 176, 179, 212
Díaz, Edwin, 192
Dick Howser Trophy, 202, 203
Diekman, Jake, 194
Doppler radar, 67–68
Driveline Baseball, xiv, 34, 185
   biomechanical approach, 149–50, 151–53, 155
   blog, 46
   bridge pitch strategy, 156–58
   Buffi's partnership with, 48
   command training, 158–59
   criticism of, 154
   examples of players worked with, 159–62
   founding of, 146–47
   Glasnow at, 150–51
   influence of, 151, 164–65
   motion capture lab, 152–53
   Paint Mixer, 157–58
   pitch-tracking technology, 55–56, 154–55
   Seam-Shifted Wake research, 170–75
   Stuff+ model, 155–56
   weighted ball training, 92, 148–49
   youth sports focus, 163–64
Dropbox, 192–93
Duncan, Dave, 118–19

earned run average (ERA), 39, 113, 135
Edgertronic cameras, xviii, 98–101, 104, 107, 152, 154, 166–68, 221, 233, 239
effective velocity, 120–22
Eliot, Charles, 139
Emotiv Flex, 152

Facing Nolan (film), 192
fadeaway, 143–44
Fangraphs, 65
farm strength, 36–37
Fast, Alex, 59
Fastball (film), 12, 21
fastballs
  Dalkowski's, 23–25
  Feller's, 21–23
  front-door, 206
  Johnson's, 19–21
  Ryan's, 11–23
  sailing, 145
  Skenes's, 203, 206
Fearing, Doug, 46
Feller, Bob, xviii, 12, 21–23, 38, 40, 184
Fetter, Chris, 48, 49–50, 176, 179, 212, 214
Fielding Independent Pitching (FIP), 113–14
finger pressure, 59–60
Fisher, Michael, 125–33
FlatGround, xiii–xiv, 198–200
football throwing, 17–18, 216–17
force mound, 207–8
force plate systems, 78–79, 163, 239
Freeman, Freddie, 208
Friedman, Andrew, 46
front-door fastball, 206

Gallen, Zac, 122, 208
Garrett, Amir, 162–63
Gausman, Kevin, 129, 193–94
Getty Images, 7
Gibson, Bob, xix, 183
Gibson, Kirk, 96–97
Gilbert, Logan, 192
Gillespie, Mike, 109
Glasnow, Tyler, 150–51, 192
Golf Swing Analyzer, 182
gratitude, 235–36

Gray, Josiah, 83
Gray, Sonny, 107, 168, 179–80, 192
Greinke, Zack, 111–14, 213
Grimes, Burleigh, 142
grip strength, 59–60
Grover, Taylor, 199

Hader, Josh, 33
Halladay, Roy, 220
Hall of Fame, 15
Hawk-Eye, 49–50, 68, 116, 132–33, 179
Hawkins Dynamics force plates, 78–79
heat maps, 124–30
Hendriks, Liam, 128, 129–30
Herschberger, Richard, 139
Hicks, Jordan, 12
high-speed cameras, 68, 98–101, 149–50, 152, 154
Hill, Rob, 153
hitters
  bat technology, 229–31
  curveballs and, 138–41
  cutters and, 225
  difficulties facing, 224–26
  evolution of, 225–26
  the fadeaway and, 143–44
  game-planning against, 123–24
  injuries to, 24
  knuckleballs and, 142–43
  pitch-tracking technology for, 222–23, 227–29
  Seam-Shifted Wake and, 224–25, 229
  spitballs and, 141–42
  sweepers and, 225
  swing data, 132–33
  technical adaptations, xix–xx
Hobbs, Matt, 232–33
Holmes, Clay, 32–33
Honeycutt, Rick, 137–38
Hosmer, Eric, 226–27, 230–31

House, Tom, xviii, 109, 184, 231, 241
  biomechanics lab, 8–9, 187
  family background, 4–5
  football throwing methodology, 17–18, 216–17
  graduate studies, 7–8
  injury prevention approach, 57–58
  Johnson's training with, 1–3, 16
  Mustard app, 186–89
  National Pitching Association (NPA), 16–17
  NFL work, 17–18
  pitching background, 5–7
  The Pitching Edge, 147
  Ryan's coaching by, 6, 14–17
Houston Astros, 119–22, 129, 130
Husband, Perry, 120

Imanaga, Shōta, 240
infrared laser devices, 11
injuries
  biomechanics analysis, 45–49, 55–58, 68
  finger pressure and, 59–60
  prevalence of, 52, 54
  preventing, 9, 46–47, 54–55, 58–59
  recovery techniques, 15–16, 58
  velocity and, 45, 48–49, 52, 54–55, 242
Inside Edge, 70, 103
Instagram, 28
Istler, Andrew, 48

Jaeger, Alan, xii, 56, 91, 107, 148
Jagers, Eric, 98–99, 153, 166–68, 170
Japan, 240
Johnson, Derek, 237
Johnson, Randy, 1–3, 16, 212–13, 220, 242
Johnson, Walter, xvii, 19–21, 37, 40, 243
Johnson, Wes, 186, 207–8, 210–17

Jones, Chipper, 220–21
Joyce, Ben, 12, 196

Kansas City Royals, 79
Kaplan, Brian, 85
Keller, Mitch, 33
Kelly, Merrill, 122
Kenny, Brian, 65
Kershaw, Clayton, 13, 159–60, 192, 194
kick change, 33
KinaTrax, 47, 234
King, Michael, 70–71, 157
Kirby, George, 192, 193–94
Kirby, Martin, 88–89
Kluber, Corey, 80–81, 82, 100–101
K-Motion, 163, 225
Knickerbocker Rules, 35–36
knuckleballs, 142–43
Koufax, Sandy, 6, 118, 121
Kurcon, Connor, 72

Lambert, Jack, 156
laminar flow, 170
Langs, Sarah, 66
La Russa, Tony, 118–19
Leanhardt, Aaron, 229–31
lemon-peel balls, 136–37, 174
Let's Talk Pitching (forum), xii, 26, 27, 147–48
Lewis, Michael, 40
Lincecum, Tim, 89–90
long toss, 87, 91, 107
Los Angeles Dodgers, 45–49, 153
Louisiana State University (LSU), 202–8
Lowder, Rhett, 205, 228, 237–38
Luetge, Lucas, 175–76
Luhnow, Jeff, 119–20
Lumiline Chronograph, 22–23
Lund, Robin, 49, 50
Luzardo, Jesús, 83
Lynn, Lance, 82–83, 119

Maddux, Greg, 69–70, 123, 124, 173, 192, 242
Magnus Effect, 169, 171, 172, 178–79
Major League Baseball (MLB)
    Baseball Savant expansion, 65–66
    bat rules, 230
    clip-sharing crackdown, 191–92
    data secrecy practices, 61–63
    influence of Cressey's training philosophies, 84–85
    pitching coaches, 86–87
    pitching training by, 74
    pitch-tracking technology, 61, 67–68, 132–33
    policy criticisms, 87
    spitballs banned by, 141
Martinez, Edgar, 123
Martinez, Pedro, 123–24, 220
Mathewson, Christy, 143–44
McAlpine, Coan, 26, 30
McCracken, Voros, 109, 113
McCullers, Lance, 129
McCullers, Lance, Jr., 138, 196
McGwire, Mark, 123
McHugh, Collin, 121–22, 194
Megill, Trevor, 230
mental training techniques, 16–17, 235–36
Mills, Dick, 147
Milwaukee Brewers, 230
Minnesota Twins, 153, 186
Momentum, 105–6
Moneyball (Lewis), 40, 146
Montero, Miguel, 97
Morgan, Deven, 164
Morton, Charlie, 122
motion analysis, 5
motion capture, xiv, xviii, xix, 30, 47–52, 152–53, 165, 234
Muscara, Corey, 205–6, 209, 227–28, 232–37
Mustard app, 186–89

National Baseball Hall of Fame, 35
National Pitching Association (NPA), 16–17
New York Mets, 11, 33, 43, 109, 117, 153, 167
New York Yankees, 83, 99, 164, 176, 179–80, 206, 230, 237
Neyer, Rob, 144
NFL, 17–18
nickel curve, 144
Nieves, Juan, 50
no-hitters, 3, 4, 13, 15, 144
Norton, Charles Eliot, 139
Nunn, Chris, 199
Nyman, Paul, xii, 26, 27, 28, 56–57, 147, 181–86

Oakland Athletics, 127, 200
Ohtani, Shohei, 160–61, 175, 240

particle image velocimetry (PIV) system, 170–71
Passan, Jeff, 54
Patterson, Nathan, 199, 200
Perry, Gaylord, 117–18
Petriello, Mike, 66–67, 69
Pfaadt, Brandon, 122
Philadelphia Athletics, 144
Philadelphia Phillies, 153, 237
Pierzynski, A. J., 222, 227, 241
Pitch-a-Palooza, 85
pitch design, xix, 166–68, 176, 224
PITCHf/x, 62–63, 67, 108, 110–11, 116, 126
pitching
    as an art, xviii, 19, 123
    evolution of, 218–19, 227
    "golden rules" of, 9
    historically, 35–39
    overhand, 36
    underhand, 35–36
The Pitching Edge (House), 147

pitching machines, xviii
PitchingNinja, xiii–xiv, 190–92, 194, 196, 198, 200, 208, 209, 226
pitching training
  command training, 41
  evolution of, 3–7
  football throwing, 17–18, 216–17
  MLB's, 74, 86–87
  Mustard app, 186–89
  Nyman's approach to, 181–86
  personalized, 30–32, 49–50, 127–32, 186–87
  role of social media, 27–28, 190–200, 208
  Wake Forest's, 232–40
  weighted balls, xiv, 48, 56, 87, 91–92, 148–49, 184, 186
pitch-tracking technology
  access to data, 71–72
  Bannister's use of, 110–14
  Baseball Savant, 63–71
  Bauer's use of, 98–101, 104
  data analysis, 62–63, 109–14
  data secrecy, 61–63
  for hitters, 222–23, 227–29
  in Japan, 240
  limitations of, 179–80
  LSU's lab, 207–8
  MLB's, 61, 67–68, 108, 132–33
  pitch design and, 166–68
  placebo effect, 130–31
  Wake Forest's lab, 232–35
pitch tunneling, 111, 120–21, 208–9, 224
Pittsburgh Pirates, 122, 202, 213
Pocket Radar, xiv
PokerStars, 147
prehabilitation, 58
pronation, 33
Proteus Motion, 77–78
PULSE sensors, 55, 152
Pupil Labs, 152

Quantifying Arsenal Effects (Lambert and Ramilo), 156

radar guns, xvii–xviii, 12, 55, 185
Ragans, Cole, 31–32, 33
Ramilo, Marek, 156
Rapsodo, xiv, xviii, 98–101, 104, 107, 154, 166–68, 179, 221
Reboot Motion, 51–52, 207, 235
recovery techniques, 15–16, 58
Remington Arms, 20
resilience, 235–36
Reuschel, Rick, 75
Rickey, Branch, 40–41, 46
Ripken, Cal, Sr., 24
Robinson, Jackie, 40, 46
Rockwell International, 11
Rodón, Carlos, 192
Roe, Chaz, 194
Rooker, Brent, xx, 224–26
Rosenthal, Trevor, 119
rotator cuff, 54
Rudd, Josh, 200
Ruth, Babe, xix, 6, 223
Ryan, Lynn, 10
Ryan, Nolan, xviii, 3–4, 9, 40, 42, 118, 184
  childhood, 10–11
  fastball velocity, 11–13
  House's coaching of, 6, 14–17, 18
  mentorship of Johnson, 1–3
  no-hitters, 13, 15
  PitchingNinja interview, 192
  strength training, 43–44

sabermetrics, 40, 109, 113
sailing fastball, 145
Sale, Chris, 176–77, 192, 211
San Diego Padres, 70, 117, 186
San Francisco Giants, 129, 177
Sato, Masahiro, 240
Sawyer, Logan, 199

Scherzer, Max, 13, 81–82, 192
Scott, Tanner, 33
Scott, Tayler, 130
scouting, 197–200
Seam-Shifted Wake, 96, 170–79, 224–25, 229
Seattle Mariners, 2–3, 6, 193
Seaver, Tom, 3–4, 5, 42–44, 117–18
Senga, Kodai, 192
SetPro, 56, 183, 185
Shove Score, 233–34
Skenes, Paul, 2, 122, 192, 202–19, 231, 239, 243
Skubal, Tarik, 49–50, 52, 161–62, 176–77, 192, 193, 194
sliders, 71, 100, 144–45, 157, 175, 195
Smith, Barton, 169–74, 178
soaking, 137
social media, 27–28, 84, 103–4, 185, 190–200, 208
Soto, Juan, 229
Spade, David, 196
spin efficiency, 169, 178
spitballs, 141–42
splinker, 209–10, 218
Sports Technology Inc., 182
Statcast, 12, 13, 66–67, 71, 114
Steroid Era, 223
St. Louis Browns, 145
St. Louis Cardinals, 40, 118–20
Stock, Robert, 185–86
Stottlemyre, Mel, 50
Straily, Dan, 125–26
strength training, 42–44, 75–79
Strider, Spencer, 71
strike zone expansion, 223
Strom, Brent, xiv, 61
  baseball career, 117–18
  Bauer's influence on, 106–7
  coaching career, 85, 118–22, 129
  family background, 116–17
  injury prevention approach, 57
  on Skenes, 213–14
Stroman, Marcus, 100, 192
sweepers, 100–101, 175, 225
swing data, 132–33
Swords, 196–97

Taillon, Jameson, 33
talent discovery, 197–200
Tango, Tom, 66, 110, 113
targeting, 102
Texas Baseball Ranch, xiv, 89–90, 106, 185
Texas Rangers, 13–14, 72–73
thermographic imaging, 58
Tips with Trev (YouTube series), 103
Tommy John surgeries, 54, 242
Topa, Justin, 199
torpedo bat, 229–30
Trackman, 67–68, 114, 132, 154, 179, 207, 221, 233
Trajekt, xix, 222, 227–29
Tread Athletics, xiv, 26, 27, 28–34, 57, 148, 185
Treinen, Blake, 83, 100, 126–27, 128, 192
Twitter/X, 28, 84, 103–4, 170, 194–95, 196

Uhle, George, 144–45
ulnar collateral ligament (UCL), 46, 54, 55
ultimate pitcher, 201–2, 217
University of Southern California (USC), 5–6, 109, 117
US Air Force Academy, 204, 206, 213
US Army, 22

velocity
  Aberdeen test, 23–25
  Army test, 22–23
  Dalkowski's fastballs, 23–25

development programs, 48
effective, 120–22
Feller's fastballs, 21–23
Johnson's fastballs, 19–21
measuring, 11–12
motorcycle test, 22
pitching injuries and, 45, 48–49, 52, 54–55, 242
Ryan's fastballs, 11–13
theoretical limits of, 47
Verlander, Justin, 13, 82, 121, 137–38, 213
video analysis, 3, 7–8
Volpe, Anthony, 230
Votto, Joey, 65

Waddell, Rube, 37–38
Wagner, Billy, 192
Wake Forest Player Development Seminar, 236–37
Wake Forest University, 232–40
Walsh, Ed, 141
Washington Senators, 20, 21
wearable technology, 102–3
Webb, Logan, 129, 177–78
weighted balls, xiv, 48, 56, 87, 91–92, 148–49, 184, 186
weight training, 14, 15
Wheeler, Lantz, xii
Williams, Devin, 196
Williams, Ted, 24
Willman, Daren, 62–63, 65, 68, 72–73
Wolforth, Ron, 89, 185
Woo, Bryan, 192

Yamamoto, Yoshinobu, 240
Young, Cy, 21
youth sports, 163–64
YouTube, 28, 103–4, 106, 185

ABOUT THE AUTHOR

Rob Friedman, also known as PitchingNinja, is one of the most recognizable voices in baseball. A former big law firm attorney and internet software entrepreneur turned pitching coach and analyst, he's built a massive social media following by breaking down pitching in a way that's intelligent, creative, and often hilarious. His videos and analysis are used by players, coaches, and fans at every level of the game, and his work has been featured on ESPN, MLB Network, Peacock TV, and baseball broadcasts around the world.